Selenidad

Selenidad

Selena, Latinos, and
the Performance of Memory

DEBORAH PAREDEZ

Duke University Press

Durham and London

2009

© 2009 Duke University Press
All rights reserved.
Printed in the United States of
America on acid-free paper ∞
Designed by Amy Ruth Buchanan
Typeset in Dante by Tseng
Information Systems, Inc.
Library of Congress Cataloging-in-
Publication Data appear on the last
printed page of this book.

For my family

Because even grief provides a living remedy.
—Marie Howe, from "For Three Days"

Contents

1. "Anything for Selenas!" Altar installation, detail, by
Dino Foxx. Commissioned by ALLGO: A Statewide
Queer People of Color Organization (Austin, Texas).
Photo by Deborah Paredez.

"Talk about... Talk about...
Talk about mo-o-o-vin'"

This is not a book about Selena, but about what it means to remember her. As her legions of fans can attest, remembering Selena often involves talking about how she moved and how she moved us. When remembering her, some fondly recall how Selena took them to "Funky Town," belting out "Talk about . . . talk about . . . talk about mo-o-o-vin'" as her rhinestone-studded, self-designed costume glittered under the Astrodome stage lights. Some remember other songs she sang at that sold-out concert as she moved from English to Spanish within the same phrase and from disco grooves to salsa steps within the same song. There are some who prefer the more official remembrance of Selena as a crossover star moving from a regional Spanish-language niche into a nationally recognized English-language market, while others insist on remembering that she grew up speaking English in south Texas and that she moved across numerous national and musical borders before moving back to English-language pop hits. Record industry executives at EMI Latin remember how their profits increased 800 percent in the three years after they signed Selena in 1989.

Millions remember 31 March 1995, when Selena, murdered by her fan club president, moved beyond the borders of the living, from her status as a superstar with promise to a slain, fallen star. Others remember responding to the announcement of her death on CNN or their local radio affiliate by asking, "Who was Selena? And how did she become so famous?" They remember her only as a posthumous icon.

Avid readers of *People Weekly* remember how the magazine moved into the Latino market with its launching of *People en Español* after its tribute issues commemorating Selena sold out overnight. Many remember their outrage when radio shock jock Howard Stern ridiculed Selena's music and those who mourned her on the day of her funeral. Tens of thousands remember descending upon Corpus Christi, Texas, to file past her casket.

Only a few thousand remember traveling to see the ill-fated touring musical based on her life. Nearly twenty-four thousand young women and girls remember auditioning for the Warner Bros. biopic of Selena. Some remember their dismay when Jennifer Lopez was cast in the movie's leading role; others recall her uncanny performance of Selena's moves. Many Corpus Christi residents remember the controversies stirred up by the construction of her memorial statue on the city's bay front. In cities across the country, other fans generously apply eyeliner and strategically placed padding to remember Selena as a drag icon. Many, if not most, remember Selena's generous rear end and her skill at moving it. Many more continue to remember Selena in their own choreographic and critical movements. To be sure, remembering Selena moves many to tears, some to political action, and a few to the bank.

This book focuses on a few of these memorial movements in an effort to understand the political, cultural, and civic meanings produced by acts of remembering Selena. What were people remembering or attempting to re-member, to mend or make whole, when they remembered Selena? What were the forces that propelled such large-scale and diverse outpourings of grief and longing following her death? How was the phenomenon of Selena commemoration that took shape in the 1990s related to other, concurrent political and cultural phenomena that both celebrated and excluded Latinas/os? Simply, what does it mean to remember Selena?

This book explores the creative endeavors that constitute what I call Selenidad, the dynamic and vibrant afterlife of the Latina superstar. Selenidad provided a pivotal arena for the growing numbers of U.S. Latinas/os to define and assert themselves, for corporate enterprises to develop a Latino marketing demographic, and for mainstream communities to police America's borders during a time of increased nativist sentiments and legislation that marked the 1990s. The decade witnessed a surge of recognition among Latinas/os and among larger societal forces that Latinas/os were emerging as a significant political, social, and cultural presence in the United States. Often embedded within or accompanying popular celebrations of a "Latin Boom" were expressions of a deep anxiety about growing Latino numbers in the nation. During this time, Latinas/os mobilized around and were moved by Selena.

Just as Selena moved Latinas/os, Selenidad moved *latinidad*—the process of Latina/o identity making—in new directions. Selenidad operated as a hinge connecting and facilitating the physical movements enacted by Latina/o bodies and the affective movements created by Latinas/os and others invested in latinidad. As such, Selenidad makes clear the relationship between emotional and political economic structures that support national, racial, and gendered identifications. In particular Selena commemoration reveals how, through the collective expression of grief, Latinas/os assembled themselves as a political and cultural constituency in the United States at the close of the twentieth century.

While Selena's tragedy offered a way for many Latina/o communities to mourn their own plights resulting from political economic struggles throughout the 1990s, numerous corporate and political forces deployed Selena's tragedy as a way to construct Latinos as hot commodities and valued consumers while denying their status as citizens. That is, Selenidad was used to efface Latina/o struggles even as it was invoked to decry them. Selenidad has thus emerged as a significant site of Latina/o cultural affirmation, as a lucrative industry, and as a disciplining force unleashed against a Latina/o body politic. It is precisely because the memorial currents of Selenidad traverse the realms of the commercial and the popular, of the officially sanctioned and the countercultural, that Selena commemoration illuminates the interplay among a range of claims to latinidad: as market segment, as political force, and as cultural process.

This book's exploration of Selenidad foregrounds the role of performance in the politics of remembering among U.S. Latina/o communities and those seeking to count, contain, or commodify them. This focus brings the fields of performance, Latina/o, and American studies into productive conversation. American studies provides models for examining the role of collective memory in the making of American culture and citizenship, while performance and Latina/o studies insist on remapping the national borders and text-based methodological boundaries of American studies by sharing a concern for the experiences of historically marginalized communities and devalued cultural phenomena. Latino studies insists that Selenidad matters, while performance studies provides the methods for understanding how and why it matters. Selena's material and symbolic body has been used to mobilize emotions, cash flow, votes, and emergent identities — from her hometown's memorial statue to drag queens and pubescent girls who continue to embody her. Performance studies helps us understand these various embodiments in nuanced ways. When examined from a Latina/o performance studies perspective Selena's Astrodome concert comes into focus as more than simply crossover entertainment devoid of political saliency, and instead emerges as a complex event that both embeds and takes part in shaping the political economic forces faced by Latinos throughout the 1990s. Moreover, because performance studies teaches that memory, like performance, is as much an act of creation as an act of citation, it encourages us to recognize how the myriad acts of remembering Selena create imaginative and literal spaces for negotiating shifting political landscapes in the present and for envisioning future possibilities. In particular, when conjoined with Latina feminist studies, performance studies positions the Latina body at the center of analysis. *Selenidad* adopts this model, revealing how Selena's body was central to the making and the managing of the Latin Boom, and suggests that Latina/o representation (as both political constituency and cultural product) in the United States cannot be fully understood without a close examination of the often highly sexualized Latina performing body.

Selenidad focuses on several moments of remembrance, revealing how, within these acts of Selena commemoration, cultural identities, political action, and economic markets coalesce or unravel. Each chapter explores a different function or effect of Selenidad among a range of Latina/o communities in the United States. I begin by addressing the questions posed by those who knew Selena only as a posthumous icon, those who might have asked themselves, "Who was Selena, and why was she so famous?" In the introduction I consider Selena's career and emergence as a posthumous icon within political and cultural transformations in the United States during the final decade of the twentieth century. I provide definitions for and an overview of the key concepts that frame the project — latinidad, performance, memory — and explore some of the forces that shaped anti-Latina/o legislation and the simultaneous Latin Boom celebrations enacted throughout the decade. The introduction positions Selenidad within the context of a prevailing national fascination with dead Latina icons that pervaded U.S. popular culture during the 1990s; I argue that this preoccupation with the dead Latina body facilitated the Latin Boom while strategically obscuring the struggles shared by many Latinas/os as they faced new forms of political exclusion and economic exploitation.

As with other late pop stars, Selena's star text, multiplatinum albums, and recording industry promotion fuel the industry of Selena commemoration, but it is her performances that serve as the benchmarks of her status as an enduring icon. In chapter 1 I argue that her performances document and serve as methods for experiencing latinidad as an affective mode of belonging. In particular I explore how Selena's final concert renditions of her frequently evoked hits "Disco Medley" and "Como la Flor" measure and direct the affective labor of latinidad, invoking the pleasures and punishments resulting from "feeling" Latina/o. These songs thus provide emotionally useful modalities that posit new possibilities for latinidad beyond the homogenized categories of market segment, political constituency, or national threat that have characterized constructions of Latinas/os since the 1990s. This chapter thereby foregrounds performance analysis as a valuable method for understanding the contours of Selenidad and establishes Selena's signature song, "Como la Flor," as a leitmotif that will recur throughout the book.

Chapter 2 focuses on how the act of memorializing Selena functions within the political economy of her hometown, Corpus Christi, Texas. How and on what terms does a city remember Selena? Specifically, how is the maintenance of Selena's memorial related to the maintenance of civic identity in the post-NAFTA borderlands? I tackle these questions by chronicling and examining the heated debates and struggles surrounding the construction, composition, and maintenance of the *Mirador de la Flor* memorial statue and pavilion erected in Selena's honor in 1997 along Corpus Christi's bay front. The Selena monument was mired in controversy since its inception, as local working-class Tejana/o fans of Selena struggled against predominantly Anglo and middle-class Mexican American city officials and civic boosters over the function and acceptable forms of stewardship of her memory. In this contested south Texas region the act of memorializing Selena provides a platform for enacting class- and race-based battles over claims to civic citizenship.

Beyond the U.S.-Mexico borderlands Selenidad has emerged as a (trans)national forum wherein a range of commercial, political, and cultural investments in latinidad converge. In chapter 3 I consider how the act of remembering Selena is imbricated within these fraught processes of latinidad. I examine the touring musical initially entitled *Selena For-*

ever (2000) and eventually restaged and remounted as *Selena: A Musical Celebration of Life* (2001) within the contexts of legislative attacks against Latinas/os in the late 1990s and of the 2000 Census projections that hailed Latinas/os as the imminent majority minority. My analysis of the public discussions and staging of the musical and my interviews and field research at performances in San Antonio, Chicago, and Los Angeles reveal the ways that mourning Selena played a significant role in the formation and policing of latinidad at the close of the twentieth century. For Latinas/os, mourning Selena through participation in the musical—as spectators, producers, vendors, and performers—provided a forum in which to decry prevailing anti-Latina/o rhetoric and legislation and to imagine a future wherein they would gain significant representational ground as voters, consumers, and cultural workers in light of the 2000 Census projections and findings.

Young Latinas frequently navigated this contested terrain of latinidad through embodied acts of Selena commemoration. In chapter 4 I explore the ways Selenidad provided young Latinas with a cultural script and a repertoire of gestures and attitudes for enacting emergent versions of Latina subjectivity within and against the grain of the representational spaces that circumscribe their lives. In particular I investigate the meanings produced by the act of "becoming" Selena for many young Latinas who auditioned for the Warner Bros. biopic *Selena* (1997). The auditions, which were held in Los Angeles, San Antonio, Miami, and Chicago, were the largest open casting call in Hollywood history since the Scarlet O'Hara auditions for *Gone With the Wind*. I rely on interviews drawn from newspaper accounts, television and radio reports, documentary film, and my own field research to argue that the act of imitating Selena emerged as a powerfully effective and affective expressive practice wherein many young Latinas negotiated prevailing concepts of and charted new mappings for Latina subject formation.

The book concludes with a consideration of the queer dimensions of Selenidad. Frequently interpreted as a legibly queer Latina/o text invoked to structure queer Latina/o self-understandings, Selenidad also operates as a queering agent within latinidad, as a repertoire of acts or performative practices that consolidate queer Latina/o cultural affiliation. Chapter 5 surveys a range of Latina/o queer engagements with Selena and culminates with an examination of two of the most frequent queer memorial practices that proliferate within the sphere of Selenidad: Latina

lesbian readings of Selena's death scene and queer Selena drag. Drawing from Lourdes Portillo's documentary *Corpus: A Home Movie for Selena*
(1999) and its companion video, *A Conversation with Academics about Selena*
(1999), and from interviews with queer organizers and artists at ALLGO:
A Statewide Queer People of Color Organization based in Austin, this
chapter reveals the ways that Selenidad offers Latina/o queer communities an intervention in the racial politics of camp culture, an alternative
vision for living with AIDS, and a platform for expressing Latina lesbian
desire and feminist critique.

In the book's epilogue I take part in remembering Selena in an attempt to reveal how Selenidad provides an expansive and performative
memorial space for commemorating other Latinas who endeavored to
cross over the transnational borders of American political and cultural
landscapes and whose critical and creative movements, like Selena's, were
halted by the quotidian forces of violence that threaten many U.S. Latina
lives. To remember Selena is ultimately to re-member these Latina histories.

Taken together, the wide-ranging memorial acts explored and undertaken by *Selenidad* underscore that just as Selena engaged in a number of
crossovers during her lifetime, she also continues to engender them. She,
quite literally, moves us. This book is moved by and follows the movements of Selenidad. It talks about mo-o-o-vin,' exploring the ways that
Selena, like those whom poet Marjorie Agosín recalls, is "not mine, not a
cadaver either, but a waterfall, a dialog, / a shore to be crossed."

Acknowledgments

Although I did not know it then, this project began in the fall of 1997, when I left graduate school for a year to return to Texas in the wake of a family tragedy. Selena was not much on my mind then, despite the pervasive elegies for her that resounded through popular media outlets and airwaves, but the workings of grief, that is, the work of the living, weighed heavily on me. In many ways I pursued this project, entering the memorial space of Selenidad, in an attempt to make sense of loss. I graciously thank all of those individuals who accompanied me on this journey.

I express my sincerest gratitude to the inhabitants of Selenidad who emerge in these pages as thoughtful cultural critics, skilled performers, and savvy spectators. *Mil gracias a* T. Jackie Cuevas, Dino Foxx, Teresa Gil, Lorenzo Herrera y Lozano, Kelly Kline, Annabelle Medina, Dennis Medina, Jerry Ortiz, Onaney Ortiz, Claudia Pérez, Ixchel Rosal, Francisco Vara-Orta, and the numerous other Selena fans who shared with me keen observations, moving recollections, and impressive archival treasures of Selena. I am also grateful to Coco Fusco and Lourdes Portillo, two visionary artists and cultural critics, for creating and sharing their artistic visions and memories of Selena. This book would have been impossible without all of these generous and insightful individuals.

In its earliest stages this project was nurtured by an exceptionally supportive dissertation committee in the Interdisciplinary Ph.D. in Theatre and Drama Program at Northwestern University. Sandra L. Richards contributed keen insights about collective memory and encouraged my poetic intrusions. Josef Barton provided a historian's perceptive attention to detail, and the late Dwight Conquergood offered lessons in the humility and attentiveness necessary for ethnographic work. In my earliest memory of Dwight, he launched our graduate seminar in Critical Ethnography in the fall of 1994 with the statement, "When I die, I want them to write, 'He was a good field worker' on my tombstone." And so he was.

Generous financial support from a range of institutions made completion of this project possible. The Committee on Institutional Cooperation Predoctoral Fellowship at Northwestern University and the Consortium for a Strong Minority Presence Visiting Scholar Fellowship at Vassar College were instrumental sources of support during the project's dissertation phase. At the University of Texas, the College of Liberal Arts Borderlands Research Fellowship and College of Fine Arts Dean's Fellowship provided valuable leave time. Additionally, a University Summer Research Award, College of Fine Arts Creative Research Stipend, and research funds from the Department of Theatre and Dance and the Division of Diversity and Community Engagement provided crucial resources for the development and revision of the book.

The community of intellectual collaborators who surround me at the University of Texas in Austin has inspired and supported me beyond measure. Special thanks go to the members of the Chapter Four Collective — Frank Guridy, Juliet Hooker, and Jemima Pierre — for offering careful readings and illuminating responses to every chapter included in this book. Thanks especially to Juliet, who was a steady writing companion during the final revisions. My colleagues in the Performance as Public Practice Program have tirelessly advocated for my work and my well-being. My gratitude to Charlotte Canning, Jill Dolan, Omi Oshun Olomo, and Stacy Wolf is substantial. Jill Dolan has taught me (and countless others) how to be a feminist spectator, how to assume power with utmost integrity, and how to inhabit pleasure in the process. Stacy Wolf sets an unparalleled standard for loyalty and incisiveness and for posing the questions aimed decisively at the heart of the matter. The Center for Mexican American Studies and the Center for African and African American Studies have created institutional home bases on which I have safely stood. I am enormously grateful to the Center directors José E. Limón, Ted Gordon, and Omi Oshun Olomo for providing valuable counsel and resources when I most needed them. Thanks also to Robert Schmidt, chair of Theatre and Dance; Richard Flores, associate dean of the College of Liberal Arts; Douglas Dempster, dean of the College of Fine Arts; and Gregory Vincent, vice president for Diversity and Community Engagement for additional financial support. I am also indebted to my students, in particular to Fadi Skeiker and Sonya Aguilar, who shared their photographs of the Selena memorial; Sarah Myers, who exchanged ideas and resources about queering Selena; and Kristin Leahey and Angela Ahlgren, who acted as meticulous research assistants during the final stages of this book's completion. I thank other colleagues at the University of Texas who responded to the manuscript in its various stages of development: Elizabeth Engelhardt, Meta DuEwa Jones, Nhi Lieu, Tiffany Gill, John McKiernan-González, Cherise Smith, and Jennifer Wilks. Thanks especially to John McKiernan-González for inspiration for the book's title. I thank Virginia Raymond for sharing materials that strengthened my chapter about queer Selena memorials.

A number of brilliant scholars, mentors, and advisors have provided intellectual guidance and career-defining opportunities for me over the years. In many ways this book began to take shape when Alberto Sandoval-Sanchez, in response to a lecture I delivered about the *Selena* auditions, succinctly insisted, "You know, it's all about Selena." I thank him for this insight, which ultimately set this project clearly on its course. Arlene Dávila's and Patricia Zavella's intellectual contributions and generous advocacy have fostered my growth as a Latina feminist scholar. And in innumerable ways, David Román has consistently provided steadfast faith in and respectful challenges to my work. The results of his critical acumen, honest appraisals, and devoted mentorship are evident everywhere in this book.

I am extremely fortunate to be part of a generation of emerging Latina scholars whose work and critical generosity regularly impress and humble me. My gratitude to and respect for Deborah R. Vargas is deep and abiding. I thank Deborah, *mi tocaya*, for sharing crucial resources and sharp insights on Tejana/o music and a mutual appreciation for divas who carry us out of bounds. I thank Dolores Inés Casillas, whose astute feedback encouraged me to listen, where otherwise I might have looked, for the answers. Endless thanks to the other brilliant *mujeres* whose work and fellowship inspire and sustain me across the miles: Maria Elena Cepeda, Cary Cordova, Cindy Garcia, Macarena Gomez-Barris, Stacy Macias, Gina Pérez, Felicity Schaeffer-Grabiel, and Sandy Soto.

This book benefited immensely from the scholars and students who participated at invited talks, workshops, and conference presentations over the years. I thank those who created opportunities for me to share my work and who generously responded to it: Jossianna Arroyo, Rosana Blanco-Cano, sharon bridgforth, Mari Castañeda, Maria Elena Cepeda, Tracy C. Davis, Judith Halberstam, E. Patrick Johnson, Arturo Madrid, Uma Narayan, Gina Pérez, Teresa Palomo Acosta, Ramon Rivera-Servera, Clara Rodriguez, David Román, Nancy Saporta Sternbach, and Rita Urquijo-Ruiz. Frances Aparicio, Paul Bonin-Rodriguez, Antonia Casta-ñeda, Coco Fusco, Larry LaFountain-Stokes, Suzanne Oboler, Joseph Roach, Angharad Valdivia, and Gayle Wald also offered valuable support and feedback. I am deeply grateful to Ken Wissoker, Mandy Early, Mark A. Mastromarino, Judith Hoover, and the anonymous reviewers at Duke University Press for their editorial insights and suggestions. This book benefited enormously from their advice and encouragement. I also thank Sonya Manes for her careful and expedient work on the index. Thanks as well to others who, in subtle or substantial ways, left their imprints on this book: Majed Abu Ajamia, Julie Bathke, Patrick John Barry, Rona Banks, Christopher Brandt, Hsiu-chen Classon, Gabrielle Cody, Paula Cooey, Marta Effinger, Christopher Grabowski, Luke Harris, Darrell James, Paul Johnson, Sarah Jones, Alice Kersnowski, Frank Kersnowski, Joy Lei, Paul B. Lyons, Leonard Nevarez, Marissa Wolf, and Bill Worthen.

Friends and loved ones in Chicago, New York, and Austin have nour-ished me and my creative and critical work in every way. In Chicago I was surrounded by a circle of four women who, in the decade since, have continued to stand by me. I am profoundly grateful to Regina Deil, who always gets straight to the point; Michelle Boyd, who incisively sharpens every point; Heather McClure, who compassionately softens the point; and Gina Pérez, who rationally considers every point. Endless thanks to each of them for regularly reminding me how all the points connect to form a constellation worthy of worship. Special thanks to Nadine George-Graves, Anthea Kraut, Shannon Steen, and Margaret Werry, a cohort of exceptionally sharp and devilishly witty women who have offered emo-tional comfort, intellectual inspiration, and retail therapy in the years since our paths first crossed at Northwestern. In New York Alejandro Crawford, Helga Davis, Gabriel Evansohn, Sita Frederick, Daniel Alex-ander Jones, Jane Pfitsch, Judy Polyné, Millery Polyné, and Stacey Sutton always welcome me home. I am especially grateful to Michele Archange, who never fails to meet me on poetic ground; Iris Morales, who reminds me to keep justice in sight; and Eva Woods Peiró, who remains a sister through changing styles and struggles. And I extend deep thanks to the remarkable people who have helped make Austin home during the long durée of this book's revisions: Phillip Alexander, Jafari Allen, Jossianna Arroyo, sharon bridgforth, Laura Cisneros Wise, T. Jackie Cuevas, Jill Dolan, Lee Edwards, Carrie Fountain, Juliet Hooker, John McKiernan-Gonzalez, Jamie Hart, Jennifer Margulies, Carna Martinez, Shoshana Partos, Jemima Pierre, Carlos Ramos-Scharrón, Diane and Richard Rodriguez, the late raul salinas, Christen Smith, Claudia Voyles, Stacy Wolf, and the artists and organizers at ALLGO and the Rude Mechanicals.

I am blessed with a family that has always encouraged my aspirations and endeavors as a writer and scholar. My Bronx family—Amparo, Francisco, and Daniel Guridy—have opened their home and their hearts to me and have taught me valuable lessons about tenacity and resiliency in the way only Bronxites can. Thanks as well to the Díaz, Garcia, and Toplitsky families, who keep the Bronx burning with love and laughter. I am deeply indebted to my Tejana/o family, to all of the members of the Bustillo, Cavasos, Salinas, and Villarreal families, who have generously supported my academic and creative pursuits. In particular I extend heartfelt gratitude to Tía Lucia Bustillo, Grandma Stella and Grandpa Frank Salinas, Uncle Frank B. Salinas, Aunt Dolores and Uncle David Lozano, and my brother and sister-in-law, Gilbert and Laura Villarreal. Their constant love, irreverent humor, and material and emotional support carried me through every phase of this project's development and completion. Above all, I offer profound appreciation and respect to my parents, whose labor cleared this path through which I have moved: my father, Gilberto C. Villarreal, who introduced me to the music through Isaac Hayes, War, and Little Joe albums, and my mother, Consuelo S. Villarreal, who taught me how to dance to its rhythms.

And then there was Frank—without warning—with so many gifts. Frank Andre Guridy, who daily offers nothing less than "a love supreme," has read every sentence in this book, and has, indeed, steered many of them toward greater clarity. I am eternally grateful to Frank Andre for hailing me back from sorrow, for teaching me how to live a life measured, not by loss, but by love.

Selenidad and Latinidad in the 1990s

The vocabulary of grievance that constitutes so much of American political discourse has ironically deflected attention away from a serious look at the more
immaterial, unquantifiable repository of public and private grief that has gone
into the making of the so-called minority subject.
—Anne Anlin Cheng, *The Melancholy of Race*

To get to the Selena Museum, you must leave the tourist district along
Corpus Christi's bay front, traveling west on IH-35, or you can take the
side streets, driving through town on Leopard Street, past the pawnshops,
past the sign for Braslau's furniture that, when lit, reads "R S AU'S," past
A & A Bail Bonds and Vick's Hamburger stand, past the Buccaneer Stadium, where on Friday nights crowds gather for local high school football
games, past the racetrack, past the Ranch Motel and La Siesta Motel and
Sunset Motel and Cactus Motel, past a billboard advertising Bud Light
in Spanish, past the Diamond Eyes and Party Place Cabaret gentlemen's
clubs, and just past the Greyhound RV Park on the right side of the street.
If you're coming in from out of town, once you've crossed into the city
limits, passing the oil refineries dotting the landscape, lit up and glimmering like the Emerald City at night or billowing smoke in the day-
light hours, you must exit long before you see the ocean, veering onto
Highway 358 from IH-35, quickly exiting and then turning left on Leopard
Street, arriving finally at Q Productions, the recording studio owned by
Selena's father and former manager and where Selena once recorded her
award-winning albums. You almost miss the building, a low, boxy, industrial structure; almost miss the sign to the left of the side door indicating
that this is indeed the Selena Museum, launched by her family in response

to thousands of fans who visited the recording studio following her death (figure 2).

Once inside the rectangular room, after you've paid your one-dollar donation, you are immediately surrounded by the soft sounds of Selena's music piped in on the intercom system and by an eclectic range of memorabilia from Selena's life and career: the second-place spelling bee award Selena won in fifth grade, gold albums, Coca-Cola ad campaign photos, promotional movie posters for *Selena*, glass cases brimming with music awards, a copy of the Texas State Senate Resolution No. 619 honoring Selena. There is a roped-off area in which her red Porsche is parked. There are magazine covers, album covers, photos of Selena with other celebrities, her famed Fabergé egg collection, and letters from fans in Jamaica, Japan, Singapore, Malaysia, Spain, Cuba, New Zealand, and nearly every country in Central and South America. Selena's famous self-designed costumes are lined up throughout the room, adorning mannequins enclosed in glass cases.[1]

In the center of the room something sparkles. You can't miss it: the geometric cut, the deep color, the flared material aching for a twirl. Here it is in its violet resplendence, the mythic purple sequined pantsuit Selena designed and wore for her final concert in the Houston Astrodome (figure 3). In the year after her death the pantsuit toured with the Smithsonian traveling exhibit America's Smithsonian before returning to Selena's hometown. A miniature replica of the outfit adorned the Selena Barbie doll, sold frequently on eBay and more officially at the touring musical based on her life. Selena's purple-spangled pantsuit has assumed a life not unlike Elvis's flashy white pantsuit, that of iconic signifier, into which impersonators and other admirers aspire to fit.

On the afternoon I visit the Selena Museum a young Latina meanders across the room, singing along to "Como la Flor," pausing in front of one of the glass cases, pointing to a black leather bustier, interrupting her singing with, "Me gusta este, este de cuero [I like this one, this leather one]." Two other Latina visitors gather around the mannequin in the purple pantsuit. One tells the other, "This is my second time [here]. I really like this one a lot." They size up the mannequin. "Selena was little. She was so . . . skinny." The other responds, "Well . . . it's fit for the mannequin. She had big legs, but, you know, they don't make mannequins [like that]. . . . Look, they are kind of *huango* [loose] in the butt." They ask a young Latino who works in the museum, "What size was Selena? A size *five*?

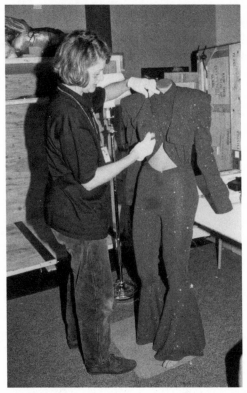

2. Sign posted outside the
Selena Museum. Photo by
Deborah Paredez.

3. Selena's Astrodome concert
costume being prepared for
museum display, Houston.
Photo by Jeff Tinsley.
Courtesy of the Smithsonian
Institute.

No! I thought she was at least a size seven or nine." The women remain suspicious as they continue to assess the official record of Selena's size.

When I approach the purple pantsuit I too am surprised by how small it looks, convinced as well that the costume has been recut to fit the mannequin. In my memory of her in that purple-spangled outfit undulating across the Astrodome stage, she seemed larger, at least larger than life, her generous rear end filling out the costume in inspiring ways. But as with many memories of Selena, my recollected image is surely a palimpsest. Is it Selena crooning her disco medley that I remember, or is it Jennifer Lopez as Selena discoing across the concert stage in the Warner Bros. biopic that pervades my memory?[2] My accretive memory suggests that the act of remembering Selena is inevitably imprinted by images taken from the phenomenon of Selena commemoration. To evoke Selena is to evoke her absence, to attend to the *huango* fit, the hollowed and hallowed spaces of her remains.

The observations about the huango fit of Selena's purple pantsuit reveal that despite its attempted alterations, Selena's proverbial measurements don't quite conform to the narrow curves of the standard-issue mannequin. The sartorial attempt to cut Selena's figure down to size is undeniably a racializing act appealing to standards of whiteness (smaller rear end, leaner thighs), and as such speaks to the larger practices in U.S. culture that police, contain, or attempt to refigure Latina/o bodies. The outfit's misfit also signals the frequent misfit of official Selena commemorations that often fail to fill out the contours of Selena as she is remembered by legions of her Latina/o fans. And yet, in spite of the labored efforts to redraw the contours of her figure, the purple pantsuit with its huango inseam persists in casting the shadow of a different outline for Selena. As the Latina museum visitors observe, these huango folds serve as a visible reminder of the critical space created by Selena's absence. The gaping material in many ways acts as a metaphor for the creative processes of memory itself, whose imprecise fit invariably provides a capacious space for the production of new subjects or countermemories.

This book follows the lead of these observant Latina fans, focusing on that symbolic space between the mannequin's silhouette and the sagging or huango folds of the glittering purple material, on that space where memory, performance, and Latina/o identity gather. It is precisely these spaces opened up by the shell or sign of Selena, what I call Selenidad, that interest me. This book explores how a range of Latina/o communities, like the observant museum visitors, critically inhabited and interrogated the memorial terrain of Selenidad in efforts to measure and create new patterns for their own lives at the close of the twentieth century.

✿ Latin Boom, Latina Tomb

In May 1991 Louise Rosenfield Noun, an art collector and feminist historian from Des Moines, Iowa, decided to auction one of her most treasured paintings from her international collection of women's art. The painting, Frida Kahlo's *Self-Portrait with Loose Hair*, sold at Christie's in New York for $1.65 million, the most ever paid for a Latin American work. Following the record-breaking sale, economic forecasters announced that Latin American art had emerged as a solid investment.[3] Noun donated the proceeds to endow the Iowa Women's Archives at the University of Iowa, the same university that had trained Ana Mendieta, another Latina artist who, like Kahlo, had suffered a tragic and untimely death and was experiencing posthumous fame in art circles across the country. In the months before the auction another of Kahlo's self-portraits graced the sides of New York City buses, advertising the monumental exhibition Mexico: Splendors of Thirty Centuries at the Metropolitan Museum of Art. In the decade to follow, Fridamania, as the cultural and commercial iconization of Kahlo was often referred to in popular accounts, exploded across the United States with biographies, exhibitions, operas, plays, documentaries, a Volvo ad, a U.S. postage stamp, countless Frida-emblazoned tchotchkes, and a battle over the coveted role of the anguished artist in the Hollywood biopic.

As Salma Hayek wrestled the role of Frida from Jennifer Lopez and Madonna, other battles ensued in Hollywood over the casting of yet another dead Latina icon, Eva Duarte Perón, in Disney Studio's film adaptation of Andrew Lloyd Weber's 1979 musical, *Evita*. When, after much protest, Madonna secured the role and began promoting the film, fashion industries ranging from vintage boutiques to runway shows capitalized on Evita's famously glamorous Dior-clad and Ferragamo-heeled image. Just a few weeks before the $60 million film's Christmas Day premiere in 1996, Bloomingdale's launched Evita boutiques in their stores, stocked with well-tailored designer suits, shoes, faux furs, and other Evita-inspired accessories. Estée Lauder soon followed with "The Face of Evita," a new line of makeup and perfumes that offered the patrician hues and scents styled after the late Argentine icon.[4]

Evita was not the only dead Latina fashion icon summoned to generate revenue for the garment and cosmetics industries in the mid-1990s. For those consumers and style mavens on a limited budget, JCPenney and Sears began carrying the "Selena" collection, inspired by the slain Tejana (Texas Mexican) musical superstar and budding fashion designer, Selena Quintanilla Pérez. Before her tragic death at age twenty-three in March 1995, Selena had achieved international success as a Grammy-winning recording artist and had become known as the designer of her rhinestone-studded stage costumes. The line of "Selena" apparel, which was unveiled in 1997, targeted a junior market that composed a substantial portion of Selena's fan base and included sassy yet affordable items such as skirts with side slits, sheer tops, and flared pants modeled after Selena's image of working-class Latina glamour.[5]

Selena's funeral occurred in the same year that Frida Kahlo's 1942 *Self-Portrait with Monkey and Parrot* fetched $3.2 million at Sotheby's and the U.S.-based publisher Knopf purchased the rights to Argentina's best-selling novel, *Santa Evita*, a fictionalized account of the abduction of Evita's corpse.[6] During Selena's closed-casket wake on 2 April 1995 rumors began spreading that the whole affair was a publicity stunt, that she was not really dead. To dispel the rumors and to appease the nearly fifty thousand mourners who had descended upon Corpus Christi, Texas, to honor the slain superstar, Selena's family agreed to open her coffin, momentarily revealing her corpse during the final hour of the twelve-hour public visitation held at the Bayfront Convention Center. Those who reverently filed past the opened casket caught a glimpse of Selena's embalmed body dressed in the self-designed outfit she had worn to accept her six Tejano Music Awards earlier that month. One popular account of the scene described her "lips and long nails done in blood red" and her "slinky purple gown" (she wore a pantsuit and jacket that revealed little skin); another emphasized the "single long-stem red rose . . . placed in her crossed hands."[7] The event was so noteworthy that the multinational Spanish-language television network Univisión interrupted regular programming with live footage from this unveiling that Sunday afternoon. This episode of exposure eerily foreshadowed countless other episodes in which Selena's body would be made public after her death, as corporate forces, political figures, and Latina/o communities mourned her passing, prompting one journalist to proclaim, "The veneration of Selena is taking on a life of its own."[8]

This generative "(after)life of its own," or what I call Selenidad, proliferated across the United States at the close of the twentieth century.
Not unlike Fridamania and Evita worship, Selenidad assumed numerous
and wide-ranging forms that included documentaries, magazine tributes,
monuments, murals, a Selena Barbie doll, websites, biographies, Selena
look-alike contests, musicals, drag shows, a ballet, a display of one of
her costumes at the Smithsonian, and, as with Frida and Evita, a well-
publicized controversy over the casting of a Hollywood biopic in her
honor. Jennifer Lopez was ultimately cast in the Warner Bros. film *Selena*,
but not before the studio staged well-publicized auditions in Los Angeles,
San Antonio, Miami, and Chicago that drew over ten thousand young
women and girls from across the country.[9]

It appeared that many Americans were invested—emotionally, politically, and financially—in the posthumous lives of Selena, Evita, and Frida.
Why did dead Latina icons figure so prominently in the 1990s? What ideas
and struggles did these dead Latina figures embody, enable, or efface?
What do we make of this necrophiliac fascination with the tragically
fallen Latina body?

Dead Latina bodies were frequently celebrated and sometimes reviled
by a range of communities throughout the 1990s to facilitate emerging
and often competing articulations of latinidad, or Latina/o identity. That
is, the Latina tomb was regularly raided to promote, to contain, and often
to capitalize on the cultural, economic, and political Latin Boom in the
United States. The decade witnessed what is commonly referred to as a
"Latin Explosion" in culture and commerce, when corporate marketing
forces understood Latinos as categories of potential capital at the same
time that a resurgence of nativist discourse and sweeping immigration
reforms saw Latinos as a potential threat to national unity. Latinos themselves engaged in acts of self-fashioning often not accounted for by the
state or by corporate tastemakers. Despite their differing investments in
latinidad, all of these constituencies frequently evoked the same symbol
to further their cause: Selena's death. In short, it was over Selena's dead
body that the Latin Boom exploded. As Selena's public viewing evocatively foretells, her dead body was frequently publicized to delimit or
to expand prevailing notions of citizenship, cultural identity formation,
and collective memory at the close of the twentieth century. More than
any other dead Latina icon, Selena's dead body repeatedly galvanized
Latina/o efforts to mourn collective tragedies and to envision a brighter

future, corporate attempts to corner the Latino market, and political jockeying for and public concerns about the Latino vote. As such, Selenidad provocatively illustrates the simultaneous recognition of and anxieties about Latinos as a growing political, economic, and cultural force in the nation during the 1990s.

This book examines some of the ways that Selenidad provided blueprints for and often remapped the terrain of latinidad. My understanding of Selenidad as a contested, creative, and critical set of endeavors is indebted to scholarship in recent years that has revealed how acts of cultural memory and collective mourning can generate and transform concepts of national, racial, and gendered identities. This focus on the imaginative nature of memory often foregrounds the role of performance and popular culture in the transmission of national or cultural histories.[10] Understood as an act of creation as well as citation, memory functions much like performance, as Joseph Roach observes, "as both quotation and invention, an improvisation on borrowed themes, with claims on the future as well as the past."[11] That is, both memory and performance defy traditional notions of temporality by simultaneously repeating *and* revising cultural scripts or scenarios. Given their improvisatory and capacious nature, sites of cultural memory such as public commemorations commonly act as contested arenas wherein what Marita Sturken calls "narrative tangle[s]" form among competing claims to a shared past, present, and future.[12] This book takes part in these efforts to explore the inventive powers and political contours of memory and mourning by examining the entangled narratives about latinidad, citizenship, and gendered and sexual identities that cross over Selenidad.

Some critics see only obsessive, often racialized hagiography in Selenidad, while others bemoan it as the prime example of the commodification of Latino culture.[13] To be sure, tracking Selenidad invariably involves following the trails of fan cultures and commodifying structures, but these forces alone cannot account for Selena's robust afterlife. To borrow a phrase from Gilbert Rodman in his work on Elvis's afterlife, I am interested in explaining Selenidad, rather than in explaining it *away* as simply the result of inevitable commodification or pathological Latino melancholia.[14] Selenidad operates in ways akin to what Raymond Williams refers to as a "structure of feeling," or a critical and affective social practice in process, that supports multiple and variant constructions of latinidad.[15] In fact, as the following chapters illustrate, Selenidad reveals important insights about the ways that assumptions about Latino consumption and mourning practices are positioned against normative standards for civic and national citizenship.

It is not uncommon for a singular figure, event, or image to emerge as a flashpoint for the constellation and transformation of cultural or national memory (think, for instance, of Stonewall, *Jet* magazine's photographs of Emmet Till, Elvis, or the planes careening into the Twin Towers). These memory circuits are charged by and in turn animate a range of collective memories.[16] Memory circuits provide complex pathways through which currents of past histories often run alongside or intersect with currents that pulse with claims to the present and hopes for the future. Selenidad acts as one such memory circuit. Dead bodies of famous figures often operate as such circuits, or what Roach calls surrogates for the transmission of collective memory or cultural continuity among communities of the living.[17] The tragically fallen, once beautiful, dead female body has its own particular cultural function, as Elisabeth Bronfen notes: "The death of a beautiful woman emerges as the requirement for a preservation of existing cultural norms and values. . . . Over her dead body, cultural norms are reconfigured or secured."[18] Throughout the 1990s dead Latinas, Selena in particular, were frequently pressed into service by a range of communities in efforts to claim or to contest the political, cultural, or economic force of latinidad. What made Selena more readily activated and frequently deployed than other dead Latinas?

Ironically the aspects of Selena that distinguish her from figures such as Frida and Evita are the very ones that seem to make her an unlikely candidate for such widespread iconization.[19] Unlike Frida and Evita, Selena was a U.S.-born Latina who grew up speaking English in a family that had lived in Texas for several generations. Although advertising executives and political parties rarely acknowledge this distinction in their homogenizing formulations of latinidad, U.S. entertainment industries — before Selena — historically ignored U.S.-born Latinas in favor of the exotic appeal of foreign-born Latin stars in the manufacturing of such cultural icons as Dolores del Rio and Carmen Miranda.[20] Selena was also affiliated with an explicitly Latina working-class style; she wasn't deployed to sell Volvos or Dior suits. She shared Evita's humble roots, but unlike the Argentine first lady she continued to promote a working-class aesthetic and allegiance after achieving fame through her fashion and her decision to continue living in the neighborhood where she was raised. This working-class aesthetic was undeniably linked to the contours and complexion of Selena's own body; she was brown, unquestionably curvy, and had black hair that hadn't been lightened—no securely held blond chignon or understated accessories were fastened to tone down her color. (Although Frida shared Selena's dark-haired and brown-skinned features, Frida's style was more frequently equated with an exotic, artistic sensibility and with the romanticized notions of revolutionary Mexico than with contemporary U.S. Latina/o culture.) Selena's age also set her apart from the others. All three women faced untimely deaths, but Selena was a particularly young woman who was clearly at the beginning of her career when she died at age twenty-three. Her status as a figure who had just begun to cross into the limelight thus resonated powerfully for Latina/o communities yearning to express a collective promise for their own future.

Selena lived, died, and was quickly canonized during the 1990s, unlike the others, who were unearthed and rediscovered years after their deaths. She was a product of and ultimately helped shape the decade. And while one could argue that all three women performed distinctive public personas, Selena was the only one who was a performer by profession. Moreover, Selena gained popularity in a musical performance form (Tejano music) that was often ignored or, at best, derided by mainstream and even many Latino communities. And yet despite the fact that all of these distinguishing traits—dark, working-class, Tejano music singer—are frequently devalued and even reviled in many communities across the nation, Selena emerged as a widely revered icon among diverse constituencies with a range of sometimes conflicting agendas. It is precisely this conundrum—how and why this unlikely young pop star became a seemingly ubiquitous cultural icon—that interests me. In the following pages I explore how Selenidad animated a range of charged, interconnected circuits, from political attempts to manage the emerging population categorized as Latinos to corporate manufacturing of Latinos as a marketing demographic, from the makings of U.S. Latina/o cultural memory to the inter- and intra-Latina/o conflicts and coalitions that arise along lines of gender, sexuality, race, and region.

The performative context from which Selena emerged and ultimately took part in reimagining is the dynamic tradition of Tejano music, which, unlike most of the Latino musical styles popularized in the recent Latin Music Boom, originated within the borders of the United States. As the ethnomusicologist Manuel Peña notes in his history of Tejano music, Texas Mexicans have distinguished themselves from other Mexican American communities of the Southwest by their "strongly innovative musical spirit."[21] Tejanos were the principal innovators in a range of musical styles, including the *corrido* (border ballads), *conjunto* (working-class dance hall music), and *orquesta* (orchestral ensembles patterned after American swing bands). Historically Tejano music has been derided by Mexicans as "too Americanized," by Anglo-Americans and other Latino communities as "too Mexican," and by nearly all as rural, working-class music. In truth Tejano music exemplifies the best of border cultural production by providing a historically resilient and innovative space wherein Tejanos have (re)fashioned an identity that transcends the bipolar categorizations of "Mexican" or "American." Within the themes and rhythms of Tejano music one can trace the legacy of occupations and negotiations over power that have marked south Texas; Mexican *rancheras* and Latin American *cumbias* collide with German polkas and mainstream U.S. country, pop, and hip-hop, often all within the same song. Tejano music thus reveals the deeply creative ways that Texas Mexicans have adapted to and often challenged the pressures that bore upon them as the result of a history of economic and political disenfranchisement in the state.

Selena mastered traditional Tejano musical conventions with a repertoire that included Spanish-language mariachi ballads, English-language pop love songs, and code-switching cumbias.[22] Like other young musicians throughout the 1980s, Selena, who grew up in the working-class neighborhood of Molina in Corpus Christi, transformed Tejano music largely as a result of her urban upbringing and her exposure to rock 'n' roll, African American funk, Caribbean reggae, Colombian cumbia, and Anglo-American pop music.[23] But unlike other young Tejano musicians of her generation, Selena reinvented the male-dominated genre with performances that highlighted the racialized and sexualized Tejana body. During her early years of touring as a teenager Selena quickly gained a reputation for the combination of her deep resonant voice, adroit dance moves, charismatic stage presence, and sexually suggestive, self-designed costumes. Her stage persona was unusual for artists in the history of Tejano music. The dominance of male performers and record label owners and the common recurrence of misogynist themes found in the lyrics of Tejano music contributed to the dearth or, at best, devaluation of female participation.[24] Selena's profound economic success, bold costumes, deft choreography, and powerful vocal skills marked a significant intervention within the masculinist space of Tejano music. That is, she represented and ultimately re-defined Texas-Mexico border culture, while simultaneously succeeding in crossing over a range of aesthetic, cultural, and national borders.

Selena also displayed wide-ranging talents and actively participated in the creation of her image in her second career as a clothing designer.[25] It was well known among her fans that she performed in outfits of her own design, characterized by their sexual suggestiveness; she would often com-bine low-cut, sequin-studded bustiers with midriff-baring, tight-fitting, flared-cut pants. These costumes led many mainstream chroniclers to (mis)label her the "Tex-Mex Madonna," when in fact Selena's style was more reflective of a decidedly working-class Tejana self-fashioning than an uninspired attempt to copy Madonna's style.[26] After years of designing costumes for herself and her band, Selena launched her own clothing line in 1993 and opened a small chain of boutiques, Selena, Etc., in 1994. This act served to bolster her status as a working woman, and more particu-larly as a young Latina actively striving to assert symbolic and material in-dependence from the patriarchal confines of her family and larger cultural forces as well. Her entrepreneurial efforts in the realm of self-fashioning also clearly set the prototype for the "star as brand" phenomenon that has emerged with artists such as Beyoncé and Jennifer Lopez.

In addition to her status as a sexy young woman, Selena was regarded as a barrio-girl-next-door, long before Jennifer Lopez's incarnation as "Jenny from the block." She was often referred to as *la reina del pueblo* (the queen of the people) or *la gran muchacha del barrio Molina* (the best girl of the barrio), due in large part to the fact that even after achieving fame and fortune she continued to live next door to her parents' home in Molina with her husband, the guitarist Chris Pérez, whom she married in 1992. Her working-class persona did not result simply from the fact that she continued to reside near her family in the barrio, but from her savvy self-fashioning. In interviews she often discussed her love of fast food or her shopping excursions to Payless Shoes, a discount franchise frequented by and often located within working-class communities. She thereby gained a reputation as a genuine, wholesome, barrio girl "who never lost touch with her roots."[27] Selena resonated with audiences not only in terms of a shared class and regional history, but in terms of color: her brown skin and unbleached black hair provided a rare and affirming representation of frequently devalued *morena* (dark) traits in a world where most Latin/a American celebrities conformed to Anglo-American standards of beauty in hair color and body shape. Selena's promotion and self-fashioning as the Tejana-in-touch-with-her-roots and the well-worn good girl/tempting siren dialectic that circumscribed her career invariably highlight the demands of authenticity placed on minoritarian communities and, in particular, on racialized female bodies. Through her constant efforts at self-fashioning she navigated both the roots (the authenticity demands) and the routes (good daughter/dangerous woman) through which her story was regularly channeled.[28]

In some ways, as a working-class musical performer from somewhere down South who exuded a sexual charisma onstage and set up home close to her roots, Selena resembles that other dead American icon, Elvis Presley. Both performers continue to enjoy a vibrant afterlife, underscoring the ways that performers act as repositories of cultural fantasies and mediums through which collective histories, anxieties, and aspirations are expressed and refashioned.[29] Frequent comparisons to Elvis proliferated following Selena's death, with one critic summarily reducing her to "a new, darker-complected Elvis."[30] While this dismissive quip ignores the historical and gendered specificities of Selenidad, it does provoke questions about the racializing work that Selena does. What does it mean to be a "new, darker-complected Elvis"? What do Selena's performances and the memorial performances in her honor *reveal* about racial understandings in the United States that Elvis's performances and his ensuing iconization in particular sought to *conceal*? Because Selena died before she dyed her hair the dark roots of U.S. popular culture show through in Selena commemoration in ways that are often strategically effaced in most Elvis worship.[31] Selena and her subsequent phenomenon opened up a space for the representation of working-class, brown women and made visible traditionally ignored Latina/o histories and the ongoing Latina/o presence within U.S. cultural, political, and economic spheres. Selenidad thus illuminates, and at times actually inaugurated, the connections between cultural memory and the shifting categories of racial and gendered identifications at the dawn of the twenty-first century.

Nativism in the 1990s

Among the most notorious and indeed most virulent reactions to Selena's death was the response of the radio shock jock Howard Stern. On the morning of Selena's burial Stern played one of her songs accompanied by the sound of gunfire while he parodied, with an attempted Spanish accent, the thousands of weeping mourners who had attended Selena's wake. He then announced, "Spanish people have the worst taste in music. They have no depth. . . . Selena? Her music is awful. I don't know what Mexicans are into. If you're going to sing about what's going on in Mexico, what can you say? . . . You can't grow crops, you got a cardboard house, your eleven-year-old daughter is a prostitute. . . . This is music to perform abortions to." Stern also spoke about having sex with Selena in her coffin and joked that starving mourners at the funeral had eaten parts of her corpse. Outraged by his actions, two disc jockeys from KXTJ, a Tejano radio station in Houston, called the show to protest. In response Stern asserted, "If you don't like it, go back to Mexico." Discussing what would happen if his Mexican American critics were to achieve political power in America, he claimed, "It's *adios*, Constitution. They'd ruin this country, too."[32] Stern issued an apology in Spanish following the deluge of complaints filed against the station, including formal denunciations from the city councils in New York, Los Angeles, and Houston and the threat of a nationwide boycott of the show's corporate sponsors issued by the National Hispanic Media Coalition, the American G.I. Forum, and the League of United Latin American Citizens, a national Latina/o advocacy group in Texas.[33]

Stern's parodic performance and the public battles it provoked reveal how Selena's death was invoked to enact competing claims to America. Here, to mourn Selena is to proclaim Latina/o purchasing power, while "not mourning" her, to borrow Richard Johnson's productive formulation,[34] redraws the borders of America to exclude Latinas/os, or, in Stern's words, "Spanish people" who should "go back to Mexico." And yet Stern's anxieties about the growing threat of Latinos are, predictably, accompanied by the desire to consume the racialized female body. His necrophiliac fascination with Selena's body highlights one instance of how the (hyper)sexualization of Latinas in the 1990s served as the launching pad for public concern about the growing numbers of Latinas/os. His reference to abortions also expresses a fear of the uncontainability—in this case, the reproductive threat—of the Latina body. Furthermore the positioning of Selena and her fans as Mexican and thereby beyond the borders of American citizenry, despite that fact that Selena was born and raised in the United States and learned Spanish as an adult, allows him to locate the source of their problems (living in a cardboard box, hunger, and child prostitution) in Mexico and not as a result of U.S. investments in transnational capitalism. Stern's comment that the Constitution would be forsaken should Mexican Americans achieve political power reveals a belief that the rising numbers of Latinas/os pose a very real threat to the national(ist) order. That is, his trenchant and labored efforts to redraw the American border to exclude Latinas/os underscores the explicit xenophobic anxiety that, in fact, the excessive displays of grief among Selena fans represent an uncontainable, indeed, a cannibalistic force in the nation. Thus Stern's act of "not mourning" Selena reflects and ultimately reinforces the new nativist sentiments that were circulating at the time and that resulted the following year in the passage of the most restrictive immigration legislation in U.S. history.[35]

The rise of a "new nativism" characterized the 1990s, manifesting in the passage of legislative acts that included California's Proposition 187 (1994) and Proposition 227 (1998), the immigrant provisions of the Personal Responsibility and Work Opportunity Act (1996), and the Illegal Immigration Reform and Immigrant Responsibility Act (1996).[36] Proposition 187 denied access to public health care and schooling to all undocumented persons; Proposition 227 banned bilingual education in public schools.[37] Even though much of Proposition 187 was overturned as unconstitutional by federal court decisions, Congress ultimately enacted national legislation that enforced some of the proposition's provisions within the welfare and immigration reform bills passed in 1996. The immigration-related provisions of the Work Opportunity Act sought drastic welfare cuts targeted at legal immigrants, while the Immigration Reform Act further entrenched the border's status as a militarized zone with increased Border Patrol agents, surveillance technologies, and fences. The initiation of Operation Blockade/Hold-the-Line in El Paso (1993) provided a model for a "territorial denial" strategy of immigration regulation that was adopted in the implementation of Operation Gatekeeper in San Diego (1994) and Operation Safeguard in Nogales, Arizona (1999).[38] These state-sponsored "enhanced boundary enforcement strategies" were preceded by anti-immigrant citizen action groups such as Light Up the Border that staged demonstrations along the border in San Diego in the early 1990s.[39] The draconian measures and subsequent racial profiling of all Latinas/os resulting from these acts and from the more quotidian expressions of xenophobia, in conjunction with the effects of NAFTA (1994), severely disenfranchised many U.S. Latina/o communities or, at best, constructed all

Latinas/os as suspect citizens, even while politicians increasingly sought to capture the Latino vote.

Howard Stern's anti-elegy for Selena emerged at the same time that government officials were honoring her in efforts to reach out to growing Latina/o constituencies in her home state. On 3 April 1995, just one day after Stern made his vituperative remarks, the Texas State Senate adopted Senate Resolution No. 619, which resolved to honor Selena's "one-of-a-kind talent" and successful efforts at "breaking through the ethnic, cultural, age and language barriers that divide people and nations":

> Whereas, Selena Quintanilla-Pérez, who as Lead Singer of the internationally famous Tejano group "Selena y Los Dinos" was instrumental in making the Texas Tejano industry vibrant and world renown, died March 31, 1995; and . . . Whereas, The loss of this special friend, who proudly demonstrated her hometown pride in every concert and accomplishment achieved, will be felt by millions of fans and young Latinos who see her not only as a peer, but as a sister who personified the coming of their generation; Whereas, With strong family support, Selena was able to stay away from the downfalls of the night life that plague many and achieved wholesome, unprecedented fame; and . . . Whereas, This enterprising young Tejana worked diligently over the years, building a multi-million dollar singing career and more recently establishing a boutique and hair salon in Corpus Christi and San Antonio; and . . . Whereas, Texas' single most important resource is its people, and the state's changing demographic composition presents both promises and challenges for our young people in the future; . . . now, therefore be it Resolved, That the Senate of the State of Texas, 74th Legislature, hereby honor the life, career and personal convictions of this self-made international star and acknowledge the impact that this young Tejana has had across the world.[40]

In the weeks following the adoption of this honorary resolution Governor George W. Bush issued a memorandum that officially proclaimed 16 April 1995 (what would have been Selena's twenty-fourth birthday) "Selena Day" in Texas.[41]

These state-sanctioned tributes underscore how Selena was evoked both as a symbol of an ominous Latin(o) invasion and as a tool for deflecting attention from xenophobic legislative acts in the very state where these measures were producing dire effects for Latinas/os. That is, at the same time that the Texas-Mexico border was being reinforced and that Latinas/os across the state were subjected to increasing surveillance, the state senate deployed Selena as a way to acknowledge Latinas/os as a potential political constituency. The wording of the senate resolution reveals as much if not more about the state's understanding of Latinas/os as it does about Selena herself. The adulation of Selena as a "one-of-a-kind" and "enterprising" Latina who "worked diligently" and stayed clear "of the downfalls of the nightlife that plague many" implicitly conveys state conceptions of Latinas/os as gang-banging, drug-addicted, nonworking burdens to society. Here Selena is honored as the exception to her (Latina/o) community and not as a representative citizen of it. The resolution's references to the "coming of their [young Latinas/os'] generation" and the state's "changing demographics" also works to efface the difficult conditions of the present moment for many Latinas/os. The future promise, not the present acknowledgment, of full citizenship is held out for Latinas/os. And while the resolution does mention the "promises" that these demographic shifts hold open, it also reveals the state's anxieties about the challenges that the growing numbers of Latinas/os pose to "our young people," who, given the syntactic shift from third-person discussions of Latinas/os to an ambiguously referenced second-person plural, do not yet include Latinas/os. The resolution's projections into the future suggest that the goal for the state is to create more Latinas/os like Selena because in the present the state is inundated by growing numbers of non-Selena Latinas/os. The resolution acts as a cautionary guide for both Latinas/os seeking acknowledgment as citizens and for "our young people" who must contend with these changing demographics.

Marketing and Mapping Latinidad

Two weeks after Howard Stern's inflammatory comments and Governor Bush's declaration of "Selena Day" in Texas, editors at People Weekly ran a split cover for the first time in the magazine's history. In seven states primarily throughout the U.S. Southwest, Selena graced the cover of the 17 April 1995 issue, while throughout the rest of the country the cover featured the cast of the NBC sitcom Friends (figure 4). The article reporting Selena's death announced, "Before her time: Touted as Latin music's Madonna, the Texas-born singer known as Selena was on the brink of crossover stardom — until a friend's bullet cut short her life."[42] Selena's murder

The friends from *Friends*: TV's hottest new faces

APRIL 17, 1995 $2.49

People weekly

A rising pop star is murdered at 23

THE DEATH OF SELENA

Grammy-winning singer Selena was shot and killed by the former president of her fan club in Texas

4. *People Weekly* covers Selena's death, 17 April 1995. Photo courtesy of *People Weekly*. Reprinted with permission.

had catalyzed an extraordinary outpouring of grief from Latina/o communities throughout the country, indeed throughout the world. Thus it is not surprising that the 422,000 copies of the issue honoring Selena sold out nearly overnight.[43] Executives at the magazine, stunned by what they suddenly understood as a sign of Latino purchasing power, responded by running two printings of a seventy-six-page special tribute issue devoted to Selena and released later that month (figure 5). This marked only the third time in its history that *People* had printed a commemorative issue; the two previous issues were devoted to Audrey Hepburn and Jacqueline Kennedy Onassis. When both printings of the special issue also sold out, selling 523,000 and 384,000 issues, respectively, *People* began plans for launching *People en Español*, a magazine aimed exclusively at what they regarded as the untapped Latino market. The first issue of *People en Español* was launched on 28 October 1996 with a cover story featuring "Las 10 estrellas latinas del momento" (The 10 Hottest Latino Stars). Other publishers took notice, and by the end of 1996 *Newsweek en Español* and *Latina* joined *People en Español* on the newsstands.

In an editorial announcing the launch of *People en Español* Landon Y. Jones Jr. explicitly links the rise of the new magazine with the fall of Selena:

> When the Tejana singer Selena was murdered on March 31, 1995, few of us at the New York City offices of *People* knew very much about her. But the outpouring of grief and anger in the Latino communities where she was already a superstar quickly commanded our attention. . . . This powerful response led us beyond short-term publishing economics to realize a startling fact: Even though America's Latino community is 27 million strong—and by 2010 is projected to constitute the largest minority in the U.S.—this country had no mass-market Spanish-language magazine that viewed pop culture at large from a Latino perspective. . . . Now we present, on Oct. 28, the first edition of *People en Español*, with four issues to follow in 1997.[44]

Jones's editorial remarks reveal how the act of mourning Selena emerged as one of the most powerful and lucrative acts through which Latina/o communities were imagined and formulated into a marketing demographic during the 1990s. The *People en Español* launching also serves as a compelling example of how, in the U.S. Hispanic marketing industry, as Arlene Dávila argues, "Spanish language is built as the paramount

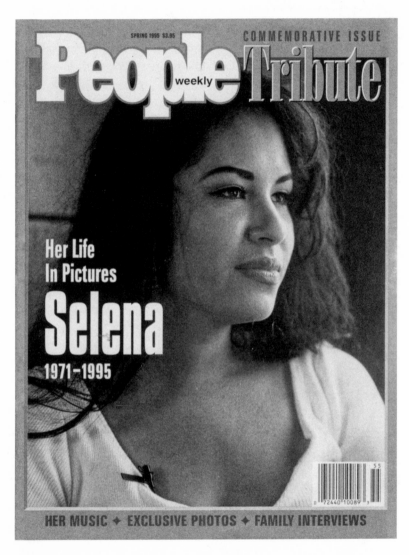

5. *People Weekly* special tribute issue, spring 1995. Photo courtesy of *People Weekly*. Reprinted with permission.

basis of U.S. latinidad."[45] The deployment of Selena's tragedy in the construction of an exclusively Spanish-speaking Latin market is ironic given that her public struggles with the language (she was a third-generation, U.S.-born Latina) were well known among her fans. That is, Selena, like the editors at *People Weekly*, also had to cross over into Spanish-language media outlets before she was able to cross back to English. So even while her career highlights that the Latin market is not reducible to Spanish-language markets, her tragedy is invoked to reify notions of Latinas/os as intrinsically excluded from English-language U.S. culture.

In its attempt to cross over into Latino territory *People Weekly* capitalized on Selena's status as a crossover Latin star. The conspicuous exaltation of the Latin crossover star marked U.S. popular culture throughout the 1990s, and Selena was touted as the prototype.[46] In the music business the term "crossover" generally implies a unidirectional, assimilationist move from a racially marked, regional genre to the realm of English-language pop music defined by a strategically unmarked Anglo-American standard.[47] As such, the notion of crossing over serves to reify hegemonic notions of whiteness by charting a teleological journey toward a so-called American culture, thereby effacing the complex dynamism of and cross-cultural borrowings among the multiple and often undervalued communities that compose the diverse range of popular cultures in the Americas.[48] This discursive frame also strategically obscures the profound impact that the multinational recording industry has had on regionalized musical genres such as Tejano music.

The story of Selena's career has been locked within this crossover narrative trajectory.[49] In official commemorations approved by her family, the narratives that frame the Selena musical and the biopic, the *Behind the Music* episode about her, obituaries, tribute shows, and magazine chronicles, Selena is often remembered as a Latin music star who was on the cusp of crossover stardom when she died. The story usually goes something like this: Selena successfully crossed over from the regional Tejano music market into the multinational Latin music market and then tragically died just as she was poised to cross into the U.S. English-language pop music market. Within this crossover frame, Selena is positioned outside of the boundaries of popular U.S. music due to the regional obscurity of Tejano music, its linguistic categorization (predominately Spanish-language lyrics), and its working-class affiliations. The tragedy of her death was thus often characterized by her inability to fully cross over into American culture.

The *People Weekly* editorial evokes Selena's tragic failed crossover attempt as the narrative through which it invites Latinos to cross over into mainstream American culture: "Not that the idea of *People en Español* hasn't generated some controversy. We have already heard some concern that a Spanish-language magazine might discourage certain members of the Latino community from acculturating fully into American society. In fact, it is our hope and expectation that *People en Español*, with its vibrant mix of stories, will help inform Latinos about mainstream culture."[50] These comments fail to account for the fact that many Latinos in the United States are already American citizens; many of them, like Selena herself, were born here and raised by families who have lived here for generations. In particular the editorial, like Howard Stern's comments, deploys Selena's tragedy as a means of reinforcing the borders of America to exclude Latinas/os. Latinos are positioned as irreducibly untranslatable, insistently monolingual Spanish speakers whose only hope for assimilation is through the well-worn path of consumer-as-citizen.

The origin story of *People en Español* is indicative of the ways that Selenidad emerged as a powerfully effective and affective arena wherein competing claims to latinidad were enacted. While Selena did not singularly set in motion the Latin Boom of the 1990s, Selenidad operated as a central forum for the historical articulation of latinidad by offering a range of constituencies a space to claim and to negotiate the Latin marketplace. The explicit connection between Selena's death and the proliferation of attempts to capitalize on the Latino market is clearly expressed by Anna Maria Arias, founder of *Latina Style* magazine: "Selena's death was a turning point for the emergence of the U.S. Latino market. It's like twenty years ago and someone is telling you to invest in the high-tech industry. The same thing can be said now for the Hispanic market. Invest now."[51] Comments such as these pervaded public discussions about Latinos during the second half of the 1990s, as the insights by Edward Rincon, a research psychologist with the market research firm Rincon and Associates, illustrate: "[Selena] demonstrated to the world that there are dollars associated with Latinos, a population that many were used to relating to negative things like poverty and voter apathy. She made the connection between Latin entertainers and economics."[52] As the genesis of *People en Español* makes clear, corporate forces and entertainment industries took part in collapsing and depoliticizing latinidad into categories of (potential) capital through the creation of Spanish-language market segments. And yet mainstream American marketing forces were not the only ones invested in mourning Selena. A diverse array of political figures, corporate sponsors, cultural workers, and minoritarian communities engaged in Selena commemorations as a means of proclaiming, reclaiming, and negotiating the terrain of latinidad.

Latinidad slips easily from one's grasp. Mercurial, it destabilizes easy identity politics. To be sure, one becomes Latina/o only within the geographical and political economic borders of the United States. And yet despite this shared geopolitical positioning, Latinas/os do not, as the performance scholar Diana Taylor writes, "occupy any *one* positionality (be it in terms of ideology, class, gender, sexual preference or race) [nor do] they occupy it in any *one* way."[53] *Latinismo* (and thus the self-proclaimed term "Latina/o") emerged among the various groups that the U.S. Census Bureau since 1980 had officially labeled "Hispanic."[54] Numerous social scientists have theorized about the ontological contours of latinidad, referring to it, in Felix Padilla's estimation, as an "expression of Latino ethnic conscious behavior," or, according to Juan Flores and George Yudice, a "new social movement."[55] Agustín Laó-Montes describes the process of what he calls "Latinization," or "the production of latinidad by both the dominant powers and the subordinate social sectors." He argues that Latinization functions as "a *power process* of social differentiation and cultural production . . . [that] signifies a mode of production and appropriation of urban space."[56] Arlene Dávila characterizes the Hispanic marketing industry as an "arena of Latino self-representation" and examines its role in the making of latinidad during the 1990s, while Gina Pérez has productively explored inter-Latina/o *dis*identifications that have marked the past decade.[57]

Scholars in the fields of theater, performance, and film studies have generally understood Latina/o subject formation as a process of political and affective (and not simply cultural, social, or ethnic) affiliation. The performance scholar David Román notes the "politically efficacious" potential of latinidad, whereby "people from quite distinct cultural backgrounds and ideological positions meet and organize under the label Latina/o in order to register an oppositional stance to majoritarian institutions."[58] The film scholar Frances Negrón-Muntaner attributes latinidad's political efficacy (what she refers to as its "constitutive materiality") to its operations as a technology that functions as "a specifically American national currency for economic and political deal making: a technology to demand and deliver emotions, votes, markets, and resources on the same level as other racialized minorities."[59] But precisely because the term "Latina/o" does not subscribe to a common racial, class, or national positionality it is often rendered, according to José Esteban Muñoz, "politically incoherent" in its "inability to index with any regularity the central identity tropes that lead to our understandings of group identities in the United States." While highlighting this incoherence, Muñoz attributes the political work marshaled by latinidad to the ways it is consolidated both hegemonically and oppositionally through the performance of affect.[60] Following Muñoz, Ramón Rivera-Servera notes that latinidad operates "as a performative modality," highlighting the processual nature of latinidad, that "through serial acts like performance . . . becomes a legible, although fluid, identity position."[61] Understood as a hegemonic category of capital, a political constituency, an affective mode, a performative process, or a necessary and momentary cultural fiction, latinidad functions in multiple locations for frequently divergent ideological goals.

Selenidad was one of the most powerful arenas in which the complex struggles over claims to latinidad were waged at the close of the twentieth century. This book is concerned with some of these multiple and often competing investments in Selena and latinidad. Before her death Selena had achieved fame and recognition across the wide spectrum of Latina/o and Latin American audiences. Her transnational Latin/o American success resulted both from her adept fusing of pan-Latina/o musical sounds and from the entrance of multinational record companies that had begun to sign and distribute a number of Tejano acts during the 1980s. Selena's success during these years coincided with and was undeniably linked to increased grassroots assertions of and multinational corporate attempts to capitalize on latinidad. As a result of these forces Selena signed a promotional deal with Coca-Cola in 1989.[62] In return the company provided crucial financial support for her touring career during this time. Months after signing with Coca-Cola she secured a deal with EMI Latin Records, which began promoting her as a Latin music star by capitalizing on the transnational Latin sound already present in her regional Tejano music and by encouraging her to continue improving her Spanish-language skills.[63] Thus EMI Latin played a large part in engineering Selena's successful crossover from a regionally identified Tejana to a nationally marketable Latina. During her tenure with EMI Latin her concert tours and television appearances throughout Latin America and her musical collaborations with the Honduran pop singer Alvaro Torres and the Nuyorican boy band Barrio Boyzz further facilitated her Latin/o American appeal.[64] The transnational reach of Spanish-language networks such as Univisión also contributed to her widespread popularity by broadcasting a number of her concerts across the Western Hemisphere. But recording and media industry engineering did not solely account for Selena's inter-Latina/o popularity. Her remarkable stage charisma, vocal power, and deft inter-Latina/o choreographic moves during her live performances contributed substantially to her widespread acclaim. Furthermore Selena's frequently discussed body, specifically her ample rear end (a trait often associated with Afro-Caribbean Latinas rather than with Mexicanas and Tejanas), also emerged as a site of obsessive racialized sexual fantasies and of identification by many women from across the Latina spectrum.[65]

Despite her cross-Latina/o popularity before her death Selena was in some ways a counterintuitive choice for launching latinidad. Her popularity among a range of Latinas/os and her promotion (both corporate and personal) as a Latina star conspicuously occurred even as she cultivated a proud Tejana persona through her style, linguistic markings, and decision to continue residing in the working-class Tejano neighborhood in which she was raised. Her simultaneous maintenance of her Tejana identity and her claims to the space of latinidad, as Frances Aparicio argues, "defy the linear conceptions of identity shifts" which have often pervaded discussions of Latino identity formation.[66] Selenidad undeniably raises critically productive questions about the tensions that disrupt and affiliations that enable latinidad. Indeed by most accounts Selena helped inaugurate the Latin Music Boom that exploded in the 1990s—an ironic fact, given the conspicuous erasure of Mexicans and Tejanos both from dominant representations and from the Latin/o music industry itself, as the controversy over the first annual Latin Grammys made clear.[67] Given that Tejanas/os historically have been (dis)regarded as decisively un-hip, blue-collar, country cousins within larger Latina/o imaginaries, how and why did Selena, with her proudly proclaimed Tejana markings, become a transnational Latina icon among often divided Latina/o communities across the Americas during the 1990s?[68] While this question underscores the "fractured and fraught" possibilities for latinidad,[69] it also points to the ways that Selenidad provides a critical map with which many Latinas/os navigated and continue to navigate these inter-Latina/o tensions. It is perhaps Selena's very unlikeliness for Latina superstardom that enables Selenidad to palpably reveal the conflicts and momentary coalitions that undergird latinidad. Thus, unlike with other sites of latinidad production, within the space of Selenidad we can observe the interplay and incoherence among the various operations of latinidad as a marketing demographic, as a countercultural coalition, as a patriarchal force, and as a political technology.

ৡৡ This Bridge Called My Corpse

In 1997, the same year that Warner Bros. released their much anticipated biopic *Selena*, the Cuban American performer and cultural critic Coco Fusco premiered her performance installation *Better Yet When Dead* at venues across the Americas: she lay in an open coffin framed by white satin and roses, remaining on view for several hours a day over the course of three to four days (figure 6). Fusco's work emerged from the American fascination with the violent and spectacular deaths of Frida Kahlo, Evita Perón, and Selena. She chronicled the impetus to her performance: "After the Tex-Mex singer Selena was shot and killed . . . and the *People* magazine bearing her image sold more copies than any other issue in the publication's history, I began to ask myself why Latino cultures in the north and south are so fascinated with female creativity once it has been forever silenced."[70] Fusco's performance highlights the spectacularization of dead Latina icons and uncannily echoes the episode of exposure at Selena's wake. Her self-conscious staging of the dead Latina body exposes and challenges the necrophiliac terms of Latina visibility during the 1990s. Her embodiment of these dead Latina figures reveals an explicitly Latina feminist critique of the political and cultural labor that Latina bodies were pressed into service to conduct at the close of the twentieth century.

Better Yet When Dead is a compelling example of the myriad and multivalent Selena memorials created by a range of Latinas/os in the years following Selena's death, and moreover provides a model for understanding performance as both an object of study and a method of analysis. In Fusco's work performance is not simply the product of her insights but the process by which she conducts her intervention. This book is inspired by Fusco's model of a Latina feminist performance methodology. In the chapters that follow Selena commemorations are understood as

6. Coco Fusco,
Better Yet When Dead
(performance), 1997.
Photo by Peter Dako.
Reprinted with
permission.

performances that embed cultural, racial, and gendered histories while simultaneously creating new constellations of subject formations. Like other performance studies scholarship, this book foregrounds the agency of cultural actors in the making and reception of performances and emphasizes the centrality of performance in transmitting cultural memory, forging identifications, and imagining alternative worlds.[71]

In recent years performance scholars have produced valuable insights about the ways that performance functions as "a process, a praxis, an episteme, a mode of transmission, an accomplishment, and a means of intervening in the world."[72] Like Dwight Conquergood, I regard performance, broadly understood as embodied practice, as a valuable hermeneutics.[73] My methods thus foreground field research that includes interviews and participant-observation at performance events in addition to archival research, close readings of periodical accounts, and feminist performance analysis. This ethnographic approach allows me to focus on the creative and resilient ways ordinary Latinas/os in a range of venues participated in Selenidad. The explicit positioning of myself as researcher, spectator, or participant that recurs throughout the book emerges from both a performance studies paradigm of critical and localized embodied practice and from Donna Haraway's notion of situated knowledges: "We do not seek partiality for its own sake, but for the sake of the connections and unexpected openings situated knowledges make possible. The only way to find a larger vision is to be somewhere in particular."[74] My attention is focused on a few particular spaces of Selena commemoration. The ephemeral nature of many of these memorials provided a useful critical countertechnology for Latinas/os negotiating increasing surveillance technologies in the 1990s. Like all performances, Selena commemorations underscore how, as Peggy Phelan notes, the political power of performance often lies in its ontology of disappearance, in its ability to elude the "economy of reproduction."[75] Yet Selena memorials also, as mentioned earlier, take on a life of their own, functioning, as Diana Taylor suggests about the nature of performance, as an "invocational practice" that summons and activates "the ghosts, the tropes, the scenarios that structure our individual and collective life."[76] Selenidad thus reveals the synecdochic power of performance to invoke and mobilize the presence of the many in the remembrance of the one.

This invocational power is central to a Latina feminist analysis of Selenidad. When paired with performance studies, Latina feminism requires an attention to both the symbolic power of Selena's spectral body and to the material consequences for actual Latina bodies that result from invoking Selena. The title of this section not only refers to the ways that Selena's corpse was deployed to link together the categories of memory, citizenship, and latinidad, but also alludes to *This Bridge Called My Back: Writings by Radical Women of Color*, a foundational work in the feminist critical genealogy from which this book descends.[77] Latina feminism enables the acknowledgment and examination of the relationships between the frequently appropriated, once glamorous dead Latina bodies of Evita, Frida, and Selena and the other, more quotidian though no less significant Latina deaths that have occurred as the result of welfare reform, border militarization, and the post-NAFTA economy. Throughout the 1990s the murders of hundreds of young women and girls in Juárez, many of them employees of U.S.-owned multinational *maquiladoras*, were conspicuously ignored by Mexican and U.S. government and corporate officials.[78] The deployments of the dead Latina icon that were used to promote and capitalize on the so-called Latin Boom strategically deflected attention from these actual Latina bodies that suffered the most devastating conse-

7. Señoras Norma Andrade and Ramona Morales, Nuestras Hijas de Regreso a Casa demonstration, Washington, D.C., 14 August 2002. Photo by Deborah Paredez.

quences arising from legislative attacks and economic restructuring during the 1990s.

As the century drew to a close these other dead Latina bodies continued to remain both literally and figuratively disappeared. In August 2002 I joined Coco Fusco in Washington, D.C., for a performance demonstration to raise awareness about the ongoing deaths and disappearances of young women and girls along the U.S.-Mexico border. We accompanied members of the international peace network Women in Black, along with Norma Andrade and Ramona Morales, the courageous mothers of two murdered girls. Señoras Andrade and Morales had formed the organization Nuestras Hijas de Regreso a Casa (May Our Daughters Come Home) and had traveled from Juárez to honor and demand justice for their daughters' lives (figure 7). Fusco and I dressed as *maquila* workers in an attempt to render visible those who had disappeared. As I fit the elastic band of a hairnet along the rim of my scalp and slid my arms into a borrowed blue smock, I felt the weight of the rubbery elastic and of the cotton-polyester fabric, felt the material weight of a Latina feminist responsibility resting upon me. Inspired by Señoras Andrade and Morales' brave and harrowing journey from the corridors of grief through the doors of the Organization of American States, I seek in this book to re-trace a particular journey of mourning, to mourn the many in the one, to chart a course of grief for the countless young Latinas, like Selena, from the border and beyond who were denied safe passage into the twenty-first century.

ONE

Soundtracks of Selenidad:
"Disco Medley" and "Como la Flor"

I do believe that the experience of performance, and the intellectual, spiritual, and affective traces it leaves behind, can provide new frames of reference for how we see a better future extending out from our more ordinary lives. Seeing that vision, we can figure out how to achieve it outside the fantastical, magic space of performance.

—Jill Dolan, *Utopia in Performance*

"Como la Flor" [tiene] algo especial, algo mágico. ¿M'entiendes? Y es por eso que—yo pienso—que todo el mundo quieren a "Como la Flor" ["Como la Flor" has something special, something magical. You know what I mean? And it's because of that— I think—that the world loves "Como la Flor"].

—A. B. Quintanilla III, Selena's brother, lyricist and composer of "Como la Flor," on *En Persona: Selena*, narrated by Joe Morales, Galavisión, 31 March 1999

Director Gregory Nava launches the 1997 Warner Bros. biopic *Selena* with a backstage scene from Selena's final concert in the Houston Astrodome on 26 February 1995. The opening tracking shot follows the frenzy of last-minute preparations as grips roll sound equipment into and out of the frame and Selena's sister Suzette calls out in exasperation, "Selena! You're still not dressed?" Selena, portrayed by Jennifer Lopez, sits at a lighted dressing room table hurriedly fixing her hair when she utters her first on-screen words: "I can't decide what to wear." The camera then makes a series of fast cuts: Selena flipping through a rolling rack of costumes; Selena plopping an off-brand suitcase on the floor and unzipping it; Selena, suitcase unzipped, exclaiming "I know which one!" as she pulls out a rumpled pile of glittering purple material and rushes off-screen in a sparkling violet blur. This series of images flash by in less than ten seconds, setting an anticipatory pace and quickly establishing Selena as a down-to-earth girl who, like so many of us, packs her bags in a haphazard way and picks out her outfit at the last minute.

This behind-the-scenes view of Selena's decision-making process, with its focus on the famous purple pantsuit, depicts a key moment in the literal and proverbial fashioning of Selenidad. The film introduces Selena's pantsuit in a conspicuously unglamorous way, stuffed carelessly in a suitcase apart from the other costumes, implying a recognition of the outfit's status as an iconic representation of her. The joke here, for those in the know, is that the iconic purple-spangled pantsuit is self-consciously introduced as simply a heap of wrinkled fabric waiting to be called into service. This opening image serves as a contrast to the vision of Selena in the following scene, when she fills out the costume in iconic ways as she belts her "Disco Medley" to over sixty thousand adoring fans. Together these before and after images of the purple pantsuit highlight the specific representational value it has come to have within the circuit of Selenidad. The pantsuit was clearly made for the stage, the very excess of its construction—the generous scattering of sequins, its synthetic stretchiness hugging the hips, the bell-shaped flare at the ankle—designed to reflect and sparkle under the stage lights and to simultaneously cling to and flow with the dancing body. As such, the costume has emerged as the most recognizable sign of Selena's skills as a performer, its aura imbued with the echoes and gestures of her performances. The opening moment of Nava's film, wherein the purple pantsuit is transformed from disheveled knot into fulsome symbol of excess, reminds us of the power of Selena in performance and suggests that her performances provide insights about how and why Selena became Selenidad.

As with other late pop stars, Selena's star text, multiplatinum albums, and recording industry promotion fuel the industry of Selena commemoration, but it is her performances that serve as the benchmarks of her iconicity. The continued proliferation of these performances across her memorial terrain suggest that they provide imaginative, collective, and affective spaces for the expression of what Frances Aparicio calls "the interlatino affiliations, desires, and conflicts" of latinidad.[1] Selena's 1995 Astrodome concert in particular circulates frequently in the repertoire of

Selenidad, deployed as video montage or staged reenactments to assert diverse aspects of latinidad, ranging from queer Latina/o style, Tejana/o working-class resiliency, and pan-Latina/o collaboration. These invocations suggest that if Selenidad acts as a memory circuit wherein claims to latinidad are negotiated and contested, then it is performance that provides the prevailing mode by which such claims are made. Selena's performances document and serve as methods for experiencing latinidad as an affective mode or, as Ramón Rivera-Servera observes, "as a sensibility, a shared feeling of placeness, and at times placelessness, within the U.S. national imaginary."[2] Selena's concerts chart the emotional registers and cultural codes of latinidad and offer insights into how and why Selenidad, like the purple pantsuit, is inhabited and transformed by the range of Latino communities that gather within its capacious measurements.

Performance accumulates much of its power as a spatial practice. Live performance, by its localized and ephemeral nature, offers a way to account for the specificity of historical, geographical, and political location: a play or a concert takes place in this venue in this city at this moment in time. But the magic of performance resides in its ability to encourage transcendence beyond discrete temporal boundaries. While performance only ever occurs in the present, it simultaneously lifts us out of this present, haunted by the ghosts of the past (invoking previous iterations of a role or a song) and gesturing toward future possibilities (creating structures of feeling or imaginative worlds).[3] Performance is thus often spoken of in terms of both effect and affect. Jill Dolan writes evocatively about how performance can capture "the attention of the audience in a way that lifts everyone slightly above the present, into a hopeful feeling of what the world might be if every moment of our lives were as emotionally voluminous, generous, aesthetically striking, and intersubjectively intense." Dolan refers to these moments as utopian performatives that "in their doings, make palpable an affective vision of how the world might be better." Utopian performatives are "most effective as a *feeling*," and, as such, their political and social efficacy resides in creating "the *condition* for action" in the spaces beyond the now of the performance.[4] Thus the most potent effects of performance are often the affective spaces it can open up for its participants.

The afterlife of Selena's concerts can be attributed to this affective spatial power of live performance and also to the ways that music creates and transcends space. In fact, Selenidad operates as one of the most frequently traversed soundtracks of latinidad. Josh Kun writes about both the spaces within and produced by music, the structural components of song and sound as well as the social, political, and imaginative worlds music makes. Kun shares Dolan's interest in the utopic spaces within artistic practice, calling our attention to what he calls audiotopias, those "small, momentary lived utopias built, imagined and sustained through sound, noise, and music." For Kun these audiotopic spaces are what enables music to "give us the feelings we need to get where we want to go."[5] Kun's work highlights the audiotopias produced by American popular music, within which we can hear and inhabit the soundscapes of racial difference and the remapped borders of America. The audiotopic spaces created by Selena's performances of two distinctively American pop songs, "Disco Medley" and "Como la Flor," afford us the opportunity to listen to the ways that the staging of racialized sexuality often provides the bass line for the sounds and gestures of (trans)national citizenship and migration.

"Disco Medley" and "Como la Flor" circulate frequently within Selenidad, in video clips posted on YouTube and tribute websites and in re-enactments performed by young girls and drag queens. These songs are, in fact, the two hits that frame the Astrodome concert re-created in the opening moments of Nava's film and documented on the 2003 DVD release *Selena Live—The Last Concert*.[6] A close look at Selena's final concert renditions of these signature songs reveals how they offer sites wherein expressions of Latina/o longing and belonging are palpably felt. Through both musical components (tempo, rhythm, lyrics, and song structure) and performative skills (easy charisma, choreographic virtuosity, velvety voice), Selena's performances of these songs create circuits for navigating Latina/o grief and survival. The songs provide emotionally useful modalities, what Dolan would call utopian performatives, that posit new possibilities for latinidad beyond the homogenized categories of market segment, political constituency, or national threat that characterized constructions of Latinas/os at the end of the twentieth century. The songs measure and direct the affective labor of latinidad, invoking the pleasures and punishments resulting from feeling Latina/o. In these performances we can hear the sounds of Latino desire, can witness the improvised steps marking Latino loss, can sing along with and follow the lead of the audiotopic possibilities for queer latinidad or Latina agency that they offer. "Disco Medley" and "Como la Flor" thereby tune us in, so to speak, to the affective frequency of latinidad and to the echoes of its lasting political effects.

⌘ Latina Hustle

In the opening moments of her now legendary Astrodome concert, Selena looks out at the record-breaking crowd, flashes her signature beaming smile, lifts her left arm in benediction, and asks in a booming Tejano twang, "How're ya doin,' Houston, Texas?" She then lowers her hand, clutching her heart as she begins to perform her version of the Gloria Gaynor song "I Will Survive." Throughout the song she gestures with her left hand, pointing her index finger for emphasis, highlighting the Band-Aid wrapped around her forefinger in place of what appears to be a lost acrylic nail. She marches rhythmically across the stage, her purple-sequined, self-designed, midriff-baring costume glimmering under the stage lights and showcasing her ample curves. After a few verses she closes the chorus with a powerfully rich "Hey Hey" and commands "¡Todos amigos, vámonos, todo el mundo! [Everybody join in! C'mon everyone!]" as the tempo shifts into a synthesizer-heavy rendition of another pop classic, Lipps Inc.'s "Funkytown." She claps her hands above her head as she moves her body to the new rhythm, shouting "¡Eso!," a popular Mexican American exclamation of encouragement akin to "Go on!" or "Preach it!" She then spins around into a step-slide-step-kick cumbia before launching into the lyrics: "Talk about—talk about—talk about—talk about it. Talk about—talk about—talk about mo-o-o-vin.' Gotta move on" (figure 8). During the synthesizer-thumping *pum-pum-pum-pum-pum-pum* between verses, she glides seamlessly from cumbia-inspired freestyling into a forward-moving flamenco-esque stomp-and-clap routine before imploring the audience, "Won't you take me to—funky town?" She then dances upstage as she delivers another command: "Let me hear you, Houston, Texas-Méjico." As the crowd goes wild, she claps her hands above her head emphatically and kicks her legs into quick-paced salsa stylings, the flared-cut material of her sequined pantsuit rippling to a blur, breaks into one of her famous 360-degree backspins—off flies one of her earrings—switches her microphone from right to left hand and tears off the remaining earring, breaks into another 360-degree turn followed by more freestyling, all on the beat, and then claps overhead again as she marches forward and

8. Selena performing "Disco Medley," flanked by A. B. Quintanilla on guitar and Don Shelton on backup vocals. Houston Astrodome, 26 February 1995. Photo by Arlene Richie/Media Sources. Reprinted with permission.

begins crooning Donna Summer's "Last Dance." Immediately following her final "So let's dance the last dance toni-i-i-ight" she declares "Do the Hustle!" as the music changes and she joins Don Shelton and Freddy Correa, her African American and Nuyorican backup singers and dancers, in the well-known Van McCoy disco routine. After a few moments she calls out, "Bring it down! Let me hear some gritos! ¡Vámonos! [shouts! Let's go!]," as her timbale player launches into a solo, during which she kicks her silver, spike-heeled boots into cumbia and salsa stylings once again. She concludes this premiere of what has become known as her "Disco Medley" with another Donna Summer hit, "On the Radio," in her trademark deep and textured voice.[7] At the close of the song, she warmly declares, "¡Muchas gracias, Houston! ¿Cómo 'stán todos? [Thank you very much, Houston! How is everybody?]," before issuing another command, "¡Manos arriba! ¡Eso! [Hands up! C'mon!]," as she dances her way out of her purple-sequined jacket, exposing a matching halter top that crosses her chest like the bandolier worn by iconic Mexican revolutionaries, and launches into the Spanish-language cumbia title track to her Grammy-nominated album, "Amor Prohibido" (Forbidden Love). She performs this complex semiotic feat in just under eight minutes.

Selena's Astrodome concert has been frequently invoked as an emblem of her stage charisma, inter-Latina/o musical range, and crossover promise. Just one month following her murder on 31 March 1995 the Spanish-language television network Univisión aired the concert as Selena's "Ultimo Adiós" (Final Goodbye). Gregory Nava depicts the opening moments of the concert to launch an American Dream narrative in his 1997 biopic.[8] In 2003 the concert was packaged and released as a DVD, *Selena Live: The Last Concert*, complete with special features that included behind-the-scenes footage from the making of Nava's film. The performance is notable not only because it set new concert attendance records at the Astrodome, but also because it occurred in the midst of Selena's well-publicized studio work on her forthcoming English-language album, *Dreaming of You*. This crossover context has framed many of the invocations of this concert, ignoring the facts that "Disco Medley" was the *only* English-language song Selena performed that evening and that Selena was doing "The Hustle" as part of "Tejano Night" at the Houston Livestock Show and Rodeo. Nava's film, for example, does not include Selena's Spanglish interjections within and between the songs. In these narratives

Selena's opening "Disco Medley," which she premiered that evening, seemed to offer a glimpse of this potential crossover career move.

But the complex semiotics of "Disco Medley," wherein Selena's "Hustle" breaks down into Tejano cumbias and Caribbean salsa kicks, clearly exceed the confines of the conventional (unidirectional) musical crossover classification.[9] Her performance undeniably crosses over a range of performative, national, racial, sexual, and gendered boundaries. Within the context of latinidad, frequently fractured by these very divisions, Selena's concert (and its ensuing circulation within Selenidad) offers a compelling space for observing the articulation of inter-Latina/o conflicts and desires. Frances Aparicio has argued, "That Selena could affirm and maintain her Tejana identity while simultaneously constructing a larger Latina/o identity through her music and audience, is evidence of the multiple subjectivities that traverse and inhabit the space of Latinidad."[10] Selena's performance of "Disco Medley" enacts an instructive negotiation between Tejana/o and Latina/o affiliations, and thereby offers us a guide for feeling our way through the gestures of belonging within the "multiple subjectivities" of latinidad.

Selena's choice to perform disco covers as her opening number at the Astrodome concert may at first appear to signal simply an unequivocal crossover moment, an uninspired attempt to conform to American pop music's formulaic demands that value sales over originality. Some might even characterize "Disco Medley" as a capitulation to the marketing of a Generation X nostalgia that strategically effaces African American and Latino traditions from and influences on 1970s popular culture. Others dismiss Selena's purple-spangled discoing body as an example of how she "inevitably succumbed to market pressures and converted her voluptuous body into a commodity."[11] These views of Selena's performance fail to account for the fact that her "voluptuous" style was part of her woman-of-color working-class aesthetic long before her purported crossover moment and that the real thrust of 1990s disco nostalgia actually didn't show its force until three years after the concert, with the release of such films as *54* and *The Last Days of Disco*, the airing of the wildly popular VH1 special series, *Seven Days on the Seventies*, and the launching of the Fox sitcom *That 70's Show*. Moreover, unlike much of the disco nostalgia that permeated the mid- to late 1990s, Selena's "Disco Medley" does not possess an ironic condescending detachment, which may have everything to do with the fact that the performance is not directed at a white audience. It is, after all, "Tejano Night" at the rodeo.

This attention to venue begs an obvious question: Why did Selena perform disco at all? More precisely, what does disco mean when performed by a Tejana at a rodeo in Houston? Why debut her "Disco Medley" at this particular historical and geographical location? Given that she was promoting her upcoming album, why not open with one of her new English-language songs? Or why not a country-western song fitting for the rodeo milieu? Or why not cater to her loyal Tejana/o fans at "Tejano Night" by opening with one of her numerous Spanish-language Tejano hits or a traditional Mexican ranchera or even an Afro-Caribbean standard? Yes, quite simply, *Why disco?*

Given its fluidity as a genre — romantic orchestrations meet electronic sampling — and its complicated history, from queer and working-class Black and Latina/o nightclubs to John Travolta's mainstreaming to racialized derision to equally racialized nostalgic reclamation, disco provides opportunities for the interaction of a range of often conflicting cultural forces.[12] Or, as Jaap Kooijman writes, "Disco offers a learning experience which accepts and invites ambiguity and contradiction."[13] What, then, does disco offer Selena? First and foremost, in its relentless 4/4 beat and what Richard Dyer calls its "whole body eroticism," disco showcases the body.[14] Disco demands moves that reveal performative skill both within and beyond traditional set choreography. That is, disco invites Selena to dance. But then so do Tejano music and country-western tunes and, undeniably, a range of Mexican and Afro-Caribbean genres. So the question persists: Why disco? Unlike country-western music or Spanish-language genres such as Tejano, Mexican, or Afro-Caribbean dance forms, disco has come to be regarded by the recording industry as a mainstream pop music form, or, to risk crudeness, disco was and continues to be frequently derided as nonthreatening minstrelsy funk for white audiences.[15] As such, disco dancing allows Selena (known for her exceptional skills as a dancer) an arena for negotiating and intervening in her positioning within corporate crossover narratives while *appearing*, at least to record company and rodeo promoters, to enact a conventional crossover move that imitates and emulates English-language U.S. popular culture. She is, after all, doing "The Hustle," that very icon of crossover-sellout musical commodity. "Disco Medley" thus symbolizes a tactic by which Latinas/os navigate and momentarily circumvent the crossover frame (positioned as they are as potential—never actual—English-speaking citizens, voting blocs, or consumers) through which they are frequently interpellated. In short, disco offers Selena an idiom sanctioned in the big house that also provides the opportunity to bring down the house in multiple ways.

During "Tejano Night" at the rodeo in Houston, a city that bears the name of one of the first Anglo colonizers in Texas, Selena appropriates or, more precisely, Tejano-izes disco as a means of momentarily articulating a critical resistance to this history of Anglo colonization while under the glaring spotlight of the dominant gaze. The rodeo's celebratory promotion of the Anglo-Texas ranching legacy with its token inclusion of its Tejana/o neighbors strategically effaces the regional history of political economic violence wherein Anglo-owned corporate ranches, composed largely of illegally confiscated Mexican *ranchos*, relied upon exploited Tejano labor to sustain their growth.[16] Set in this context, Selena's soaring and soulful rendition of "I Will Survive" asserts an enduring Tejana/o presence and continued struggle within the circumscribed borders of these historic colonizing practices. In one breath she calls out, "I will survive! Hey! Hey! ¡Todos amigos, vámonos! ¡Todo el mundo!," and her Tejana/o fans join in and respond to the call, momentarily reclaiming the rodeo's space. They will survive, and they want the global audience, *todo el mundo*, to know it. Selena's Spanglish phrase embodies and asserts the dynamic language of the Tejana/o borderlands;[17] her opening benediction to the inhabitants of "Texas-Méjico" spatially remaps the Texas border to foreground a Tejano history that predates the region's Anglo-American economic colonization largely brought about through a ranching economy worshipped at the altar of the rodeo. The audiotopic sounds of Tejana/o voices in this call-and-response and the collective labor of their performing bodies symbolically reworks the spatial foundations of the rodeo, unearthing the Tejana/o laboring bodies central to the origins of the region's ranching economy.

The fabulousness factor of disco coupled with its acceptance of ambiguity also allows Selena to go public at the rodeo in ways that Tejano and country-western music have not historically allowed for women of color.[18] Disco's unabashed aspirations of glitz and glamour historically enabled communities shut out of the mainstream the opportunity to assert "flamboyance [as] a political statement [wherein] the displayed body becomes a fundamental site from which to claim social space."[19] For Selena disco encourages an unapologetic assertion of racialized sexuality on her own terms despite the narrow confines of studio career engineering, Tejano music conventions, and the rodeo setting—the very emblem of a hegemonic Texas history that strategically erases both the labor of and violence enacted against Tejanas/os in the establishment and projections of Texas cowboy traditions. Disco's potentially politicized flamboyance provides her with a choreography through which to assert a particularly dynamic Tejana subjectivity within the historically male-dominated space of Tejano music. Her glittering disco fashion sensibility also visually disrupts the gendered style of Tejano music best symbolized by the other headliner that evening, Emilio Navaira, known for his signature outfit of jeans, cowboy hat, boots, and belt buckle and for his role as a spokesperson for Wrangler jeans and Stetson hats.[20] Selena's skillful control of her performing body may appear in many ways like that of Madonna or Janet Jackson, both of whom owe a great deal to disco; Selena openly acknowledged Jackson as an influence. But within the context of Tejano music Selena's performing body marks a significant departure from tradition. Although her backup dancers occasionally cross downstage to join her, she predominantly commands the stage by dancing *alone*. Disco allows Selena to boldly stage the solitary Tejana dancing body within Tejano music—a tradition wherein women rarely occupied the stage at all and in which their presence at performances was historically circumscribed by the sexually exploitive transactions of the *bailes de negocios* popular during the first half of the century or the masculinized cultural politics of contemporary *conjunto* dance halls.[21] Her embrace of this aesthetic in her purple-spangled glory as well as her improvised movements across the stage mark a conspicuous contrast to the stationary balladeer style of her Tejana music predecessors, Lydia Mendoza and Chelo Silva.[22] Selena's act, combined with her star text as an economically successful clothing designer who exerted substantial control over her own image, moves beyond the historical positioning of Mendoza's desexualized-singer-of-the-poor persona or Silva's staging of the sultry nightclub siren.

Even as Selena's solo disco dancing encourages the expression of Tejana agency, it simultaneously expands the parameters of Latina/o belonging by inviting Latina/o queer interpretations of and affiliations with her act. Disco's whole-body eroticism and the freeform solo dancing discothèque culture of the 1970s offered women of color and gay men an arena for fashioning and celebrating nonnormative sexualities.[23] Selena's solo disco choreography, executed with flair as she is flanked by her black-leather-clad male backup singers and dancers, circumvents the heteronormative coupling frequently imposed on disco in the process of its mainstreaming (think John Travolta), and instead evokes the "queer affective ethos" of gay nightclubs.[24] This vision of her dancing among (and not partnered with) her backup dancers, Correa and Shelton, symbolically reinserts men and women of color into disco's history, validating them as the very foundation of disco. Her movements (direct address, effortlessly bold) combined with the hyperfemininity of her costumed body—the rhinestone-studded bell-bottoms, the ample curves, the vermillion shock of lipstick, long dark mane—convey a queer musical aesthetic described by Suzanne Cusick that combines masculine and feminine elements in efforts to destabilize traditional, essential notions of gender.[25] In this way Selena's solo discoing body is available to *all*, which may explain the subsequent recording of the "Disco Medley Club Remix" and the preponderance of drag performances of this song.

Selena's choice to cover the long-established gay dance culture anthems "I Will Survive" and "Last Dance" by the African American disco divas Gloria Gaynor (crowned by gay DJs and dancers in the early 1970s as "Queen of Disco") and Donna Summer also contributes to her queer appeal. The identificatory relationship between gay male dancers and the racialized disco diva whose songs expressed outrage at betrayal, bold assertions of survival, and undisguised sexual longing played a large part in the rise of disco. The repeated refrain of "Last Dance," for example, suggests a longing for one last intimate encounter, a pleading that reveals a resigned farewell, while the song's propulsive beat insists on forward motion beyond the discothèque and beyond those darkened corridors left empty by the ravishing sweep of AIDS and other losses. Tim Lawrence describes how the lyrical "critique of the happy veneer of heterosexual romance," the "lung-busting improvisations" of the diva vamp, and the "double underdog status" of disco divas (as women of color) encouraged identification among gay men.[26] Selena, commanding the stage in her figure-hugging purple pantsuit and vamping soulfully in her full and textured voice, embodies the essence of the brown disco diva. Particularly when she growls the "I" in the verse "'cause when I'm bad, I'm so so bad" in her upbeat rendition of "Last Dance," her voice evokes the throaty vocal style of the Latina diva La Lupe, a well-known Latina/o queer icon. Selena's growl invites a specifically Latina/o queer identification by registering the crosscurrents of Latina diva vamping and staged suffering that have historically provided affective and performative models for the simultaneous expression of Latina/o queer mournfulness and resiliency.

The breakdown of Selena's improvisatory command of her disco choreography—that is, both our attempt to break it down for analysis and her own skill at breaking it down and breaking it apart—evocatively charts the strategies for Latina/o survival amid the tragedies of colonization, AIDS, and immigration reform and maps out a place for Latina/o belonging within and against this history of struggle. In particular, Selena's dance moves clear a space for Tejanas/os within the landscape of Latina/o belonging. Her choreographic deftness and choreographic departures in "Disco Medley" highlight how, even at the moment of her apparent enunciation of English-language crossover, her performing body is crossing back and forth across a range of musical genres and cultural imaginaries. In the opening percussive riffs of Lipps Inc.'s "Funkytown" she executes forward-marching, silver-spiked flamenco steps that, as the additional instrumental layers of the song are added, break apart into lateral movements of cumbia and salsa freestyling. The easy match between steps and beats highlights disco's indebtedness to and resonances with Afro-Latin/o rhythms. The seamless progression from Spanish flamenco to Tejano cumbia and Afro-Caribbean salsa symbolically charts a genealogy of colonial history while also staging the ways that Tejano and other Latina/o communities maneuver through and rechoreograph these set routines of colonialization. Selena's harmonious shifts between Tejano cumbia and Afro-Caribbean salsa also position Tejanos within the dynamic space of latinidad. This maneuvering constitutes an important intervention in conventional formulations of latinidad that often exclude Tejanas/os, or at best deride them as decisively un-hip, blue-collar country cousins with limited dance moves. Thus Selena's adept choreographic fusing of the traditionally regarded rural Tejano cumbias with cosmopolitan salsa stylings embodies a continuum of latinidad that insists upon the inclusion and performative skill of Tejano/a bodies.

In "Disco Medley" the explosion of the timbale breaks "The Hustle" down, and by defying the containment of its set choreography Selena's improvisatory moves rhythmically chart the traditions of transculturation that has marked the history of Latina/o social dance forms. When her "Hustle" transforms into impressively executed cumbia and salsa stylings she is not simply staging, as Manuel Peña suggests, a "diluted transnational Latino 'flavor' largely divested of the power to galvanize . . . communities."[27] Rather, a creative Latina fury and not a "diluted Latino flavor" attacks the right angles of "The Hustle" in a manner evocative of the ways that the deliberate shuffle and counterclockwise glide of the Tejano conjunto dance *el tacuachito* of the 1940s challenged European dance forms. Selena's quick-paced improvised kicks during the percussive solo that transitions her from "The Hustle" to "On the Radio" are also evocative of the complicated open footwork practiced by the Nuyorican dancers redefining the mambo at the Palladium in the 1950s.[28] Her choreography through this transition marks the Latina/o migrations — the hustles and side steps and polycentric moves — that have forged the pathways for so many contemporary popular musical forms. Her timbale-propelled kicks and flares also provide a metaphor for the everyday migrations of Latinas/os as they move creatively within and in moments beyond the daily hustle to earn a living in the aftermath of NAFTA and the new nativism of the mid-1990s. Moreover, her migration across instrumental orchestrations, musical styles, and English and Spanish languages offers an audiotopic possibility for Latinas/os whose own movements within and across a range of borders are regularly policed.

Selena's display of a Latina creative aesthetic is not surprising given the historic ways that disco's "tacky sumptuousness" showcased a specifically working-class woman-of-color style and sensibility.[29] Her performance of disco's working-class aesthetics and racialized flamboyance — the flashy pantsuit, the broken acrylic nail — reclaims and proclaims the origins of disco that have been frequently elided in the wave of disco's return to mainstream popular culture. That is, Selena not only infuses Tejano with disco, but she also Tejano-izes disco — evident in her growl, her bilingual encouragement of participation from her Tejana/o audience, her unironic homage — in ways that intervene in whitewashed reclamations of disco in recent years. Her efforts to Tejano-ize disco within disco's set rhythmic and structural boundaries are emblematic of the ways that Latinas/os often remake the spaces they inhabit within the set geopolitical boundaries that circumscribe their lives. Her Tejana infusion into disco surfaces even in her design of the bell-bottoms on her purple pantsuit.[30] The inseam of each pant leg does not simply arch out into a symmetrical bell, one seam on either side; instead each bell is gathered at its head by generous pleats, crowned by silver dollar–size rhinestones. The extravagance of the pleating that fans out in voluminous twirls and the eye-catching sparkle of the rhinestones not only showcase her deft footwork, but also exemplify a racialized reworking of popular fashion, or what Catherine S. Ramírez defines as style politics, "an expression of [racial, sexual, class, and/or gendered] difference via style."[31] The extra fabric and flashy accessorizing of the bell-bottoms are markers of the unabashed self-fashioning of working-class women of color whose creative stylings, often derided as excessive, frequently serve as inspiration for mainstream trends. Selena's "Disco Medley" outfit ultimately recovers the black and brown roots of disco style.

Selena's vocal quality also takes part in this recovery of disco's racialized origins. The rich timbre and the ranchera-infused longing and power of her voice in the "Whoa oh oh oh ohs" in "On the Radio" restores the texture and agency of the racialized female's voice of disco's most popular hits. The fullness and undulations of her voice cannot entirely be contained by the pop constraints of the songs; like her bell-bottom design, there is more here than the customary pattern requires. This vocal quality is important given the recording history of disco that often exploited black female sexuality for commercial gain and flattened or attempted to "tame" the black voices of performers such as Donna Summer.[32] Selena's deep ranchera sound, its longing and pathos, that permeates her renditions of "I Will Survive," "Last Dance," and "On the Radio" reinstates the woman of color's voice into disco's story and thus serves as a crucial counterweight to the early stirrings of 1990s disco nostalgia.

Selena's insertion of Afro-Latino percussive sounds and dance moves into her "Disco Medley," in conjunction with the presence of Don Shelton, her African American vocalist and dance partner, semiotically restores the often effaced sources of African (American) performance traditions appropriated by disco and Tejano and other Latino music. Selena may not have been the first Tejana/o musician to collaborate with African American artists or to partake in a black diasporic sound, but she was the first to make those connections so visible.[33] Like Tejano *orquestas* of the 1960s and 1970s, Selena acknowledges her influences from African American musical styles.[34] In fact, in one interview conducted just before her concert she positions herself within a genealogy of pop stars of color; she remarks that performing in the Astrodome held a special significance for her because, seeing Michael Jackson perform there when she was young, she dreamed that one day she too would perform on that stage.[35] But unlike her Tejano music predecessors, Selena stages this indebtedness in corporeal ways onstage. During the slotted steps of "The Hustle" she is joined first by Correa and Shelton, but after a few back-and-forth steps Correa retreats to his microphone, leaving Selena and Shelton to their playfully coordinated cross-steps and rock steps. These moves provide an unprecedented metonymic representation of this history of exchange between Tejano and African American performance traditions and recalls the black and Latina/o origins of and collaborations in disco.

Selena's body, or, more precisely, her much discussed rear end, also signifies the presence of, as Frances Negrón-Muntaner notes, "Africa in(side) America."[36] Certainly her hustle with Shelton may also serve to authenticate her crossover into the U.S. pop music market since the historic appropriation of African American forms have often been required for pop music stardom. But again, Selena does not represent the "Tex-Mex Madonna," a crossover comparison that also effaces blackness, but instead, to appropriate Ilan Stavans's term, she more closely resembles "a darker-complected Elvis" who tactically reveals rather than strategically conceals the African (American) sources to which she is indebted.[37] In this way Selena's discoing body does not simply foreground the historic resonances among and collaborations between black and Latina/o artists, but also expands Latino belonging by insisting on the inclusion of blackness within the parameters of latinidad.

Like many of the disco moves historically executed in gay and black and Latino working-class discothèques, Selena's performance showcases the way marginalized people come out in audaciously fabulous ways. The fabulousness of her choreography and her costume, its excessive sparkle and generously filled proportions, offer a sign of unabashed arrival and not, as the concert has come to stand in for, of her departure. "Disco Medley" is Selena's coming out as a legitimate subject in Texas history, as a new generation of Tejanas, as a Latin(a) star whose very Tejananess creates an expansiveness within the scope of latinidad, extending its reach beyond the urban centers of the nation's coastal cities. As such, "Disco Medley" reveals disco's romanticism or utopic possibilities; there is within its open breaks and inviting choruses a promise of unforeseen collectivity.[38] But perhaps the most persuasive reason this moment continues to live on for many of Selena's fans as what Dolan calls a "utopian performative" is the structural components of disco. Disco's relentless repetitions and cyclical drive refuse harmonic closure, suggesting that it has "no particular endpoint."[39] In the same way, the slick transitions of "Disco Medley" allow for the possibility of no particular endpoint in Selena's life. It is impossible to watch footage from or participate in re-enactments of this performance without casting the shadow of Selena's violent and unjust end upon it, in much the same way that one cannot hear tales from the Sanctuary without hearing also the echoing silences caused by AIDS. But Selena's seamless shift from "Last Dance" to "On the Radio" to "Amor Prohibido," her smooth move out of her bolero jacket while staying on the beat, and her adoption of disco's refusal of closure invite the possibility of another ending, of another life beyond the radio and the rodeo, beyond the hustle, beyond funky town, beyond the Astro-dome. The participants of Selenidad stage and restage this scene; they cut the pattern of the costume to fit their own silhouettes with the hope that if they cannot turn the beat of her tragic demise around then at least they can ensure that the beat goes on.[40]

Beyond Disco, beyond *Dolor*

Selena closed her 1995 Astrodome concert with "Como la Flor," the hit that has circulated throughout Selenidad as her trademark song. Most of the songs Selena performed between "Disco Medley" and "Como la Flor" were drawn from her 1994 triple-platinum album, *Amor Prohibido*.[41] A few weeks before the concert, she was nominated for a Grammy in the Mexican-regional category for *Amor Prohibido* (the previous year, she had won the "Best Mexican American Performance" award for her album *Selena Live*, making her the first Tejana artist ever to win a Grammy).[42] Given the number of hit singles cut from *Amor Prohibido* and from Selena's previous albums, the positioning of "Como la Flor" as the concert's closing song underscores its special status within the repertoire of Selena's song-book. As the final song in her final concert, "Como la Flor" has emerged as Selena's swan song, as the aural signifier for both her creative vitality and her untimely death. Given its literal translation (Like a Flower) and its clichéd associations with beauty and ephemerality, the song title has also become Selena's posthumous epithet, inspiring the name of her biog-raphy, a drag contest tribute, and countless other commemorative acts, including the musical tribute *Selena: A Musical Celebration of Life* (2001) and the ten-year anniversary tribute *Selena ¡Vive!* (2005), both of which show-cased the song as their rousing final number.

A pivotal scene in Gregory Nava's biopic re-creates an iconic staging of

"Como la Flor" that depicts both the effects and affect of Selena's concert versions of the song. In the scene Selena and her band are performing before an unruly crowd at an outdoor concert in Monterrey, Mexico, in 1993. In an effort to manage the massive crowd, Selena turns to her brother as they huddle backstage and says, "Let's do 'Como la Flor,' but start it slow, okay?" She demonstrates for him, singing the traditional cumbia melody of the tune in a soothing, elongated tempo: "Co-o-o-mo la flo-o-o-r." They walk onstage, and after the opening chords crest and fall, she starts to croon the song's chorus, taking her time with each phrase. Just before the final line she pulls the microphone away from her mouth and deliberately pauses. In this interlude she lifts her hand and waves sweetly to the audience, then draws her hand to her mouth, pressing her index finger against her lips, asking for silence. The audience, entranced, stands together peaceably, listening intently as she finishes the chorus in a measured cooing — casting her performative spell — before gently guiding the crowd back to the song's trademark cumbia rhythm.

In the narrative arc of the film the concert follows a frequently chronicled scene from Selena's biography: at a Monterrey press conference she defied the odds, overcoming her lack of Spanish-language fluency and the prevailing stereotype in Mexico of Tejanas/os as assimilated, uncultured Latinas/os, and charmed Mexican reporters with her charisma and gracious decorum.[43] Following the "Como la Flor" performance scene, the camera cuts to an image of Selena's tour bus crossing a river, presumably the Rio Grande, semiotically representing the movement of successful crossover. The next scene takes place inside the bus, where Selena's band and family are reading several Mexican newspapers that feature Selena on the front page. Her father, Abraham, who reads from a paper with the headline "Provoca Selena Hysteria en Baile" (Selena Provokes Hysteria at Dance), exclaims, "Listen to this: 'Selena is a genuine artist of the people.'" Selena responds giddily, "¡Que viva Mexico — Monterrey!," as the rest of her band and family squeal with delight. This series of scenes collectively conveys the preliminary moments of Selena's transformation from a regional Tejana into a transnational Latina star. Within this process of cross-border acceptance, "Como la Flor" emerges as the auditory marker of *pocha/o* triumph, its drawn-out chorus momentarily invoking a community of listeners across various divides.[44]

The placement of "Como la Flor" within the film's story of Selena's transnational achievements underscores the transformative power of the song (the rowdy audience quelled, the Tejana girl accepted in Mexico) and the song's own transformation (from synthesizer-driven pop cumbia to captivating ballad) in performance. As an amalgam of various live versions of "Como la Flor," Nava's concert re-creation specifically alludes to Selena's Astrodome concert at the moment when Selena waves coyly to the audience. The scene highlights the emotional investments and interactive participation encouraged by the song and enshrines the song securely within Selena's memorial terrain. But how and why exactly did "Como la Flor" achieve this status? What is it about Selena's performances of "Como la Flor" that has inspired such valedictory reverence, pleasurable engagement, and gestures of identification across the space of Selenidad?

A pop cumbia written by A. B. Quintanilla and Pete Astudillo, "Como la Flor" was Selena's first hit single when it was released on her 1992 album, *Entre a Mi Mundo*. The lyrics, like those of many pop tunes, ramble along with a tale of heartbreak, the catchy chorus crowing "Como la flor (Como la flor) / Con tanto amor (con tanto amor) / Me diste tú / Se marchitó / Me marcho hoy / Yo sé perder / Pero, ay-ay-ay, cómo me duele / Ay-ay-ay, cómo me duele [Like the flower / With so much love / You gave me / It withered / Today I leave / I know how to lose / But, oh, how it hurts me / Oh, how it hurts me]." The song invites participation; the call-and-response lyrical structure of its chorus and the narrow range of its tessitura seduce listeners into singing along, while its transnational cumbia beat welcomes a wide range of Latina/o dancers to move in the side-to-side slide of its galloping tempo. The upbeat pop cumbia melody works as a crosscurrent against its self-abnegating and lovelorn lyrics, not unlike a number of cumbia, salsa, and other dance tunes within Latin/o music whose melodic tempos and the quick-paced choreography they inspire seem at odds with lyrics of unrequited love, political commentary, or tragic loss.[45] As a result, there is a tensive pull built into the song as the aching proclamations of loss strain against the cumbia's playful pop synthesizer-driven charge.

The song's melodic classification as a cumbia was a large part of its inter-Latina/o appeal. Many Latin music industry executives and experts agree with the Arista Records producer Cameron Randle: "Cumbia's what opened the door for Selena. . . . It's considered the musical passport to Latin America, you know—the cumbia."[46] Indeed by the 1980s cumbia had emerged as a transnational symbol of working-class latinidad. Whereas in Colombia the cumbia was often played in a big-band style, Tejano musicians stripped the form down into an accordion-driven conjunto sound. Selena and her band continued to transculturate the Tejano cumbia with elements from ska, reggae, hip-hop, and funk, thereby revealing one of the ways Selena's music represented an "index of interlatino articulations and of the transnational circulations of sounds that made them possible."[47] As Selena's brother and band mate, A. B. Quintanilla, stated, "They call us Tejano, and yes, we are from Texas. But a lot of the music we're playing is from Mexico and South America [and is] a mixture of tropical, reggae, cumbia, all these things. It's got pop influences to it, too."[48] This synthesis of sounds from across the Americas is not altogether surprising given the Afro-diasporic cultural roots shared by the cumbia, tropical, and hip-hop music and dance styles. In this way Selena's music also, as Deborah Vargas notes, "captured the underexplored cultural dialogue between Mexican American and African American communities" in addition to other Latin/o American musical traditions.[49] In its transculturated structural components and lively tempo, "Como la Flor" ultimately exemplified a contemporary, classic pop cumbia crafted from and aimed at a range of Latina/o aesthetic tastes.

Selena often began her live renditions of "Como la Flor" by singing the chorus as a mournful attenuated cadenza, breaking from the song's pop cumbia melody (as depicted in the scene from Nava's film). In concert "Como la Flor" pulled its audience in the undertow of its marked Latina sorrow only to buoy them up on its bouncy cumbia rhythm. The sing-along seduction of its emotive opening, with its direct address, "Me diste tú," and its easy-to-follow dance beat, called upon the audience to interact with their whole bodies as harmonizing chorus and as exuberant dancers. Selena often expanded the song's participatory ethos by using it as the moment in performance when she engaged directly with the crowd, encouraging a call-and-response echo or moving beyond the borders of the stage to share the microphone with her adoring fans. In one such engaging moment during a 1992 concert at Rosedale Park in San Antonio, Texas, Selena invited young women onstage to sing the chorus, offering them a moment to showcase their own talents and performative aspirations. After assembling the girls in a line onstage, Selena instructs one of them, "You know the words? Okay. You wanna take it by yourself? I want you to put emotion into it. This is your debut. Tonight you are a star!" When she turns to the final girl, who appears to be no older than five, she proclaims to the audience, "All right, can y'all see her? This is the next Selena-to-be! Está chiquita pero picosa [She's small but she's spicy]."[50] Throughout the solos Selena claps encouragingly, standing close and guiding them on the beat when necessary or standing outside the spotlight when they hit their marks. These interactive moments staged repeatedly during live performances of the song are suffused with an almost prescient sensibility, as Selena appears to be conducting rehearsals for her own replacement. The song continues to carry this sense of promise and loss. The performances of "Como la Flor" have thus come to signal the capacious and participatory space for self-assertion created by Selena's stardom and her death.

Selena's Astrodome performance of "Como la Flor" evocatively captures this sense of Latina/o belonging that arises from the "affective investments" the song encourages from its audiences.[51] Her fans had already come to associate the song with a multivalent emotional register and communal sensibility. As a result, an anticipatory energy and a self-conscious theatricality pervade the performance; Selena and her audience know their parts: she knowingly beckons, and they gather. In the crosscurrent pull from emotive chorus to ebullient choreography "Como la Flor" captures and conveys what Roland Barthes calls "the grain" of Selena's voice, or the "body in the voice as it sings."[52] Jose Behar, president of EMI Latin Records, called it "that teardrop . . . in her vocal chords."[53] Precisely because of its residue of materiality and its melodic shifts, the song successfully evokes Selena's presence in the elegy marking her absence, and thus offers an auditory — or, as Kun would say, an audiotopic — space for moving through tragedy and occupying the afterward of survival. But the song not only carries the body of Selena's voice — the sensuous textures of her style, the violet blur of her back spins, the unleashed teardrops in her voice; in its interactive ethos "Como la Flor" also carries the *bodies* in her voice, or, to paraphrase the legendary Abbey Lincoln, the song carries the people in her. "Como la Flor" provides an anthem for a collective Latina/o grief, lyrically offering its plangent expressions of loss, while marking the time, in pop cumbia tempo, to the other side of sorrow.

In the closing moments of her Astrodome concert Selena introduces "Como la Flor" as her final song. She speaks rapidly: "Ahora, me gustaría dedicar esta canción a todos ustedes porque ustedes hicieron esta canción un exito — el primer exito para nosotros aquí en los Estados Unidos, igual como en Mexico. Espero que se recuerden esta canción [Now, I would like to dedicate this song to all of you because you made this song a hit—our first hit here in the United States and in Mexico. I hope you all remember this song]." She then slows her pace, shifts her gaze to her raised right hand, and begins her signature move associated with this song: a flamenco-inspired *floreo* hand gesture, turning her wrist in three beckoning waves, elbow to fingertips twisting in serpentine motion, fingers elongated, as she languorously croons, "Como la flo-o-o-o-o-r." The crowd roars as she continues, "Con tanto amor," taking her time with each line, "Me diste tú," drawing us languidly through the chorus to the phrase "Yo se perde-er-er-er-er." Then she pauses. She pulls the microphone slowly away from her mouth and the crowd roars once again as she smiles, inviting us to stand with her a while in this musical rest. When she breaks the pose it is to acknowledge the future, as she turns directly to the camera recording the event and waves with her right hand, index finger bandaged, thumb encircled by a gold ring. She is smiling broadly and waving knowingly in an aside that conveys intimacy and anticipation. She finishes the chorus: "Pero," another pause, "Ay-ay-ay," left hand clenched into a fist over her heart. "Cómo me duele." The tempo quickly shifts into the recognizable gallop of the synthesizer-driven melody as she repeats her signature hand gesture and the lights brighten to showcase her famous back spins and shuffling steps that smoothly mark the 4/4 time of the cumbia. She then launches into the first verse of the song, carrying us along toward the chorus again, inviting a response to her call, "¡Con animo, raza. Vámonos! [With feeling, my people. C'mon!]," and the crowd echoes, "Como la flor."

This performance of "Como la Flor" captures the affective tenor of Latina/o belonging. Before the song begins Selena marks out a space for latinidad with her Spanish-language introduction, spoken without the traditional twang of a Tejano Spanglish or the rapid-fire cut vowels of Caribbean accents. Both the pace and the pitch of her sentences evoke a hybrid U.S. Latina/o Spanish that offers a familiar invitation to listeners from across the transnational divides of latinidad. Her Spanish introduction, with its cross-border signification ("el primer exito . . . en los Estados Unidos, igual como en Mexico"), discursively marks the song as a space for transnational Latina/o identification. This moment highlights how, even while she is performing at the rodeo's designated "Tejano Night," Selena deftly navigates the affirmations of Tejana/o culture and identifications across the spectrum of latinidad.

Having established the pan-Latina/o parameters of the song, the performance proceeds to embody the emotional register of Latina/o mournfulness. The achingly melancholic tone of her opening improvisatory vocal stylings is evocative of the doleful, booming voices of Mexican female ranchera singers who sang with melodramatic flair about themes of longing and despair.[54] The elongated cadenza, with its self-consciously exaggerated grieving punctuated by dramatic pauses, also resonates with the *filin* styles of female *bolero* singers such as Chavela Vargas and La Lupe, whose powerfully throaty vocal styles and hyperbolic stagings of sorrow and betrayal historically served as outlets and templates for Latina/o grief.[55] The tempo of this introductory improvisation and its lyrics of exposed heartbreak combined with Selena's repeated flamenco-esque *floreo* gesture suggest both the overwhelming force of Latina/o sorrow and the staggering power of the Latina diva to guide us through it. The incorporation of flamenco choreography does not signal an attempt to gain cultural capital with a gesture toward Spanish performance forms; rather, in its transculturated fluidity, it evokes the emotional landscape of the *duende*—the "shadowy, palpitating," soulful, creative force—central to flamenco practice.[56] This moment of performance is thus aurally and visually saturated with the intense, emotive colorings of Latina/o longing that pulse in the closing phrase of the chorus, "Yo sé perder," the final word made performative with the aching, attenuated moan of its second syllable.

And then there's the pause. The breath taken in the midst of so much loss. The dramatic silence before the final enunciation of agony, "Pero, ay-ay-ay, cómo me duele." The moment perched on the brink of sorrow's end. The unpredictability of the pause and the uncertainty of its duration grip the audience in the magic of the performance's present tense and emotional presence. The pause takes its time, suspends the audience in the now. But the pause also provides a break from the temporal space of the now in the instant when Selena shifts from her mournful, anguished pose to smile at the audience and then wave at the camera recording the event. Her knowing smile, a clear and self-conscious break in character, acknowledges the act, the deliberate staging of grief performed, and creates an opportunity for reveling in self-reflexive appreciation of her skill. The aside of her wave, like the song itself, is imbued with juxtaposed meanings, signaling an assurance in a time and space beyond this moment of sorrowful lament, while also presaging her imminent death. The wave acknowledges and welcomes an audience beyond the Astrodome even if only to offer them a way to say goodbye. The pause is infused with generosity, inviting its spectators to join in — to applaud at the virtuosic skill, to beg with knowing anticipation for the finish, or to bellow out their own cries of grief. In this way the pause maps out an audiotopic space wherein Latina/o voices are encouraged to resound.

The movement from pained outcry to playful pop melody is what makes this performance of "Como la Flor" especially conducive to the expression of Latina/o sorrow. Selena's break from her melodramatic belting into her signature cumbia backspins not only charts a path through and beyond Latina/o sorrow, but also conveys an irreverence toward grief itself. As the song's self-abnegating lyrics are repeatedly undercut by her self-assertive skills as a performer, the performance increasingly appears to be winking at itself, self-consciously turning its back on its themes of despair in a way analogous to the repeated 360-degree turns she effortlessly executes throughout the song. This irreverence toward loss is evocative of the playful mockery of death expressed in Mexican and Mexican American rituals commemorating the Day of the Dead and other Latina/o mourning practices. The interplay between reverence and reverie thus registers as a recognizable template for and mode of expressing Latina/o grief.

The citational style of the performance and its dancerly approach to longing and loss are also, of course, what make this version of "Como la Flor" decidedly queer. The unabashed delight with which Selena appears to be quoting her own exceptional skills as a performer — the plaintive tone and measured pace of the opening chorus and the kinesthetic verve of the cumbia choreography, which together showcase her range as both mature, full-voiced songstress and dancing pop star — the knowing sense with which she plays up her range, establishes her as an undeniable diva within a queer pantheon.[57] In its queer aesthetics "Como la Flor" possesses a particularly disco sensibility, and not simply because Selena performs the song while still costumed in her purple-spangled disco diva pantsuit. The performance's simultaneous articulation of deliberate lament and propulsive pop beat resonates with, as Walter Hughes observes, "disco's representation of desire [that] always included the element of loss." Relinquishment to the "disciplinary, regulatory discourse" of disco's insistent four-on-the-floor beat was, according to Hughes, a performative practice by which gay male identity was produced and wherein gestures of mourning and survival in the fallout from AIDS has been enacted: "The lyrics [of disco] remind us that grief can control us as tyrannically as desire, and so our submission to the beat is still a necessary practice."[58] "Como la Flor" shares this queer dialectic of lyrical longing and conditioning beat. The song's cumbia gallop rides roughshod over its grieving lyrics, providing a disciplinary practice whereby Latinas/os dance through and beyond *dolor*. In particular, the disco ethos that permeates this performance of "Como la Flor" foregrounds queer ways of knowing within a sonic and kinesthetic practice of Latina/o belonging. Through its disciplining beat, grieving diva excess, and gender-ambivalent vocal address, "Como la Flor" queers the cumbia, that "musical passport" to pan-Latina/o affiliation, recalibrating the heteronormative logic that often constrains the rhythms marking latinidad.

"Como la Flor" makes room for a multitude of Latina/o bodies in Selena's voice, rehearsing their arrivals in the capacious space of her "Last Dance." The performance history of the song reveals the way it had been preparing Selena's audiences for her departure all along; it is therefore no surprise that participants in Selenidad take up the song, partake in its offerings, swoon and slide and succumb to its sorrow as a way of feeling their way through latinidad. To perform the longing of "Como la Flor" was to share in the collective grief around which latinidad cohered at the close of the twentieth century. In its simultaneous enunciation of arrival and loss, the song expresses and modulates the way latinidad felt in the years marked by English-only propositions and immigration and welfare reform. The Astrodome performance captures the grain of Latina longing in Selena's voice as she achingly elongates the *perder*, and in its kinesthetic directives to survive the *duele* by audaciously occupying the dance the song also continues to carry the pantsuit in her voice. In the years since the Astrodome concert, in the midst of celebrations of Latin culture and legislation against Latina/o bodies, many Latinas/os accepted the invitation to fit within and fill out "Como la Flor"'s generous dimensions. For even as the archival machinations of Selenidad may have altered Selena's purple pantsuit for museum display, Selenidad also illuminates the stages where the expansive measures and measurements of these performances remain.

TWO

Colonial Past, Tejano Present:
Civic Maintenance at Selena's Memorial

The long poem of walking manipulates spatial organizations,
no matter how panoptic they may be.
—Michel de Certeau, *The Practice of Everyday Life*

If I hoist my body up like some sort of graceless gymnast, pressing my
pelvis at just the right angle on the top railing, and then carefully shift
my weight to my right side, my right hand clenched around the rail supporting me, and then if, after securing my balance, I stretch my left arm
out as far as I can, palm wide, fingers splayed, I can almost touch her. But
not quite. I am standing beside, or, more accurately, leaning against the
four-foot-high stainless steel barrier that surrounds the *Mirador de la Flor*
memorial statue and pavilion erected in Selena's honor in her hometown
(figure 9). The statue, a life-size bronze replica of the Tejana superstar,
also leans, or rather is constructed to create the appearance that the body
is casually leaning against a white cylindrical column that extends above
her (figure 10). The bronze body, right knee bent, head turned to face the
tide, appears weathered from the salty air that rides up off Corpus Christi
Bay. The column's surface immediately to Selena's right is recessed and
covered by a mosaic of small square tiles from which protrudes a large
ceramic white rose sculpture (figure 11). Underneath the white rose is a
plaque with the following inscription:

> Selena was referred to as *La Flor* [The Flower]
> and identified with *La Rosa Blanca* [The White Rose].

When you view *La Rosa Blanca*, you feel her presence nearby.
Selena's stage is now silent.
Yet her persona enriched the lives of those she touched
and her music lives on.

Weary from such awkward leaning and futile reaching, I step back
and move around to view the rest of the column. I am surprised to find
its gleaming surface unadorned except for a small square plaque hanging
from the column just to Selena's left. This plaque asserts in both Spanish
and English, "Out of respect to the memory of Selena and as requested by
the Quintanilla family, please do not write on any part of the monument.
Thank you." I take note of the message but initially am more preoccupied
by its placement within the monument's overall design (figures 12–13).
This small plaque hanging on the column opposite the busy mosaic and
white rose seems out of place, seems to render the memorial somehow
off balance. I am struck by this design, by what seems like a lopsided composition. Why adorn two adjacent areas of the column with sculptures, as
opposed to two opposing areas? I return to my own leaning pose against
the silvery steel encircling the monument. This railing bears not only my
weight, but also the weight of several small metal signs in both English
and Spanish that say, "Show your respect. Please—no markings."

Like most signs, these signs and the small square plaque represent
more than they mean. Their bilingual pleas assert more than simply their
prohibitions, reveal more than simply the bicultural identity of the many
Selena fans who visit here. The signs also point to a performance history
concealed but not entirely absent from this monument. Most memorial
statues do not require the posting of signs that plead "Please—no markings." Thus the signs must be a response to the previous presence of markings. The signs may in fact speak directly to my unsettled response to the
memorial's lopsided composition. They actually suggest that something
might be missing, or perhaps even *erased* from (and replaced by the small
square plaque on) the unadorned part of the column. The signs ultimately
reveal that the memorial may not have always looked like this. These
prohibitory assertions ironically prompt me to search for traces of now
absent markings, for moments that contradict the memorial's inscription,
indeed mandate that Selena's "stage is now silent."

The Selena monument was mired in controversy from the moment of
its inception, as her local working-class Tejana/o fans struggled against

9. *Mirador de la Flor* memorial statue and pavilion (2001). Photo by Deborah Paredez.

10. *Mirador de la Flor* memorial (2001). Photo by Deborah Paredez.

11. White rose sculpture, *Mirador de la Flor* memorial (2006). Photo by Sonya Aguilar.

12. Unmarked column, *Mirador de la Flor* memorial (2001). Photo by Deborah Paredez.

13. Plaque admonishing markings, *Mirador de la Flor* memorial (2001). Photo by Deborah Paredez.

Anglo and Mexican American city officials and civic boosters over the function and acceptable forms of stewardship of Selena's memory.[1] The *Mirador de la Flor*, its whitewashing, and the suggestion of markings that persist, reveals the very processes by which civic identity is often forged in cities throughout the U.S. Southwest, wherein elite and aspiring Mexican American and Anglo leaders (re)construct city landmarks or areas that ostensibly honor their imagined Mexican or romantic Spanish past only to render invisible the cities' working-class Mexican American present. It is precisely through the maintenance of Selena's memorial, and the public battles it inspired, that the maintenance of civic identity and public memory in Corpus Christi is conducted and challenged. The struggle over the appropriate modes of memorializing Selena is ultimately a struggle about racialized and classed codes of behavior for claiming and performing civic citizenship.

Across the U.S. Southwest many city walls are conspicuously slathered with adobe-colored stucco, others covered with mission-inspired red-tiled roofs, and still others stand resiliently against sandblasted whitewashing. Anglo and Mexican American city leaders and civic boosters in Santa Fe, San Antonio, and Los Angeles have literally and symbolically covered the surfaces of the city with what Carey McWilliams refers to as a Spanish fantasy past that serves to conceal the historical contributions and current concerns of the city's working-class Mexican American inhabitants.[2] This Spanish fantasy past is strategically deployed, as William Deverell observes, to create and reinforce cultural, economic, and temporal distance between Anglos and Mexican Americans, and moreover is central to the promotion of the tourist economy.[3] In many southwestern urban areas the maintenance of the tourist industry relies on the labor of working-class Mexican Americans and their simultaneous absence from civic representations. Thus even when an imagined Mexican past is acknowledged and promoted—San Antonio's downtown *mercado*, Los Angeles's Olvera Street, or Corpus Christi's *Mirador de la Flor*—such civic commemorations serve to create a public memory that excludes the very bodies that labored over its making.

Public memorials often provide literal touchstones for these processes of civic selective forgetting. And yet, as Joseph Roach notes, despite the whitewashing function of these memorials, other nonofficial memories often persist, their corporeal retentions and reinventions hauntingly perceptible, precisely at the site of the very modern memorials that are supposedly responsible for their erasure.⁴ That is, sometimes these civic memorials misbehave. Selena's *Mirador* is one such unruly memorial, for inasmuch as its gleaming white walls are used by the city to promote Corpus Christi's white image of itself, the memorial renders visible racialized and class-based battles over claims to urban space and civic belonging. In this way the *Mirador de la Flor* is unlike most civic monuments across the U.S. Southwest that actually succeed in obscuring the historic and ongoing conflicts between working-class Mexican Americans and city leaders.⁵ In particular the actual contours of the memorial, with its full white blossom and the polished curves of Selena's statue, underscore the gendered labor of civic maintenance by staging the sexualized Tejana body as a mediation between labor and leisure within the political economy of the city.⁶

Corpus Christi: "Between a Fierce Plain and a Ferocious Sea"

The *Mirador de la Flor* is one among eight other miradors, or Spanish-style gazebos, that line the bay front along Corpus Christi's Shoreline Boulevard.⁷ All the miradors were funded by a local Anglo philanthropist and Budweiser beer distributor, William "Dusty" Durrill. Part of Durrill's fortune arose from misfortune: following his daughter Devary's death in an automobile accident in 1978, he established the Devary Durrill Foundation in 1986 with the $8 million insurance settlement.⁸ This foundation ultimately funded the construction of the eight miradors erected atop the city's seawall, a promenade known for heavy tourist traffic. In conjunction with the dedication of the miradors and in commemoration of the 1992 quincentennial celebration of Columbus's voyage to the Americas, the Spanish American Genealogical Association (SAGA) in Corpus Christi published a slick spiral-bound document describing the significance of each episode depicted within the miradors (figure 14). Inside each mirador hangs a plaque honoring a purported key figure or episode in Corpus Christi and south Texas history. The miradors descend in a linear progression from the northernmost plaque, describing the area's "First Inhabitants," the Karankawa Indians, "circa 1500s," to the southernmost plaque, honoring the "First Cattle King: Captain Richard King" and the founding in 1853 of his King ranch. On the walk in between I seek shade among a number of Spanish and Anglo "firsts": the "First Explorer: Captain Alonso

MIRADORES
DEL
MAR

A QUINCENTENARY S A G A PROJECT

COORDINATED BY

CLOTILDE P. GARCIA, M.D.

14. Cover of informational booklet about the bay-front miradors. Collection of the author.

Alvarez de Piñeda" (1519), the "First Chronicler and Healer: Alvar Núñez Cabeza de Vaca" (1528), the "First Shipwrecks: Spanish Treasure Galleons" (1554), the "First Colonist: Captain Blas María de la Garza Falcón" (1762), the "First Missionary: Padre Jose Nicolas Balli" (1800), and the "First U.S. Flag: General Zachary Taylor" (1845). Selena's memorial, which was constructed and dedicated in 1997—five years after the original eight miradors—is situated between the shipwrecked Spanish treasure galleons and Captain Falcón's colonizing forces. The *Mirador de la Flor* thus semiotically interrupts the romantic Spanish and Anglo settlement narrative of Corpus Christi's history set forth by the original eight. Selena's *Mirador*, located at the corner where Peoples Street meets Shoreline Boulevard, reinserts Tejanos—the very "peoples" conspicuously absent from the "key episodes" depicted in the other miradors—into the official history that punctuates this well-traversed tourist path. Her presence as a Corpus Christi Tejana, her body immortalized in bronze relief, unlike the other "key figures," insists upon the inclusion of the other Mexican American bodies who labored over the building of the city.

Walking south from Selena's mirador, past Captain Falcón and Padre Balli and in between Zachary Taylor and Richard King, I come upon a dismantled wooden bench, the weathered white slats and loose bolts half piled, half strewn in mid-deconstruction (figure 15). It is late Saturday afternoon in the off-season so there are few tourists on the promenade, but traces of other bodies are clearly discernable. The bolts are gathered into mounds near the stacked slats—remnants of the interrupted labor of off-duty workers, the gathering of materials suggesting imminent return. Until then, the sea-worn slats and rusting bolts await a new configuration; until then, the dismantled bench honors a history of a Corpus Christi laboring class silenced in the monuments that flank them.

Corpus Christi, a seaport located just south of where the Nueces River spills into Corpus Christi Bay, is the largest city on the south Texas coast. Much like the history of the greater south Texas border region in which it is situated, the city's history is marked by the interdependent processes of occupation and segregation and a colonial economic structure. Its history is thus also the history of social and economic struggle among Mexicans and Mexican Americans in Texas. The power struggles that ensued in Corpus Christi as the result of Anglo American expansionism during the second half of the nineteenth century and the establishment of a powerful Anglo elite in the area set in motion new forms of political authority, mar-

15. Bay-front bench under construction, Corpus Christi (2005).
Photo by Deborah Paredez.

kets, and land laws often implemented against the resident Mexicans by force and by fraud.[9] During this time Corpus Christi emerged as the first Anglo-American settlement in the disputed territory between the Nueces River and the Rio Grande. This region, now referred to as south Texas, served as a crucible for conflict during the years following annexation, in which the United States claimed the Rio Grande as Texas's southern border, while Mexico asserted that the border was marked by the Nueces River. This dispute reached its height in 1845, when U.S. General Zachary Taylor and his troops occupied Corpus Christi. In the year that followed Taylor asserted Texas's claim to the Nueces strip and used the area as a training ground for the Mexican-American War, which began in 1846 and ended in 1848 with the signing of the Treaty of Guadalupe Hidalgo.

During the years following the war Texas Rangers regularly threatened Mexicans in Corpus Christi with imprisonment if they voted. Indeed, throughout the state Mexican voting rights were denied and the people's land confiscated by law enforcement officials who were granted the license to kill Mexicans without recourse.[10] The power inequities between Anglos and Mexicans were further solidified by the rise of mechanization during the cattle boom of the 1870s and the explosion of cotton production into the 1880s that coincided with the emancipation of slave labor following the Civil War (1861–1865). Anglo ranchers responded to both the rise of mechanization and the decline of slave labor with increased reliance on Mexican labor.[11] During this period Corpus Christi emerged as an important shipping center for cattle, transforming the area from an isolated outpost to a regional market center dominated by landowning Anglo families and syndicates who were responsible for the area's economic restructuring. The injustices promoted by this political economic structure ultimately gave rise to Mexican cattle raids against the large, Anglo-owned ranches during the early 1870s, culminating in the Nuecestown raid (also referred to as the Corpus Christi raid) of 1875. In response to this raid, Anglo residents in south Texas retaliated against all Mexican residents by looting their property, intimidating and at times murdering Mexican merchants and farmers. This wave of violence caused many Mexicans to flee or to avoid Corpus Christi and its surrounding area and further secured Anglo dominance in the region.[12]

Large corporate ranching and farming interests as well as Anglo government officials capitalized on the increased number of Mexican immigrants following the Mexican Revolution (1910–1920) for an exploited labor base, while keeping Mexicans locked within this subjugated political economic position through the practice of segregation. Much of Corpus Christi's growth during the first half of the twentieth century was underwritten by powerful Anglo elite families such as the Kings and Driscolls, who sought to secure their prosperity and promote the growth of their ranches (located in the area surrounding Corpus Christi) by financing railroads, hotels, banks, and the eventual construction of a deepwater seaport in 1926 following a 1919 hurricane that devastated Corpus Christi's central business district.[13] As a result of these factors the population nearly tripled between 1920 and 1930 as Anglo and Mexican (and Mexican American) immigrants flooded into area.[14] The city continued to experience economic growth and a population surge from the 1930s to the 1970s due to the discovery of oil in 1930 that ushered in the petrochemical industry, the establishment of the naval station in 1940 that secured income from the military, and the promotion of Corpus Christi as a tourist destination, where "Texas meets the sea."[15] This economic growth was accompanied and in fact enabled by institutionalized and later de facto segregation and the continued relegation of Tejano residents to service industry jobs and second-class citizen status. These practices were decidedly pronounced in Corpus Christi, for even though the city passed a desegregation ordinance in the 1950s it remained one of the most rigidly segregated cities in Texas during the 1960s, with most Tejanas/os and Mexican immigrants residing in the Molina neighborhood. While Corpus Christi passed an open housing ordinance in 1968, in 1970 its Molina residents were still fighting for equal access to public school busing, as the court case *Cisneros v. Corpus Christi Independent School District* reveals.[16]

Given its reliance on the petrochemical industry throughout the century, Corpus Christi was especially hard hit by the decline in oil prices that shook the Texas economy during the 1980s. In response the city diversified its economic base to include greater reliance on electronics, steel fabrication, and health services industries, in addition to continued reliance on agribusiness, the military, and tourism.[17] This economic diversification still relied heavily on manufacturing and service industry jobs relegated primarily to the area's Latina/o residents, who by 1990 composed 52 percent of Corpus Christi's population and by 2000 had grown to nearly 55 percent.[18] While a small Mexican American middle class had emerged by this time, most of the city's Tejano residents were in the working class, with roughly one-third occupying the semi- and unskilled labor market.[19]

The beleaguered status of Corpus Christi's working-class Tejano residents was undoubtedly compounded by the Illegal Immigration Reform and Immigrant Responsibility Act (1996). As a result of the act, the McAllen sector of the border that includes Corpus Christi received the greatest increase in Border Patrol agents in the nation.[20] Despite this, additional immigration policy changes followed that allowed local police to arrest undocumented immigrants for crossing the border, thereby permitting local police to enforce federal law.[21] This policy change continues to prompt concern that local police use the measure as an excuse for racial profiling of Latina/o south Texas residents.[22] Thus for many Corpus Christi Tejanas/os, these legislative acts "put Hispanics back in the 1940s," as Dr. Xico Garcia, chairman of the Corpus Christi chapter of the American G.I. Forum, asserts.[23] The history of working-class Tejanos in Corpus Christi is not one of linear progression from peaceful Spanish settlement to agribusiness triumph, but one of continued struggle for resources and recognition.

The sun is beginning to set as I turn away from the expectant slats and bolts and begin my northward walk back toward the *Mirador de la*

16. "Building a Better Future," *Mirador de la Flor* memorial (2005).
Photo by Deborah Paredez.

Flor. The globed lamps that frame each mirador begin to flicker on; a
few burned-out bulbs refuse illumination, so several miradors stand in
half darkness. Construction debris blocks long stretches of the promenade, forcing me to reroute my stroll onto a makeshift and meandering
path that winds alongside the tourist walkway. The official path opens
up again near Selena's mirador, which, unlike the others, is alight with
people snapping photographs in the violet glow of dusk. How did Selena,
this Tejana from Corpus Christi with working-class roots, arrive here, so
well lit and pristine? The answer may require less of a look backward than
a look ahead. The angled arm of a crane hovers nearby. A sign posted on
white slats, anchored by sandbags, reads, "Building a Better Future. City
of Corpus Christi" (figure 16).

✂ Corpus Christi: Between the Valley and San Antonio

By the twentieth century's end, Corpus Christi continued to rely on the
petrochemical industry, the military, and tourism for most of its revenues.
Although the city shared the fallout from immigration reform with the
rest of the Texas-Mexico border region, Corpus Christi did not share in

the post-NAFTA economic boom experienced by other south Texas cities. Following the passage of the North American Free Trade Agreement in 1994, the border city of Laredo experienced "double-digit growth," and trade activity in the Port of Houston increased substantially. Corpus Christi, a gulf coast town closer to Mexico than Houston and a city larger than Laredo, felt only "isolated effects" from NAFTA largely due to the fact that the city is not located on a convenient transportation corridor with Mexico.[24] As a result, the sentiment felt by many Corpus Christi residents was that the city was "being left behind."[25] As one resident observed in an editorial in the local newspaper, "It would appear that companies are playing leapfrog and Corpus Christi is the loser. We seem to be in the no-man's land between the NAFTA-generated boom in the Valley and the NAFTA-tourism-medical-and-everything-else-related boom in San Antonio."[26] Corpus Christi faced the twenty-first century in dire need of innovative ideas for increased revenue.

Throughout its history Corpus Christi, like other Texas cities, attempted to build its civic identity and tourist industry on the narrative promotion of a Spanish-explorer-meets-Anglo-cowboy past. Anglo civic boosters such as Dusty Durrill along with city officials and aspiring-class Mexican American civic and commercial organizations like SAGA and the Westside Business Association (WBA) have funded a number of projects that imagine the city's past through the exaltation of Spanish exploration. While their motives may sometimes differ—for example, the WBA and SAGA have frequently recuperated Spanish myths as accommodationist correctives to prevailing narratives of Anglo Texan progress and land ownership—city officials and Anglo and Mexican American civic boosters have all contributed to the construction of this romantic past that strategically ignores the history of working-class Corpus Christi Tejanos.[27]

Despite these efforts at linking Corpus Christi to a Spanish explorer or Anglo cowboy past, the city has struggled with little success to articulate and thus promote its urban history in lucrative ways. This predicament is due in large part to the actual history of Corpus Christi's development and to its urban geography. Unlike San Antonio, to which it often compares itself, Corpus Christi did not emerge as a city under Spanish colonial rule. While many south Texas cities possess a history prior to Anglo-American immigration into the state, Corpus Christi emerged as a city after annexation following the U.S.-Mexican War, primarily as a result of Anglo-American occupation and industrial—not agricultural—expansion. The urban historian Alan Lessoff observes that the city's historic reluctance to reconcile the facts of its urban history has contributed to its self-promotion as part of Texas's Anglo rural and/or Spanish colonial, mythic past.[28] Sagas of and monuments dedicated to Anglo ranchers and Spanish explorers, such as Durrill's miradors, dominate Corpus Christi's civic imaginary and physical landscape, despite the fact that Spaniards did not settle in the city until the middle of the eighteenth century (two hundred years *after* Spanish conquest) and despite the fact that the city's economic history is based on urban industrial development. The city's investment in promoting mythic versions of civic history reflects the fact that more accurate representations of history would unmask an Anglo history of violence and segregation toward working-class Tejanos still very palpable in the present. And this narrative is simply not a marketable one.

The current shape of Corpus Christi continues to reflect its postannexation, industrial emergence. Precisely because the city is "unpunctuated by plazas" or downtown *mercados* and Spanish missions like San Antonio or long-established Mexican thoroughfares like Los Angeles's Olvera Street, it has had a harder time appropriating its urban geography and architecture to reclaim a mythic Spanish or authentic Mexican past.[29] The infrastructure, the contours, the actual structure of the city resist the claims it attempts to make. As a result, Corpus Christi has struggled to succeed in what has become common practice for promoting civic identity and public memory in many southwestern cities: showcasing a romantic Spanish or Mexican past while striving to render invisible the Mexican American and Mexican immigrant workers in low-wage, service industry jobs that ensure the tourist industry's maintenance. Given the challenges posed by its geographical layout, as Lessoff agues, Corpus Christi civic boosters invested in a Spanish explorer or Anglo cowboy past have relied on public sculpture to assert these narratives.[30]

One of these sculptures stands just south of the *Mirador de la Flor*, near the corner of Shoreline Boulevard and Lawrence Street. In 1989 the WBA secured financial support from the Spanish Embassy and from Dusty Durrill to fund the construction of the *Friendship Monument*, which features a statue of none other than Captain Blas María de la Garza Falcón, the "First Explorer" honored in mirador number 5, who in the 1760s led an expedition that settled Nueces County (figure 17). The statue, designed by a local artist, Sherman Coleman, and dedicated in 1992, depicts Cap-

17. Friendship Monument along Corpus Christi's bay front. Photo by T. Jackie Cuevas.

tain Falcón on horseback, his back soldier-straight, feet secured in stirrups, left hand grasping the reins, right hand lifted, conspicuously holding his hat instead of his sword. Three of the horse's hooves are grounded on the statue's base, its right front leg bent and head bowed slightly as if in midstep. But there is something static about its composition: posture too erect, front left leg too straight, hooves too firmly planted to suggest forward motion.[31] Despite its seemingly conciliatory midmotion equestrian benediction, the statue still somehow remains too tense, too stuck, unable to move in the direction of a usable past, unable to convincingly convey momentum toward the future.

Turning away from the statue, beyond the Selena memorial and the shipwrecked Spanish treasure galleons, toward the northernmost point of the tourist promenade where the ship basin spills into the bay, I discover what looks to be two antique-looking sailing ships. They seem out of place among the industrious tugboats and ocean barges cutting through the water. As I approach I see that the ships are docked outside of the Corpus Christi Museum of Science and History. The eight-dollar museum entrance fee grants me access to the ships and to a corresponding exhibit called Seeds of Change: 500 Years of Encounter and Exchange. Sponsored by the Smithsonian's National Museum of Natural History, the exhibit commemorates the five-hundredth anniversary of Columbus's voyage to the Americas by focusing on the "seeds"—potatoes, corn, diseases, horses, sugar—exchanged as a result of the colonial encounter. In the hallway leading to the outdoor plaza are small-scale models of the ships docked outside. Here I learn that the vessels are actually painstakingly reconstructed life-size replicas of the *Santa Maria* and the *Pinta* (figures 18–20). My first thought is, of course, what happened to the *Niña*?

Once outside I am struck by how small and forlorn the vessels appear, the small-scale models indoors suggesting a glory absent from the actual replicas. The ships seem, well, shipwrecked really, stranded here below the 250-foot Harbor Bridge and across the basin from where the USS *Lexington* is docked—another symbol of a military encounter displayed to forge civic pride. On the concrete area in front of the ships a few children gather, poking their heads through life-size wooden cutouts of Columbus, King Ferdinand, and Queen Isabella. On my tour of the ships I learn that the larger one, the *Santa Maria*, is called a *nao*, and the smaller, the *Pinta*, is referred to as a *carabel*. The guide cheerfully instructs me and the handful of other tourists that the ships are authentic replicas of the originals—from their riggings and rope ladders to their hulls, constructed from lumber taken from the same forest that supplied Columbus's ships, and secured by hand-forged nails—and that the ships regularly draw visitors from across the country. It appeared that since Corpus Christi could not rely on its land for a lucrative Spanish fantasy past, then, as a city where "Texas meets the sea," it sought tourist revenue and civic pride from the tales and machinery of Spanish seafaring exploration. But, as the Seeds of Change exhibit clearly charts, Columbus never traveled anywhere near Corpus Christi. So how did the *Santa Maria* and the *Pinta* arrive here? And where is the *Niña*?

The Devary Durrill Foundation funded what was to become Corpus Christi's most well-known attempt to promote its mythic Spanish history as a lucrative tourist draw. In 1993 the city made a deal with Spain to lease life-size replicas of the *Niña*, the *Pinta*, and the *Santa Maria*. Spain had constructed and toured the ships, known as *Las Carabelas*, in 1992 in honor of the five-hundredth anniversary of Columbus's voyage. Their initial visit included stops in eighteen U.S. cities, including Miami, New Orleans, Baltimore, New York, Boston, and, after a journey across the Panama Canal, San Francisco, Los Angeles, and San Diego. The ten-day stop in Corpus Christi during March 1992 was one of the most successful stops on *Las Carabelas'* journey, with more than a hundred thousand visitors and over $160,000 in ticket and souvenir sales.[32] In response to the turnout Corpus Christi's mayor pronounced, "[The arrival of the ships] brought my city together as I have never seen it united."[33] Soon after the visit city boosters formed an organization called the Columbus Fleet Association (CFA) and began negotiations with Spain to bring the ships back to Corpus Christi permanently.[34] With a loan secured from Durrill's foundation, the city successfully wooed Spain with an offer of $1.6 million, a profit-sharing arrangement, and a letter-writing campaign by schoolchildren from across Texas. Corpus Christi offered its residents the promise not to use taxpayer money to support the ships and the hope that the investment would boost the local economy.[35] Guided by these hopes of increased tourist revenues and by the need, as the mayor asserted, for a unifying symbol of civic pride, the city planned to dock the replicas near the Bayfront Plaza and to offer tours through these vessels of discovery.[36] Newspapers across the country as well as abroad reported on the ships' departure from New York to their new home in Corpus Christi; reports as far away as London commented on Corpus Christi's hope that "the gift would help to bring together the town's Anglo and Hispanic populations."[37] In an interview with the *New Yorker* Dusty Durrill proclaimed, "I thought the ships and the museum would be a major visible flag-flyer for our tourism industry. Columbus' name is known by every child in the United States, far more than the city of Corpus Christi."[38] Thus, through the celebration of the technology of Spanish conquest, Corpus Christi would make its mark on the map, would no longer be "left behind" in the "no-man's land" between the Valley and San Antonio, but would sail into the future in the hull of a Spanish fantasy past.

Unfortunately these hopes were soon shattered. One week after the ships' arrival a tropical storm blew in. Concerned that their bay-front location left the ships too vulnerable to fierce weather conditions, the city, with funds provided by Durrill, moved them to the navigation channel. This shift in venue caused a sharp decline in tourist revenues since the navigation channel, unlike the bay front, was less accessible and inviting to tourists. In fact, the ships drew only slightly more visitors and revenue during all of 1993 than they had during their initial ten-day visit in 1992.[39] City officials and the CFA hoped to recover these losses during the high-revenue summer season in 1994, but once again their hopes were dashed.

18. Advertisement for Columbus ships exhibit at Corpus Christi Museum of Science and Industry (2005). Photo by Deborah Paredez.

19. Life-size replica of the *Pinta* dry-docked at the Corpus Christi Museum of Science and Industry with the Harbor Bridge in the background (2005). Photo by Deborah Paredez.

20. *Santa Maria* (foreground) and *Pinta* replicas dry-docked at the Columbus Exhibition Plaza behind the Corpus Christi Museum of Science and Industry (2005). Photo by Deborah Paredez.

During an early morning in April 1994 two tugboats towing an empty 430-foot ocean barge collided with the *Pinta*, putting a hole in its hull above the water line. The force of this impact pushed the *Pinta* into the *Santa Maria*, causing substantial damage to the two ships.[40]

The CFA proceeded to dry-dock the two ships behind the Museum of Science and History after the city council voted in December 1994 to raise bonds for the construction of a concrete plaza to display the ships during their repair. The decision to build this exhibition plaza was an attempt to continue making money on the ships while they were being repaired instead of risking lost revenues by sending the ships out of town for repairs. The city and the CFA hoped that profits generated from the museum's increased ticket prices (from three to eight dollars) would generate the income necessary to pay for the $2.9 million plaza. Early on in the exhibition tour guides braved the south Texas summer sun dressed in fifteenth-century costumes, and the museum hosted educational Weekend Discovery Days for children and conducted courses on fifteenth-century boat construction and navigation. But the ships' repairs remained conspicuously unfinished, their exhibition on dry land actually worsening their condition by promoting dry rot and rusting hinges. The damage to the ships was exacerbated by the fact that their design as authentic replicas wasn't so authentic after all. The ships were constructed in part with pine, a less expensive and less durable wood than the oak used in the originals, and the *Santa Maria* was painted with a primer that trapped moisture and promoted rot, unlike the unpainted originals. When Spanish shipwrights visited the ships to conduct some of the repairs in 1998 they noted, much to the city's dismay, that it had not been necessary to move the ships out of the water after all. The $2.9 million debt on the unnecessary concrete exhibition plaza mounted. The ships still needed 400,000 dollars' worth of repairs to make them seaworthy. And Spain was demanding answers in addition to its $1 million lease payment.[41]

The CFA had apparently misspent the insurance settlement funds from the barge accident, directing the money instead toward the debt for the plaza construction and for the loan from Dusty Durrill. Outraged by these actions, the WBA filed a suit demanding to view the CFA's financial records. The CFA filed for bankruptcy in 1998, halted tours to the ships in October 1999, and sought to bring an end to its ensuing battles with the Spanish government and with other local civic groups by asking Spain to take its ships back.[42] But in a plot twist evocative of a *telenovela*, Dusty

Durrill, who had invested a substantial amount of money in *Las Carabelas*, placed a lien on the ships late in 1999 to prevent Spain from seizing them and proposed that local Latino leaders raise money to keep and repair the ships. In response one local Tejano leader remarked, "Dusty, I think, is well-meaning. But unfortunately, because he's put up all the money, he wants to call all the shots, and that turns off a lot of folks on my side of town. All those things he's built and paid for around here — in the final analysis, they constitute monuments to Dusty Durrill. We don't need a patron — we watched all those movies, and those days are gone."[43] Ultimately the ships that were destined to unite the citizens of Corpus Christi as they had never been united before only served to further entrench historic civic divisions between Anglo and Mexican American residents. As the *New Yorker* reported, "The wounded feelings exposed by this debacle, it seems, are less rooted in the conflict between Spain and a citizen of Corpus Christi than in Corpus Christi's conflicts within itself."[44]

The ships continued to languish, and reports on the saga of this "blemish on the city's history" continued to litter the newspapers.[45] By 2001 the city's Convention and Visitors Bureau (CVB) resorted to paying the exhibition plaza debt with taxpayer money, drawing from the city's hotel-motel room tax for the annual payment. Berney Seal, vice chairman of the CVB, bemoaned the fate of the ships: "The termites are holding hands, that is why they are still standing."[46] The ships reopened for tours in May 2001, but local residents continued to express their exasperation with the city's inability to rid itself of this Spanish fantasy past: "The expense of the ships has been a burden and costly for taxpayers. How long is the city to remain hostage to Dusty Durrill? . . . Every time I think it's resolved, the ships are back in the news. The city keeps saying let's move ahead, but it seems we remain dry-docked in 1492."[47] The ships had undoubtedly sunk the city's annual budget, which was ranked the lowest of all Texas cities' as a direct result of the annual $245,000 concrete plaza debt payment.[48] In the spring of 2006 Dusty Durrill finally released his lien and Spain relented on its demand for the return of the marooned ships.[49] But the battle left Corpus Christi beleaguered. The city was left not unlike the seventy-foot *Niña*, which had once proudly displayed her three stout masts and had operated for a while as a sailing school but now remained docked at the Lawrence Street T-Head, admonishing visitors with her "No Trespassing" signs, precariously afloat as a result of the slow leak she had sprung years before (figure 21).[50]

21. *Niña* replica docked along the Corpus Christi bay front (2006). Photo by Deborah Paredez.

A Multihued Mirador

As the dry rot and termites spread through the wooden planks of *Las Carabelas* in a scene that surely would have caused Queen Isabella to recoil in horror, Selena was securing her reign as the "Queen of Tejano Music." In fact, the month before the *Corpus Christi Caller-Times* reported on the now legendary *Pinta* and *Santa Maria* collision, the paper announced that Selena had garnered a coveted Grammy award in the Best Mexican American Performance category for her 1993 platinum album, *Selena Live*. Despite her international fame and rising fortune, Selena continued to reside next door to her parents in Molina, the working-class Tejana/o neighborhood in which she was raised and which some residents referred to as "Corpus Christi's Bronx."[51] As a result, many fans in her neighborhood and in neighborhoods like hers across the country admired Selena as a down-home girl who provided inspiration for success while never forgetting her roots. One twenty-year-old Molina resident said, "People think if you're from Molina you're not going to accomplish anything. But just because I'm Hispanic doesn't mean I can't do it. She proved I could."[52]

After her murder in 1995 Selena's status as "la gran muchacha del barrio Molina" (the best girl of the barrio) was further solidified, as the principal of her high school, expressed in the days after her funeral: "She was a celebrity. But she was still a Molina girl—somebody who doesn't forget where they come from."[53]

Selena as the embodiment of the Molina girl was made strikingly clear when, in the days following her death, thousands of her fans flocked to Molina and drove by her home in a somber procession, bearing messages such as "Selena Lives On" shoe-polished on their car windows. By the following day thousands more made the pilgrimage to Corpus Christi, transforming the six-foot-high chain-link fence surrounding Selena's home into a canvas of banners, photos, flowers, flags of the United States, Mexico, and El Salvador, and notes penned by visitors from throughout the continental United States, Puerto Rico, Colombia, and Canada.[54] In the years to follow local Selena fans and visitors from all over the world regularly paid their respects by visiting her Molina home, her gravesite, and her recording studio in Corpus Christi. In response to the high numbers of visitors, Selena's gravesite became the only memorial marked on Corpus Christi's tourism maps.[55]

This influx of visitors and the expressions of grief among Corpus Christi's working-class Tejanos caused alarm among many of the city's Anglo residents, who were, as a local Hispanic studies professor, Leonardo Carillo, noted, "fed up with what they perceive[d] as an excessive period of mourning for the star."[56] These concerns conveyed not simply a cultural misunderstanding regarding appropriate mourning rites, but exposed the long-standing tensions among Corpus Christi residents resulting from the city's political economic history that required both the physical presence and the representational invisibility of a large sector of Tejana/o laborers. Selena commemoration revealed these existing struggles precisely because it made the city's Tejana/o presence so publicly visible. As Carillo observed, "The Selena craze is even more startling to Coastal Bend Anglos, who are unaccustomed to Hispanic culture taking such a high profile. San Antonio milks the Mexican American culture for all we can get. But in Corpus Christi, people have been satisfied with it being in the background."[57]

Despite local Anglo dismay, city officials and local news reporters could not deny the potential tourist revenue that the "Selena craze" might draw.[58] Indeed, remembering where Selena came from became exceedingly important not only among Corpus Christi's working-class Molina residents but also for city officials tangled in the scandal of the Columbus ships debacle. Desperate for a united civic image and for a source that could recover tourist revenues lost from the damaged ships, city officials seized upon Selena's memory in an effort to repair Corpus Christi's tarnished—or, more precisely, dry-rotting—civic image. The city thus turned to Selena, that is, to its heretofore unacknowledged Tejana/o history, as a potential site of civic pride and tourist promotion. The Spanish fantasy past, like Falcón's horse mounted on its statue's base, had failed to carry Corpus Christi into the future, and as a result the city was forced to rely on its Tejano history for civic boosterism. Once again, albeit in an unprecedented form, Corpus Christi called upon its working-class Tejanos to clean up the proverbial mess of civic maintenance.

A short walk from the Corpus Christi Museum of Science and History is the Corpus Christi Visitor Information Center, where tourists can receive, free of charge, a special "Selena Sites" map (figure 22). In addition to her memorial, the map highlights the location of her gravesite at Seaside Memorial Park, her museum at Q Productions Recording Studio, and her clothing boutique and beauty salon, Selena's Etc., Inc. The city began issuing these maps in response to high demand and as a way to capitalize on the unofficial market of Selena site tours offered by cab drivers and other locals familiar with the routes of Selena's memory. The Selena memorial isn't far from the Visitor Information Center; it is, in fact, the only "Selena Site" located in the tourist district of the city. How did Selena, the Molina girl whose memorialization incited such ire among many Anglo Corpus Christi residents, arrive here, such a short walk from the Columbus ships and the (other) shipwrecked Spanish treasure galleons, within sight of Falcón's half-hearted wave and the flag-waving triumph of General Zachary Taylor?

Shortly after Selena's death, which took place in the midst of the Columbus ship fiasco, Dusty Durrill, perhaps in an attempt to divert attention from the ship scandal, initiated plans and provided most of the financial backing for a monument dedicated to Selena. Ever the astute civic booster, Durrill understood both the promise and the challenge of honoring Selena: "In Corpus Christi, a larger vision could coalesce for honoring Selena if more Anglo residents understood the importance of Selena in Hispanic culture."[59] Thus in an act of shrewd political maneuvering, Durrill circumvented the Municipal Arts Council, the civic office respon-

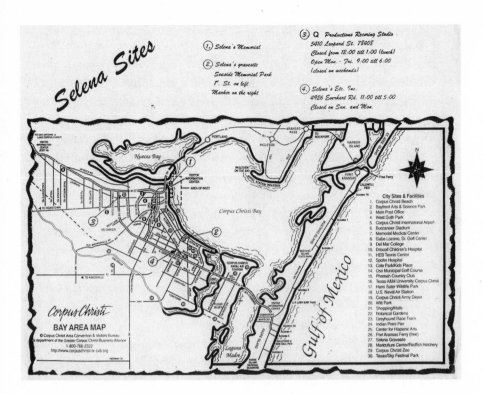

22. "Selena Sites" tourist map (2005). Collection of the author.

sible for vetting public art projects and largely known for its Anglo elitist artistic sensibilities. Instead he approached city council directly, playing on the city's need for a successful tourist attraction, and swiftly secured permission and additional city funding for the memorial's construction and bay-front location.[60] In response to the city's decision to provide financial support for a memorial dedicated to Selena, proudly displayed on the city's major tourist thoroughfare and not tucked away on the streets of Molina, many Anglo residents flooded the local newspaper with "rancorous letters" and Mayor Mary Rhodes's office with phone calls "of an ugly, racist nature."[61] One Anglo resident, Betty Brandesky, pronounced, "The Quintanilla family has a lot of money. Why aren't they building any memorials? I don't mean to sound heartless, but I just don't think we need to build a bunch of memorials every time someone dies. Who will be the next one they want to honor?"[62] Brandesky's discursive and derisive reference to "they" (local Tejanas/os? the Quintanillas? city council?)

signals the ongoing racialized and class struggles over competing claims to civic space that are embedded in the debates over Selena's memorial. For Brandesky and many other Corpus Christi Anglo residents, *they* who would remember Selena and thereby fund her memorial surely do not constitute a part of *our* public; civic citizenship is thus circumscribed to include only those who would choose not to publicly honor Selena. Brandesky's comment belies Anglo anxieties about the possibility that the city council's approval of the memorial might actually uncover and ultimately unsettle prevailing Anglo and Spanish mythic constructions of the civic history.

The dedication of the *Mirador de la Flor* memorial statue and pavilion on 26 May 1997 drew more than 250 people, including Selena's family, civic officials, and fans from as far away as Michigan. In his speech at the memorial's unveiling Durrill asserted, "I wanted to create a memorial to an incredible citizen of this community, who through her work ethic was an outstanding model to our children."[63] In addition to providing most of the $600,000 necessary for the project's completion, Durrill had enlisted a local sculptor, H. W. "Buddy" Tatum, to design and construct the memorial. The resulting monument features a life-size bronze statue of Selena standing against a column that extends above her. Immediately to the statue's right, a large white rose sculpture and plaque were affixed to the column. To the left of the statue, twelve wooden planks were attached along the length of the column to provide a space on which fans could leave messages of grief and admiration. Bricks engraved with the names of additional donors were inlaid into the pavilion's paved floor, and at the statue's base, a lengthy inscription included the following passage:

> Along with her beauty and energy, Selena's talent became a magnet for fans to identify with and emulate. Selena wanted people to live a wholesome life free of fear, drugs and gangs and she influenced admirers to get an education, attend church and respect families. Selena Quintanilla-Perez was a role model all communities need for their youth, and we are proud she was a citizen of Corpus Christi. — William Durrill

Throughout the afternoon and in the years to follow, visitors approached, running their hands along the surface of the memorial, posing for snapshots while standing near the statue, leaving flowers or hand-

23. Tile mosaic, *Paseo de la Flor* walkway (2005). Photo by Deborah Paredez.

written notes, and writing or carving testaments of longing and remembrance on the planks. The majority of the markings were characterized by brief, personalized messages, such as "We miss you, Selena," followed by the signatures or carved initials of visiting fans. Five months after the memorial's dedication the *Paseo de la Flor* (Flower Walkway) was unveiled. Over five hundred children from cities across south Texas had created the *Paseo*, a mosaic tile mural of white roses in honor of Selena, that stretched along the memorial's walkway leading toward the piers (figure 23).[64]

The monument's conspicuously interactive design set it apart from all other public sculpture in the city, and indeed transformed it from simply another mirador honoring a civic citizen into a memorial stage much like the Vietnam Memorial, where visitors could come to enact their grief.[65] The engraved bricks also encouraged visitors to linger, to adjust their posture as they bowed their heads in solemnity to read the messages underfoot—some officially engraved, others scrawled in marker—that paved the pavilion's floor. The memorial invited the gestures of loss and the detritus of remains: arched bodies, carved initials, handprints on the bronze from those who posed, arms encircling the statue for a photo keepsake. And the pavilion's walkway, with its proliferation of blooming white roses, provided a literal path, like the curtained wings extending beyond the proscenium's frame, from this mourning stage toward the future, as emblematized by the suggested presence of the five hundred children artists.

Durrill's written statement along the statue's base, in particular its reference to Selena's desire for "people to live a wholesome life free of fear, drugs and gangs," did not simply exalt Selena's wholesome, exemplary citizenship, but offered an instructive, cautionary tale to her fellow Tejanas/os, who are implicitly linked here with criminality. Here, as in many other official Selena memorials, the gesture of honoring Selena is deployed as a strategy for othering Latinas/os. The inscription echoes the rhetoric of the Texas State Senate resolution drafted in Selena's honor by celebrating her as the exception to her working-class Tejana/o community rather than one of its representative members. But since the *Mirador de la Flor* invited visitors to inscribe their own statements on it, Durrill's inscription was but one of a number of messages conveyed. In fact, in this initial design the informal conversations— "Selena Lives On," "Amor Prohibido [Forbidden Love]," "Stay cool, Selena"—along the planks and spilling over onto the white column consumed substantially more visible space than Durrill's comment on the step beneath Selena's statue. These other, multivocal comments, many of them written as present-tense directives ("Stay cool"), semiotically and rhetorically overwhelmed Durrill's references to Selena in the past tense.

Durrill's spoken statement at the unveiling, which was printed and circulated in the news coverage of the event, actually contradicted the exceptional positioning of Selena projected by his written inscription. His statement about his motivations for funding the memorial in some ways reflects simply the standard, officious rhetoric delivered at such occasions. But given Durrill's status as a prominent and well-known financial contributor to such civic projects as the miradors and *Las Carabelas* that sought to increase tourism by promoting a mythic Anglo or Spanish past, his acknowledgment of Selena's status as "an incredible citizen" and his emphasis on her "work ethic" (and not, for instance, her fulfillment of the American Dream or her extraordinary talents as a performer) carry significant weight in this region, where the work and citizenship of most working-class Tejanas/os have not historically been acknowledged. While the memorial undoubtedly contributes to the process of transforming Selena into an icon, this very iconization is not contingent upon celebrating her only as an exceptional Tejana, but as a working citizen not too unlike many of the city's other Tejana/o working-class citizens. Thus even while the Selena memorial perpetuates a practice of relying on the labor of the Tejana/o body to promote the city's status as a tourist destination, Durrill's comment at the monument's unveiling calls attention to this very practice. Instead of simply commodifying and packaging its Mexican culture (although this too is certainly occurring), the city promoted itself through the acknowledgment of the labor, the "work ethic" necessary for that process. In this way the memorial's unveiling actually unveiled, as it were, the very mechanics by which civic maintenance is achieved.

In the years following its dedication the memorial and pavilion became not only a destination for loyal Selena fans from across the world, but also a space of civic gathering for Corpus Christi residents, as Nick Jimenez, a local newspaper columnist reported: "Many cities have a place where people naturally gather. New York has Times Square. Mexico City has the Zócalo. San Antonio has Alamo Plaza. If any place in Corpus Christi comes close to being the spot where folks congregate more than any other, it's the area around the Selena memorial and statue on the bayfront."[66] Along with this congregation of bodies, the messages on the Selena memorial proliferated, refusing to be contained on the wooden planks. The written memories, proclamations of love and longing, scrawled messages in lipstick pronouncing "We Love You, Selena" across the outer petal of the white rose, and, more commonly, the etchings of fans' names and initials soon spread to the column and the statue itself.[67]

City officials responded by removing the wooden planks, despite protestations from Durrill: "The boards are serving a purpose. It gives people a place to write. Without the boards, they'll write all over the statue." When the markings persisted, City Park and Recreation employees were assigned to clean up and paint over the messages up to three times a week: "Each week, they rub a special solvent on the memorial in an effort to keep the personalized messages off the white center column." Other civic groups, such as the Junior League, joined in the cleanup efforts, arming themselves with gallons of white paint and brushes and organizing a two-day repainting event. When these efforts failed at preventing further markings the city reinforced its efforts—once again, against Durrill's protestations—by accepting bids for and eventually affixing three bronze plaques admonishing visitors against leaving their mark.[68] Throughout this protracted, three-year-long struggle, the markings continued to appear, transforming the *Mirador de la Flor*, according to Durrill, into "an emotional message center that we are unable to deal with. . . . The memorial is one of the city's major attractions, and we've got to keep it looking nice."[69]

This "emotional message center" sparked a series of editorials and public discussions about legitimate forms of "stewardship of [Selena's] memory."[70] An editorial in the *Corpus Christi Caller-Times* asserted, "Some seem to feel this is the only way they can communicate their love of Selena's music, and the sense of loss they experienced when she was fatally shot. . . . That, however, doesn't stand up under close scrutiny. Such acts bespeak more a hey-look-at-me attitude than they do true respect for Selena's life and music. What we have here, however well-intentioned it may be, is not veneration but vandalism."[71] In one editorial Nick Jimenez lamented, "The scribbling began on wood planks that were once attached to the column. Those planks, set up for fans to leave messages, were a mistake. Once begun, the notes took on a life of their own. . . . The bronze statue would have naturally taken on a uniform greenish patina as the metal weathered. But because the statue has had to be cleaned numerous times to remove writings, the metal has instead taken on a multi-hued look."[72]

In an effort to deal with this "multi-hued" "emotional message center" city officials, after meeting with Durrill and Selena's father, approved the construction of a four-foot-high steel barrier surrounding the monument. The barrier, which was designed with rounded surfaces to discourage writing, gained approval from city council in the summer of 2000 and was erected on 26 September of that year. For Durrill the "friendly barrier" made "trespassing very awkward" and reconfigured the memorial as "more of a sanctuary than an exhibition."[73] For many local residents, for whom the barrier was as friendly as Falcón's colonizing wave atop his horse, the barrier prompted public debates over the city's right to render Selena inaccessible.

Some fans, such as Sylvia Morales, expressed dismay over the barrier's construction, defending the markings: "'I think it's good for people to express their love for Selena,' said Morales, who compared the sentiments people write on the memorial column to those written on the walls surrounding Elvis Presley's Graceland mansion in Memphis, Tenn."[74] Some who shared Morales's convictions considered the markings "humble tributes from those fans who didn't have the $100 to buy an engraved brick in the pavilion's paved floor."[75] One concerned fan from the neighboring coastal town of Rockport, suggested installing chalkboards in place of the

24. Markings that persist at the *Mirador de la Flor* memorial (2006).
Photo by Fadi Skeiker.

removed planks as a compromise solution.[76] Others, like Ysmael Ybarra, expressed support for the need to "protect" the monument: "It's a memory. Why should somebody just come and mess it up?"[77] Ybarra's question is significant. What is it about Selena (and her memory) that invites its own messing up? What kind of work is this messing up doing?

The performances of messing up and cleaning up enacted upon the *Mirador de la Flor* constitute the racialized and classed battles waged over claims to civic history and citizenship. At Selena's memorial, my hips sore, teetering act forsaken for the moment, I shift my weight as I lean against the silvery railing and turn away from the statue to face the low walls and columns that enclose the monument. I notice at once the scrawled messages—"We miss you 4ever," "We keep your memory alive," or simply "Jonathan"—that persist along the whitewashed surfaces (figures 24 and 25). It appears that I am standing in the middle of an ongoing and spirited conversation. The improvised markings on the Selena memorial constitute what José E. Limón describes as an "urbanized working-class expressive culture" among south Texas Tejanas/os.[78] The continued inscription of messages, in defiance of the labored whitewashing, literally insist on

25. Markings of continued devotion, *Mirador de la Flor* memorial (2006). Photo by Deborah Paredez.

rewriting the history projected within the miradors that line the bay front to include Corpus Christi's conspicuously ignored Tejana/o presence. Remembering Selena at her mirador, especially in light of the Anglo outcry admonishing such remembrances, thus acts as an expressive cultural form through which working-class Tejanas/os (re)insert their presence within a city and region that historically has disregarded their citizenship rights.

The relentless whitewashing supported and undertaken by Anglo and Mexican American civic boosters constitutes an attempt to whitewash the racial and class conflicts that marked the city. Unlike the instructions for behavior offered at other memorial sites (e.g., Graceland, Villa Grimaldi, Oklahoma City National Memorial), the posted signs and the assiduous scrubbing on the *Mirador de la Flor* not only belie the city's fear of racialized crime (graffiti) but also suggest that the statue is not in fact a memorial stage for Selena's fans but a staging place for the city to promote a whitewashed version of itself. The imposed steel barrier separating visitors from the object of remembrance undermines the interactive impulse of most civic memorials; the steel fence surrounding Selena's statue reflects both civic attempts to control the unruly bodies of its own racialized underclass and national xenophobic anxieties that provoke the construction of more daunting fences and other technologies of containment.

Corpus Christi was, after all, eager to promote itself after being leapfrogged by NAFTA and after having its image sunk into the rotting ships of conquest. As Nick Jimenez's editorial remarks make clear, the city attempted to use the Selena memorial literally to put itself on the map alongside New York City, Mexico City, and San Antonio. In many ways Jimenez's tone echoes the despair heard earlier in editorials by other citizens who bemoaned the city's location in the "no-man's land" between the NAFTA booms felt in cities surrounding Corpus Christi. For Jimenez the memorial enabled Corpus Christi, a predominantly blue-collar gulf coast town, to reimagine itself as a more cosmopolitan locale, one certainly worthy of NAFTA attention and revenues. But, as Jimenez lamented, the memorial—its emotional messages and gathering bodies—also enabled the unprecedented visibility of the city's working-class Tejana/o citizenry, made visible the local reality of the city precisely at the site where the mythic past of the city presided. Suddenly, amid the effacing forces of the other miradors, the community messages of Selena remembrance took on a life of their own that demanded, "Hey, look at me." Jimenez's sentiment is echoed in Durrill's frustration over how the monument's emergence as an "emotional message center" was at odds with its function as "one of the city's major attractions." Thus for Durrill, Jimenez, and other civic boosters the desire for a "uniform" and not a "multi-hued" memorial is ultimately the desire for a uniform city, especially in the context of its concurrent, divisive struggles over the *Las Carabelas* controversy. The monument thus emerged as a metonym for a uniformly non-working-class-Tejana/o, cosmopolitan city where civic boosters strove to conceal its Tejana/o "mess" even as it exploited its Tejana/o "culture" in the name of tourism.

In fact city boosters capitalized on Selena's image of white rose chasteness, her "wholesome life," and hard-working purity as a way to continue the city's tradition of promoting its own pure, as opposed to "multi-hued," identity. Once the city elided its own ethnic and class purity with Selena's sexualized purity, it then leveraged this purity against the "emotional mess[ages]" of Selena's working-class Tejana/o fans, whose markings attempted to disrupt this very fiction of a projected pure or whitewashed city. Thus embedded in the debates over the appropriate ways

26. Selena statue faces the sea, *Mirador de la Flor* memorial (2006). Photo by Sonya Aguilar.

of honoring Selena are competing constructions of civic citizenship. In Corpus Christi civic boosters interpret the "excessive" displays of mourning Selena—markings that refused to remain contained on the wooden planks—as inappropriate performances of civic citizenship. The city then relies on this characterization of what José E. Muñoz would call "affective excess,"[79] of "an emotional message center we are unable to deal with," as justification for the exclusion and the erasure of the working-class Tejana/o presence from the "uniform" city. Selena, not unlike Devary Durrill, whose foundation following her death helped launch efforts at civic beautification, emerges here as the iconic dead city daughter, the Iphigenia, ensuring the maintenance of the polis.[80]

But the monument's overall composition unsettles the white rose purity so emphasized by civic boosters. I cease my leaning pose for a moment and walk slowly along the perimeter of the steel barrier, pausing near the narrow space between the white rose sculpture and the statue's own leaning pose. Selena's statue faces away from the white rose, turned toward the inscribed mirador walls and beyond them toward the sea

27. Selena statue leaning, with inscription, *Mirador de la Flor* memorial (2006). Photo by Sonya Aguilar.

(figure 26). The conspicuous turn of the head, the faraway look, the leaning repose all evoke a sense of aloof detachment—the figure standing alone in reflective thought—from the rest of the memorial. This staged isolation is compounded by the steel barrier that, in a gesture at odds with the ethos of Selena's persona, literally separates her from her fans. But inasmuch as the placement and design of the statue seem to sideline Selena from her own memorial honoring, the statue's seaward lean actually creates a semiotic tension that troubles the white rose purity narrative proclaimed by the rest of the mirador. The statue portrays Selena in one of her signature outfits: tight pants, studded jacket opened to reveal a studded bustier from which her breasts heave in a multihued patina, the faint trace of an inscribed and erased message persisting (figure 27). The statue's suggestive pose and outfit unbalance the virginal purity suggested by the white rose and by the inscription describing Selena's "wholesome life" encircling its feet. Here Selena's sexualized body—her white rose purity appropriated by the city or her heaving breasts, which provide a cleavage in civic history into which working-class Tejanas/os write themselves—is (re)produced through the struggles over claims to identity and citizenship. In this way the racialized and sexualized female body, the "very material of history," as Elizabeth Grosz writes, bears the consequences—the multihued breasts, the white rose against which the face seeks to turn—of the political economic struggles emerging from this urban south Texas context.[81] But the allure of the statue resides not so much in its various postures of sexualization as in the tension between the working-class aesthetics of Selena's dress and the conspicuously leisurely lean into which her body is posed. This working girl is not captured in the act of singing or dancing or any other labored act for which she became famous; the microphone she clasps in her left hand remains at her side while she casually leans in a moment of leisure. This posture, this mediation between labor and leisure provides a pose of aspiration for working-class fans seeking momentary leisure in the midst of their own laboring lives.

I continue to look over the mirador, the overlook, and ponder what it is I am overlooking. I look up at Selena's face, follow the direction of her gaze, toward the shrimp boats docked at the pier and selling their loads to the tourists who wander down from the pavilion and toward the replica of the *Niña* docked in disrepair. I shift my gaze back again to the bronze statue and observe that even as the memorial produces a civic identity contingent upon the exclusion of its Tejana/o citizenry, its multihued patina and off-balance composition also succeed in unbalancing this very construction of the city. That is, even as the memorial produces Corpus Christi it calls attention to the processes of erasure necessary for the city's identity to be forged. For the spectator produced here is also the Tejana/o citizen whose very evocation undermines the city's traditional construction of itself. We have climbed over steel barriers, twisted our bodies into defiant positions, written ourselves onto her—and the traces of our labor remain: the plaques admonishing markings, the whitewashed column, the multihued patina, the sore hips. The *Mirador de la Flor* requires a certain labor of its spectators, requires them to interact, to react, to enact their own subjectivity within the shelter of its walls. The reasons the monument provides an inviting stage for the enactment of civic citizenship become clear if we recall Durrill's comment at the unveiling, when he acknowledged Selena as an "incredible citizen" and honored her "work ethic," or if we simply read the inscription encircling the statue's base announcing the city's pride that Selena was "a citizen of

28. Messages of admiration amid official donor inscriptions, *Mirador de la Flor* memorial (2006). Photo by Deborah Paredez.

Corpus Christi." If the city promotes and attempts to refashion itself by honoring Selena primarily for her working-citizen status, then it is not surprising that those communities struggling for recognition as working citizens in the city or in cities across the nation would choose the Selena memorial as the site upon which to perform this very citizenship. The monument—composition off-balance, multihued patina persisting, bent bodies arched in acts of marking—thus acts as a repository for the labor that links mourning rites to the making of citizenship.

The *Mirador de la Flor* memorial statue and pavilion productively misbehave as a modern memorial. More precisely, the Selena memorial produces the misbehaving Tejana/o citizen who disrupts the city's fictions of mythic Anglo history and instead insists, "Hey look at me!" The memorial invites the frequently *overlooked* and disenfranchised to write themselves onto her, rendering visible working-class Tejana/o citizens who, by the very act of revealing themselves, misbehave according to the traditional operations of civic maintenance. Bowing in a posture of reverence, I see the bricks laid underfoot, notice how the engraved names of official donors are written over with Sharpie-markered messages by Selena's fans, a plane of interlocking palimpsests marking the contested terrain of memory formation (figure 28). Indeed, the spectator produced here is the misbehaving spectator, the spectator who seeks not simply to see but *to be seen*, thereby attempting to make visible the racial and political economic tensions embedded within the operations of civic maintenance.

The multihued patina, the off-balance composition, the defiant citizens climbing over the steel barrier all reveal how the monument acts as an index of the mimetic structures that produce notions of memory and identity. The monument bears the marks of the emotional mess(ages), of the attempted erasures, of the *processes* by which civic histories and identities are forged and reimagined. The Selena memorial, its sculpture weighted too heavily to one side and its white walls gleaming under the coastal sun, unbalances the very act of remembering—and forgetting. For even while city officials attempt to prevent the monument from being a palimpsest for working-class Tejana/o citizenship, traces of this act of erasure persist. And while the memorial may render Tejana/o citizens visible only to provoke the policing and attempted erasure of their presence, it provides the critical space to act out against this very practice precisely because of the ways the monument also points to its own process of erasure.[82] Indeed, while the statue's face points us toward the shrimp trawlers hawking their goods to tourists and toward the sisterless *Niña* docked just beyond the outstretched pier—that is, toward the operations of civic maintenance—it also forces our gaze toward the body of the Mexican Gulf supporting their weight.

Selena Forever, Latino Futures

By examining the relationship between collective popular memory and commercial culture, we may be on the threshold of a new kind of knowledge, one sensitive to contestations over meaning and capable of teaching us that a sideshow can sometimes be the main event.

—George Lipsitz, *Time Passages*

Arriving on the steps outside the Municipal Auditorium in San Antonio, Texas, for the official premiere of the musical *Selena Forever* on 23 March 2000, the crowd was surrounded by television cameras and crews reporting for English- and Spanish-language media outlets, representatives from the San Antonio Convention and Visitors Bureau distributing tourist information packets, and knots of young Latinas in Selena-inspired outfits shepherding their families through the crowd. On one of the landings Selena's father, Abraham Quintanilla, posed for a photo-op alongside two women laden with Selena paraphernalia—Selena-style caps atop their heads, Selena buttons pinned onto their blouses, Selena album covers in hand—as enterprising photographers knelt and clicked a few steps below them.

Once inside the auditorium, under the imposing banners advertising Coca-Cola and PMG (a retail and entertainment service aimed at Hispanic consumers) that loomed over the length of the lobby, spectators mingled among the musical's merchandise displays and a towering cardboard stand promoting *Estylo*, a bilingual magazine aimed at Latina readers that was launched among a slew of others in the years following the publication of the legendary *People Weekly* special tribute issue honoring Selena upon her death in 1995. *Estylo*'s editor in chief, Elia Esparza, stood in front of the display handing out free copies of the magazine's own Selena tribute issue, published to coincide with the fifth anniversary of Selena's death.

Across the expanse of the lobby the predominantly young Latina/o crowd performed a range of commemorative acts: girls pleading with their parents for a Selena Barbie, teenagers humming lyrics to Selena songs, mothers granting interviews with newspaper reporters, others pausing to peruse their complimentary copy of the *Estylo* special issue. Browsing through the magazine, amid the Selena homage and Latina beauty tips and Spanish-language Avon and Toyota ads, readers encountered a conspicuous two-page, bilingual spread sponsored by *Estylo* and the U.S. Census Bureau (figures 29 and 30).[1] On one page a humorous list enumerates "12 Good Reasons Why Latinos Should Participate in the Census 2000": "With the Middle Eastern crisis—so that they can distinguish the Joses from the Habibs"; "So that the border patrol and INS know not to deport Americans to countries they've never even heard of"; and "So Howard Stern knows how many people applaud his wife for dumping him on his ass." On the facing page a Spanish-language advertisement depicts a domestic scene of Latina/o aspiration: a young girl sits before an open notebook, guiding a ruler along a page as her doting father watches over her shoulder. The cozy living-room scene with its warm hues is framed by contrasting white letters:

> Ella necesita un lugar para estudiar. Lástima que no hay una biblioteca por aqui. . . . Su futuro está lleno de oportunidades. Y ahora que su interés por estudiar es más grande, lo que más necesita son libros, enciclopedias y acceso a computadoras: cosas que nosotros nunca tuvimos. . . . Por eso es importante llenar el Censo 2000, porque la información revela las necesidades educativas de su comunidad. [She needs a place to study. It's a shame that there is not a library nearby. . . . Her future is full of opportunities. And now that her interest in studying is greater, what she needs most are books, encyclopedias, and computer access: things that we've never had before. . . . For these reasons it's important to complete the Census 2000, because it reveals information about the educational needs of your community.]

After the lobby lights flickered and spectators settled into their seats in the darkened theater the musical began with the sound of a single gunshot and a wail of sirens, followed by a multimedia montage featuring

Census 2000
LATINOS!

Stand Up & Be Counted!!!
Estylo drives home points about Census 2000

¡Latinos!
¡Participen y háganse contar!!!
Estylo presenta puntos importantes sobre el Censo del 2000

In the early '80s, the Census Bureau couldn't tell the differences among Cubans, Mexicans and Puerto Ricans, so they coined the term "Hispanic" in order to count Latinos as one lump entity. With the Census Bureau's track record, it's no wonder that they still don't have a clue as to what it means to be Latino, much less how many Latinos are living here. This is your opportunity, Latinos, to be counted and demonstrate your strength in numbers.

12 Good Reasons Why Latinos Should Participate in the Census 2000

✔ So that the Republicans know exactly how many people aren't voting for them." — Entertainment attorney Jim Blancarte

✔ "So that when you win the top prize on 'Who Wants To Be A Millionaire?' they know where to send your money."

✔ "So that Paul Rodriguez knows which house to deliver your El Pollo Loco."

✔ "With the Middle Eastern crisis—so that they can distinguish the Joses from the Habibs." — Veteran comedian/TV writer Danny Mora

✔ "So that the Treaty of Guadalupe Hidalgo gets ratified by the U.S. Senate."— Film producer Moctesuma Esparza

✔ "So that the border patrol & INS know not to deport Americans to countries they've never even heard of." — Estylo editor Elia Esparza

✔ So the Gringo National Bank will build an ATM in your neighborhood instead of someone else's.

✔ So those dim bulbs at the English-language TV networks will finally figure out that Latinos not only watch TV but also spend money.

✔ So they'll build a library on that vacant lot down the street instead of another liquor store.

✔ So your district won't be represented by another old white guy.

✔ So the world will know exactly how many Latinos are not on welfare.

✔ So Howard Stern knows how many people applaud his wife for dumping him on his ass.

A comienzos de la década de los 80, el Census Bureau no podía distinguir entre un cubano, un mexicano o un puertorriqueño, por lo que decidieron utilizar el término "hispano" para contar y agrupar a los latinos dentro de un solo grupo étnico. Hoy en día, el Census Bureau aún no tiene idea de lo que significa ser latino y mucho menos sabe cuántos latinos viven aquí. Latinos: ésta es su oportunidad de que los cuenten y los valoren por sus méritos.

12 Buenas Razones por las que los Latinos deben participar en el Censo del 2000:

✔ "Para que los republicanos sepan exactamente cuántas personas no van a votar por ellos". – Jim Blancarte, abogado del espectáculo y "part-time" comediante.

✔ "Para que cuando usted gane el premio mayor de 'Who wants to be a Millionaire'? ellos sepan a dónde enviarle el dinero".

✔ "Para que Paul Rodríguez sepa dónde entregar su orden de Pollo Loco".

✔ "Con la crisis del Medio Oriente, para que puedan distinguir a los 'Josés' de los 'Habibs'". –Danny Mora, veterano escritor de comedias/TV.

✔ "Para que el 'Treaty' de Guadalupe Hidalgo sea ratificado por el Senado de los Estados Unidos". –Moctezuma Esparza, productor cinematográfico.

✔ "Para que la Patrulla Fronteriza (la migra) sepa que no debe deportar latinoamericanos a países de los cuales nunca ha oído hablar". –Elia Esparza, editora de Estylo.

✔ "Para que el Gringo National Bank construya un ATM en su vecindario en vez de hacerlo en otro vecindario".

✔ "Para que los ignorantes de las redes televisivas en inglés finalmente se den cuenta de que los latinos no solamente ven televisión, sino que también gastan dinero".

✔ "Para que construyan una biblioteca en ese lote vacío al final de la calle, en vez de otra licorería".

✔ "Para que otro cínico anglo no represente su distrito".

✔ "Para que el mundo sepa que los latinos no son los que abusan del sistema 'welfare'".

✔ "Para que Howard Stern sepa cuántos latinos aplauden a su esposa por haberlo botado a la calle".

29. Census 2000 promotion, *Estylo*, Selena tribute issue, March/April 2000. Courtesy of *Estylo*. Reprinted with permission.

"ELLA NECESITA UN LUGAR PARA ESTUDIAR. LASTIMA QUE NO HAY UNA BIBLIOTECA POR AQUI."

Su futuro está lleno de oportunidades. Y ahora que su interés por estudiar es más grande, lo que más necesita son libros, enciclopedias y acceso a computadoras; cosas que nosotros nunca tuvimos.

Por eso es importante llenar el Censo 2000, porque la información revela las necesidades educativas de su comunidad. Es para todos -ciudadanos o no- y la ley asegura que el Censo es confidencial; nadie tiene acceso a su información. Cuando reciba el formulario, llénelo y envíelo.

United States
Census
2000

ES NUESTRO FUTURO. HAGASE CONTAR.

30. U.S. Census Bureau public service announcement, published in *Estylo*, Selena tribute issue, March–April 2000. Courtesy of U.S. Census Bureau. Reprinted with permission.

highlights from Selena's life and career. As the overture came to a close audiences sat raptly as two Selenas, Young Selena and Adult Selena, sang the opening number, "A New Show's about to Begin." Following the show's second number, when the ensemble gathered as a chorus of "Los Sueños del Pueblo" (The People's Dreams) to sing "The Ballad of Selena," the musical turned quickly to flashback. Within its episodic chronicle the show uncannily staged the father-daughter mise-en-scène depicted in the Census 2000 advertisement, as Selena's father's own (failed) dreams of aspiration propelled Selena's journey from girlhood to the culminating moment of her crossover stardom. While the production showcased eleven of Selena's hits along with nearly twenty original songs, the first solo that audiences heard Young Selena sing as she gazed wistfully skyward on her front yard swing was the well-worn standard, "Over the Rainbow."[2]

Within this semiotically rich scene of Selena commemoration a range of commercial, political, and cultural investments in latinidad converge. To commemorate Selena on the opening night of *Selena Forever* is to cater to the Latina/o consumer, to cultivate Latina/o theater, and to lay Latina/o claim to the nation. The musical thus offers the opportunity to witness the dynamic interplay between dominant interpellations and self-generated assertions of latinidad. Latinas/os emerge here as a distinctly non-Arab, bilingual, musical-loving, consumer-oriented community rightfully positioned on this side of the border, a community that cohered in its collective devotion to Selena by sharing disdain for Howard Stern, whose derisive response to Selena's death was widely chronicled. In particular the resonance between the Census 2000 promotion and the musical's narrative framework foregrounds the centrality of young Latina aspiration in assertions of Latina/o dreams and desires. The slippage of pronouns within the wording of the census ad—the shift from third-person singular ("her needs") to first-person plural ("we've never had") to second person ("your community")—discursively constructs young Latina needs as the stand-in for both collective and individual Latina/o needs. The ad reinforces prevailing assumptions about Latino family values by positioning its readers as a community united in its custodial guardianship of a collective Latina daughter. As the iconic young Latina aspirant, Selena appears onstage as the surrogate par excellence for the failed dreams of her father's youth and, indeed, for the emerging *sueños* of her polis.

The details of *Selena Forever*'s premiere underscore the ways Selenidad was at the center of formations of latinidad—as market segment, as political force, as cultural process—at the close of the twentieth century. *Selena Forever* operated as a surrogational field for the convergence of claims to and contestations over latinidad. The process of surrogation, what Joseph Roach defines as "the enactment of cultural memory by substitution," is a common practice through which a community remembers and reproduces itself. This memorial process is invariably fraught with struggles over assertions of the community's past, present, and future. According to Roach, "The principle of surrogation clearly operates [when] . . . a powerful sense of affiliation pervades the community on the occasion of its most consequential single loss." Within this place of affiliation, "there also exists an invisible network of allegiances, interests, and resistances that constitutes the imagined community . . . a breeding ground of anxieties and uncertainties about what the community should be."[3] Spaces of surrogation thus cut across ideological and temporal divides, offering an illuminating view of the processes by which communities re-member themselves through the act of mourning one of their fallen members. As a site of surrogation *Selena Forever* held open a space for articulations of affiliation and anxieties about the collective history, representational presence, and future force of latinidad.

Selena Forever not only provided a platform for proclamations about what latinidad was, is, or will be, but also created a forum for the assertion of what latinidad could or should be. Inasmuch as the musical promoted Latino consumption or appealed to Latino patriarchy in its management of the aspiring daughter, the production also offered a space for expressions of the subjunctive possibilities of latinidad. In this way *Selena Forever* resembled nineteenth-century African American commemorative ceremonies wherein, as Geneviève Fabre notes, "the mood was *subjunctive*, the *ought* and *should* prevailed over the *was*. . . . As such, these commemorations [operated] as a *political gestus* which contributed to the development of the collective memory — not just memory of past events but the *memory of the future*."[4] Young Selena's opening rendition of "Over the Rainbow," the musical paragon of wishful thinking, sets the subjunctive tone of the show. The song's lyrical evocation of alternative spaces beyond the temporal bounds and geographic borders of the present offers an auditory (and all-American) cue for ruminations on what the history and future of U.S. latinidad could be.

Selena Forever was able to provide such an expansive surrogational space for latinidad in large part because of its genre classification as a musical. The U.S. American musical play has long been the place where artistic innovation meets commerce, where heterosexist plot lines are undone by queer identifications, where assimilationist lyrics about America are overshadowed by show-stopping rooftop mambos, where active and unruly spectatorship reigns — a place rife with pleasurable contradictions.[5] But given that Latinas/os have historically made up only 2.5 percent of touring Broadway musical audiences, why were Latina/o theater artists invested in transforming the memory of Selena into a musical?[6] In short, musicals are symbols of America; more precisely, musicals have emerged as cultural pathways to American citizenship. Historically the act of staging musicals was the process through which immigrant communities in the United States sought acknowledgment as Americans.[7] As such, the musical play offers elaborate expressions of the delights and divisions that shape U.S. American culture.

At the dawn of the twenty-first century Latinas/os enacted their collective histories, future force, and subjunctive possibilities as the nation's imminent "majority minority" on the stages and in the balconies and lobbies of the theaters whose marquees announced the arrival of *Selena Forever*. For Latinas/os, mourning Selena through participation in the musical — as spectators, producers, vendors, and performers — provided a compelling forum in which to decry past tragedies and concurrent anti-Latino sentiments that marked the 1990s and to imagine a future wherein they would gain significant representational ground as voters, as consumers, and as cultural workers in light of the Census 2000 projections and findings. In this political context Latinas/os mounted latinidad and engaged in national dialogues about the ways that latinidad counted.[8]

℘ The Census, Selenidad, and the Changing State of Latinidad

A year following our initial meeting at *Selena Forever*'s San Antonio premiere, sixteen-year-old Francisco Vara-Orta reflected on his thoughts about the musical and about the cultural force of Selenidad:

> If I could have changed something about the musical, I would have focused more on what happened after she died. [The play] needed to move past her murder. Many people think of Selena's death as just another tragedy, but Selena was not killed due to her own fault. I mean, it *was* a tragedy, but there was some triumph in what she achieved in death. When she died, this phenomenon happened. Because of her contribution to Tex-Mex culture, [Latina] girls felt someone like them was on TV — and not just for being a whore, a drug addict, a politician who forgot where they came from, or a Hispanic wannabe. Because of her work, I started to learn Spanish. Her *Amor Prohibido* album was the first album I ever bought with lyrics in the language my blood is rooted in. Because of her . . . Hispanics are on the stage and are drawing a crowd that many never believed would enter a theater unless they were going to sweep the floors. Catch my drift? Selena . . . made a lot of Americans wake up and smell the *frijoles*.[9]

Vara-Orta's rhetorical movement from his memory of Selena to a commentary about Tex-Mex culture, Hispanics, and ultimately all Americans not only underscores the scope of Selena's impact but signals how her tragedy offered many Latinas/os a narrative framework by which to critique the political economic positions of Latinas/os within the theater and indeed throughout the United States. In the context of xenophobic English-only campaigns launched throughout the 1990s, Vara-Orta's statement that Selena's music encouraged him to learn the language his "blood is rooted in" highlights the battles against "linguistic terrorism" many Latinas/os face as they struggle to maintain or acquire connections to cultural identity through the Spanish language in a nation that has historically legislated racist language policies.[10] Vara-Orta's desire for and subsequent articulation of an alternative narrative closure for the story of Selena's tragedy reveals how the act of mourning her invariably begets the imagining of a future for Latinas/os that moves "past her murder" and past a present rife with other tragedies to a space of cultural and political reclamation.

Vara-Orta's comments echo Roach's insights about the structure of classical tragedy and its relationship to the performance of memory: "The choreography of catastrophic closure—Fortinbras arrives, Aeneas departs, Creon remains—offers a way of imagining what comes next as well as what has already happened. Under the seductive linearity of its influence, memory operates as an alternation between retrospection and anticipation that is itself, for better or worse, a work of art."[11] Both Vara-Orta and Roach display the nuanced understanding that embedded within the classical tragic narrative structure as well as within the enactment of memory is a consideration of the future as well as the past. Roach ultimately derides the "restrictive linearity" of this Western narrative structure, wherein he posits the future as inevitably invested with the "fatality of the past," in favor of non-Western spirit-world ceremonies that refuse closure through an open-ended "euphoria" and not through "obligatory fifth act carnage."[12] Yet his insights about the classical tragic structure also suggest that the imagined future is not entirely circumscribed by fated catastrophe. Indeed, while the closure of Western tragedy requires that, as Roach notes, "the die is cast, the cast must die," it also invariably portends a particular future event: the subsequent change of state that will follow from the "fifth act carnage."

The act of mourning Selena, as Vara-Orta's comments suggest, constituted one of the most provocative and generative ways that U.S. Latinas/os articulated critical formulations of latinidad during the 1990s and in which they asserted Fortinbras's—or rather, Francisco's—arrival in the millennium. These hopes and anxieties were palpably evident in a now defunct website, "Forever Selena, Census 2000," one of the hundreds of websites that proliferated in Selena's honor following her death. The site appropriated the rhetoric of the U.S. Census, urging fans, "Show everyone that you were counted." Within the context of the widely publicized problems faced by official Census 2000 takers to count Latinas/os, the site's conflation of Selena commemoration with the machinations of the census carried significant, symbolic value for many Latinas/os.[13] Given that Selena was often revered as an embodiment of the traditionally undervalued aspects of latinidad, the *morena* (dark-skinned) and the working class, an affiliation with her, the website suggested, encouraged the traditionally undervalued Latinas/os in the nation to "get counted" and thereby proclaim their growing numbers. Ultimately the site's pairing of Selena with the census not only configured the space of Selena's memory as a safe and affirming place to register Latina/o presence within America, but also demanded that America take notice of the most often ignored and disenfranchised segments of Latina/o communities.[14]

Launched during the Census 2000 undertaking, the promotional process of *Selena Forever* captured the prevailing sentiments of Latina/o arrival. In an interview publicizing the musical's opening Fernando Rivas, the composer of *Selena Forever*, claimed that his score attempted to capture the ways that Selena's death "not only becomes a symbol of tragedy and failure, but also of hope for a lot of people that this type of thing [crossover success] can be achieved by Hispanics."[15] This crossover success can be understood not simply as a misguided assimilationist gesture but as a reference to the change of state that could follow from Selena's death, a change that permits other Latinas/os greater national representation. Rivas's reference to "this type of thing" signals not just a yearning to be included within existing national boundaries but an imaginative reconfiguring of the state for and by Latinas/os.

During the course of *Selena Forever*'s promotion and tour the U.S. Census Bureau's Special Publicity Office was spending more than $160 million on a promotional campaign aimed at Latinas/os, Asian Americans, African Americans, and American Indians. These efforts included the Bureau's own touring production, the carefully orchestrated Census 2000 Road Tour, which sought to increase minority population awareness about and participation in the first census of the new millennium. This ambitious promotional tour launched a fleet of Census 2000 Road Tour vehicles that collectively traveled to more than four hundred cities, reaching two million people at festivals, parades, schoolyards, shopping malls, and libraries during the ten-week tour, generating local and national media attention from small-town newspaper features to a spot on the *Today Show*. A number of Census 2000 Road Tour destinations specifically targeted Latinas/os, who, according to population projections, were estimated to constitute the new largest minority population in the United States, with continued growth over the next fifty years. Determined not to repeat the notorious undercounting of Latinas/os that occurred during the 1990 census, the Census Bureau also partnered with Hispanic advertising agencies and Latino advocacy groups such as the Mexican American Legal Defense Fund to create print and radio ads and other specially coordinated outreach measures directed at Latina/o communities. When, for example, the sight of the Census 2000 Road Tour vehicle caused undocumented migrant workers to flee, the Bureau enlisted Latina/o entertainers to perform at neighborhood rallies and set up assistance centers in predominantly Latina/o neighborhoods where Spanish-speaking communities could seek information and guidance about the function and process of the census.[16]

The Census 2000 projections and published reports about Latinas/os figured prominently in ongoing debates about the scope, nature, and contours of latinidad. Within this rhetoric Latinas/os were simultaneously touted as the nation's imminent majority minority population, gaining representational ground as a burgeoning market and a political constituency on the rise, and posited as a vexing demographic that failed to fit within the existing U.S. racial framework. Reports that 42 percent of Latina/o respondents refused to racially identify as either "Black" or "White" (opting instead to mark the "Other Race" option that debuted on the 2000 Census form) ignited debates about ongoing transformations of U.S. racial categories and sparked public anxieties about the uncontainability of the Latina/o population.[17] In response to the significant number of Latinas/os who marked "Other" for national origin, conversations about the consolidation of a pan-latinidad identification proliferated in a range of media: "Some observers believe that group [Latinas/os who marked 'Other' for national origin]—more than 6 million of the nation's 35 million Latinas/os—may be the first significant sign of a different kind of identity, that of the American Latino."[18] And while the census results reinforced prevailing constructions of latinidad as an established market force, the findings provoked clarifications about latinidad as a political force that was not yet empowered: "'We are still the sleeping giant,' of past decades, U.S. Rep. Charles Gonzalez (Dem.-TX) said at a press conference. 'The numbers don't translate into political power.'"[19] Within these conversations the power of latinidad ultimately emerged as a future force, as Cynthia Tucker asserted in the *Atlanta Journal-Constitution*: "The United States is a country not much given to looking back. It looks forward, and Latinos represent the wave of the future. Their sheer numbers—their clout at the ballot box, their spending power in the marketplace—will make them the people of color to whom public policy responds."[20]

In the midst of the Census 2000 rallies, road tours, and radio spots, the press release for *Selena Forever* offered its own claims about the transformational power of Latina/o representation: "Selena Quintanilla was one of the first Latin music artists to break into the American mainstream radar. Her amazing rise to fame in the music business is the classic 'American Dream' tale that makes a great musical. . . . Selena, poised to make the leap into English pop, had captured the hearts and minds of her Latino fans long before registering on the mainstream map. She became, in essence, a glimmer of the future, a testament to the changing character of the mainstream itself."[21] The tone of the press release captures both the anxieties and the anticipation that marked broader public discussions about the state of Latinas/os, or, more precisely, about Latinas/os and their role as citizens of the state. Latinas/os are depicted here as reliable barometers for predicting broader U.S. cultural tastes—as fans of Selena prior to her mainstream success—and are thus apt candidates for entry into the American Dream. The press release offers a sense of promise for the imminent incorporation of Latinas/os into the mainstream, not in an assimilative process, but as agents of transformation that will change the very character of the mainstream.

During the course of the musical's brief national production tour census reports indicated that more than 35 million Latinos—three million more than anticipated—were living in the United States.[22] Nearly half of all Latinas/os resided in Texas and California, the two states that bookended *Selena Forever*'s tour.[23] One striking fact that received prominent attention was the youthfulness of Latinas/os: "'More than a third of the Latino population (nationwide) is under 18,' said Sonia Pérez, a researcher at the National Council of La Raza. 'That's extremely significant. These kids are going to be the future taxpayers. They're going to be the future work force.'"[24] In this context the $2 million musical proclaimed its own record-breaking labor: "The title role is one of the most demanding ever written in American musical theatre. The leading lady is given more than 14 solos to sing during the two-hour show—compared with eight given to Ethel Merman in *Gypsy*—a new record."[25] To evoke Ethel Merman is to evoke the "queen of Broadway," whose performance as Momma Rose in the 1959 Broadway production of *Gypsy* is widely considered to be one of the greatest in musical history.[26] Merman was renowned for her unrestrained, belting voice; the theater critic Martin Gottfried described her as "so innocently obsessed with gripping the audience she felt no embarrassment as she strode downstage, planted both feet squarely beneath her, reared back, and blasted the back wall of the balcony."[27] The comparison between *Selena Forever's* leading lady and the powerhouse Ethel Merman situates Latinas/os securely within the pantheon of American culture workers and, in light of public discussions about Latinas/os as the nation's future workforce, insists that Latina/o labor be valued. Here exceptional vocal power becomes a way of showcasing Latina/o labor power.

Selena ~~Forever~~ for a Limited Run

As an ambitious attempt to combine elements of a Tejano music concert with recent pop opera conventions of the Broadway musical, *Selena Forever* was the first nationally touring Latina/o production in the history of U.S. musical theater (figure 31). The play's producers, librettist, composer, and director were all seasoned professionals in the theater business.[28] Casting calls were broadcast on the popular Univisión talk show *Cristina*, and a national search for the cast was conducted in Los Angeles and New York, in addition to San Antonio, Dallas, and Corpus Christi. *Latina* magazine even featured a story about young women auditioning for the role of Selena in its March 2000 issue.[29] The show's press release announced that the musical was originally scheduled to tour eight cities, concentrated in the Southwest and Chicago. Following this preliminary tour the production team hoped the show would eventually make it to Broadway; as one news article announced, "They're banking on a barrio-to-Broadway phenomenon that doesn't lose touch with its roots, said director Bill Virchis."[30] But despite these Broadway-bound aspirations *Selena Forever* was abruptly canceled after a six-city tour throughout Texas and in Chicago.

The musical's book follows a formulaic biographical narrative, chronicling Selena's life from childhood aspirations to her crossover musical success as an emerging adult. As such the plot fits squarely within official narratives that frame Selena's career as a journey, complete with product

31. Program cover for *Selena Forever* (2000). Collection of the author.

placements positioned like billboards along the way, toward the American Dream. Like most touring musicals *Selena Forever* relied on corporate sponsorship—in this case, from Coca-Cola and Southwest Airlines—to finance its $2 million budget.[31] Its thirty-member cast, of whom 95 percent were Latinas/os, persuasively demonstrates that the lack of Latina/o representation throughout mainstream media is by no means due to a dearth of Latina/o acting talent. In fact, as a result of the lead role's demanding requirements, two promising Latina actresses, Veronica Vazquez and Rebecca Valadez, shared the role of the Adult Selena. The set resembled a concert stage with platforms framed by scaffolding and backed by screens that showed both video footage of Selena and live-action projections of Vazquez and Valadez as Selena during the staged concert scenes. According to the costume designer, many of the costumes were drawn from Selena's own renderings.[32] The lighting design, with its multihued pyrotechnic displays, followed the stage design's attempt to evoke the atmosphere of a concert tour. The musical's thirty-five songs included a number of Selena hits interspersed among original compositions influenced by and often derivative of the styles of other big-budget musicals such as *Pump Boys and Dinettes* and *The Wiz*. And while the musical sought to create a stage hybrid through its mixture of Selena's Tejano repertoire and Fernando Rivas's original score, the conspicuous lack of intermingling of Tejano rhythms and traditional American musical styles within the score served ultimately to reinforce the discrete categorization between Tejano and American music.[33]

As much of the press coverage about *Selena Forever* noted, the musical's audience was composed largely of intergenerational Latina/o families, many of whom were not regular theatergoers.[34] A number of news features focused substantial attention on how the production sought to deal with (this traditional absence of) Latina/o spectatorship within the theater. One description of the scene at the musical's premiere in San Antonio noted, "The crowd at the preview show Wednesday night certainly was not typical for a stage musical. . . . A [Latina] woman . . . gingerly approached an usher and, pointing to the programs in his hand, asked in a soft, uncertain voice, 'Sir, can I have one of . . . those? Whatever they are.' She said she had never been to the theater."[35] Another news report acknowledged that the musical had succeeded in accomplishing what other mainstream theatrical endeavors had heretofore been unable to do: "Broadway or not, the musical's opening in San Antonio brought a large number of Hispanics into Municipal auditorium — quite a feat as producers across the country are trying to figure out ways of getting Hispanics and other minorities in the seats. Many fans at the opening night said that it was their first time to a real theater. . . . 'I don't usually go to the theater,' said Myra Martinez of San Antonio. 'I get that feeling from a lot of people here — the only reason we're out here is because it's Selena. . . . We loved her and this is our way of mourning.'"[36]

These depictions of Latinas/os as neophyte theatergoers eventually figured prominently in the debates over the show's abrupt cancellation in May 2000 in Los Angeles, as a comment from the *San Diego Union-Tribune* makes clear: "Unlike any tried and true musical productions where there are strong advance ticket sales, *Selena Forever* was aimed at a market that wasn't so theater savvy."[37] The show's cancellation ostensibly resulted from a dispute over marketing between the show's producers and the Los Angeles promoters at the Universal Amphitheatre, where the musical was scheduled for a five-day run; however, interviews published in news features covering the controversy pointed to Latinos' inability to perform proper theater etiquette as the source of the show's woes. Both the show's production team and the Los Angeles promoters frequently evoked this depiction of Latino spectatorship in their criticisms of one another. When promoters used low advance ticket sales as evidence that Latinos were unreliable and unskilled theater audiences, the show's representatives rebuffed their claim by arguing that advance ticket sales were an unreliable gauge because Latinos were "last minute ticket buyers."[38] Unfortunately in the production team's efforts to call for a different marketing strategy, they ironically directed the blame for poor sales onto Latina/o failure to adequately perform as appropriate theater spectators.

These discussions about the purported lack of theater savvy among Latino audiences relied upon and reinforced the assumption that Latinas/os operate outside dominant norms for cultured behavior and, by extension, for proper citizenship.[39] The theater operated in this context as a disciplining force attempting to condition Latinas/os to appropriate codes of (spectator, consumer, and citizen) conduct, but Latinas/os purportedly lacked the savvy, appearing instead as a constituency that not could not be counted (i.e., by census machinations) nor counted upon. Moreover, the preoccupation with etiquette, a behavioral code historically deployed to reinforce class and racial hierarchies primarily through the disavowal of its own racialized and bourgeois markings, strategically obscured the ways that larger political economic forces may have prevented many Latinas/os from purchasing tickets in advance or the ways that theater's historical exclusion of Latinas/os may have contributed substantially to their purported lack of theater savvy. We need only recall Francisco Vara-Orta's earlier comment that within the theater's traditional history Latinas/os have generally been invited in only to "sweep the floors." Unfortunately the production team's attempt to promote Selena and those who flocked to remember her as aspirants of the American Dream was undermined by these depictions of Latinas/os as beyond the borders of America(n theater). These discussions act as examples of the ways that Latinas/os are constructed, as Arlene Dávila observes, as authentic and marketable but ultimately foreign subjects.[40]

This preoccupation with Latinos' lack of theater savvy obscured the more feasible reasons for the show's failures. The musical's premiere drew approximately three thousand audience members; at performances following opening night in San Antonio, Los Angeles, and other cities audience numbers did, in fact, decline, but this decline was not necessarily due to a lack of Latina/o theater savvy. One of the members of the touring production team, Jerry Ortiz, observed the generational and class standing of many audience members from his position as concession vendor:

> We noticed a lot about the show from where we were. As people came in, mostly Mexican, it was obvious [that] they were not wealthy. They would come in with their entire family to see the show . . . it could be expensive for a family . . . sometimes tickets were thirty or forty dollars each and the things at the concession stand cost a bit also. . . . Imagine! At some shows, one of the producers would lower the prices to make it more affordable or would give tickets away to local high schools. The audience that came to the show was made up of the people that loved Selena, her fans, down-home people, many young kids came with their parents and grandparents. They paid whatever it cost.[41]

Precisely because the event may have been understood by many as a family activity, even the least expensive ticket prices ($19.95) may have been prohibitive for a number of working-class Latina/o families, or, as Ortiz notes, the "down-home people" who constituted a large part of Selena's fan base. A possible reason for the low turnout in Chicago, for example, may have been the fact that its venue, the Rosemont Theatre, is difficult to access by public transportation.

Following the show's cancellation director Bill Virchis decried the fact that the producers had neglected to inform him that the musical would be a nonunion production employing amateur actors and had begun casting the show before he was hired on as director. He noted that preliminary casting was conducted without a director, musical director, or choreographer being present, a scenario virtually unheard of in the professional theater world. Virchis also disagreed with the producers' decision to open the show in south Texas (the region Selena called home) rather than in a major city outside of Texas: "That's literally like starting in Graceland and doing Elvis."[42] His comments suggest that a lack of professionalism and vision among the show's producers and not among the show's spectators may have contributed substantially to the musical's ultimate demise.

Eduardo Cancela, general manager and vice president of KLAX-FM, a popular Spanish-language radio station in Los Angeles, claimed that the show's cancellation was due solely to poor marketing: "[Cancela] said he knew nothing about the show, even though KLAX is one of the few stations that still play Selena's music. 'I can't believe in a city with 5 million Latinos, you can't find an audience for a show like that. She's huge. . . . Something like this, it's all in the marketing. I don't think they got the word out very well. We didn't get any ads. I haven't seen ads anywhere.'"[43] Cancela's remarks, like Virchis's complaints, undermine the premise that the ultimate source of the production's problem was Latinos' inability to master theatergoing etiquette.

The musical was ultimately resurrected and remounted as *Selena: A Musical Celebration of Life* by the Ricardo Montalban Nosotros Foundation, which sought to restage the production as a way to launch a Latino performance center at the Doolittle Theater on Hollywood Boulevard (figure 32).[44] Jerry Velasco, the Foundation's president, proclaimed, "[Establishing a Latino-run theater] has been 31 years [in the making]. It's Ricardo Montalban's dream that is at stake here."[45] Alas, Selena would live on as the surrogate through which Montalban's dreams of asserting a Latina/o presence within the Los Angeles theater scene would be realized.

Despite prevailing attention to the Latino market in such major U.S. cities as Los Angeles, marketing problems also plagued the remounted version of the musical. According to Margarita Martinez-Cannon, the production's general manager, the show was "overproduced to begin with, and there wasn't much money left for advertising."[46] These financial constraints invariably led to what amounted to a "low-profile marketing campaign" that relied heavily on word of mouth, free publicity in the city's Spanish-language newspapers, and a limited promotional deal with Coca-Cola. Throughout March 2001 promotional messages were attached to Coke bottles offering $10 tickets when four or more were bought. Additionally, coupons offering two-for-one ticket deals on weeknight performances were mounted near Coke displays in twenty-five to thirty Vons supermarkets. Unfortunately the Coke promotion ended weeks before the show's official premiere on 19 April 2001.[47] These efforts reveal the operations by which latinidad is often understood as, and indeed reduced to the category of capital.[48] The musical's unsuccessful reliance on the city's Spanish-language newspapers belies the assumption that Latinos are served exclusively by Spanish-language media outlets, while the ill-coordinated Coca-Cola promotion highlights that Latinos are overdetermined as consumers and not as potential arts patrons within American culture.

32. Program cover for *Selena: A Musical Celebration of Life* (2001).
Collection of the author.

The musical's plot also projected Latinas/os within consumerist frames and ultimately succumbed to the patriarchal impulses that sometimes circumscribe the process of surrogation. Young Selena expresses her aspiration for success and for greater representational visibility for all Latinas as a wish for a commodity: "I wish they'd make dolls that look like me!" Given the prevalence of Selena Barbies sold at the show, Young Selena's articulation of her dream actually operates as an advertisement for Selena merchandise. Latina/o dreams are thus channeled through the marketplace, as both Young Selena and the audience to whom her "dream" is advertised are constructed as aspiring consumers. Furthermore Selena's dreams are narratively and musically channeled through the dreams of her father. In one of the play's early musical numbers, "Abraham's Dream," Selena's father details the racism faced by his doo-wop band in their attempt at stardom many years before. When, during the song's reprise near the middle of the first act, Selena takes up and completes the final bars of "Abraham's Dream," she is positioned as the surrogate through whom her father's unfulfilled desires will be enacted. Through this staged overlap, the progressive fight against racism is achieved by the father's discursive or melodic management of the daughter. In fact the musical number near the play's close, "You're Too Trusting, Selena," suggests that Selena's tragic flaw and eventual downfall emerged as a result of her *refusal* to heed her father's warnings about her fan club president. The musical thereby attributes the blame for Selena's death to her deviance from her father's management and reveals how capitalist values and Latino patriarchy converge within the production.

Even in its depiction of Selena's momentary rebellion against her father and her achievement of musical stardom the plot continues to position Latina aspiration squarely within marketplace values. When Selena, much to her father's dismay, falls in love with her guitar player, Chris Pérez, the two lovers meet for a clandestine rendezvous at a local pizza parlor. Upon her return from the restaurant, where they consummated their desire with a kiss, Selena relates the story to her sister in a song titled, "Pizza and Coke."[49] Escape from the strict Latino father is permitted, and love is achieved, through the consumption of all-American commodities. Thus even Selena's romantic narrative is framed within an assimilationist narrative of crossover into the U.S. market. In a scene depicting a pivotal moment in Selena's rise to crossover fame, the actress playing Selena takes a telephone call from Coca-Cola representatives seeking her as a spokesperson while a video of the real Selena accepting a 1987 Tejano Music Award for Best Female Vocalist is projected above her. This narrative and visual frame resonate with mainstream celebrations of Selena that explicitly link her success to an attachment to market forces and that acknowledge Latinos within the U.S. American imaginary primarily as consumers.

The musical's patriarchal plotting relies heavily on surrogational scenarios. Given that Selena and Pérez eloped, her biography does not fit neatly into the conventional marriage plot often coerced by many traditional biographies. Despite this deviation the musical insists on staging Selena's sister's wedding in lieu of staging Selena's own illicit adventure. Suzette's wedding, a seemingly superfluous scene that serves no narrative purpose in the development of the plot, thus clearly acts as a proxy for (the lack of) Selena's wedding. Another moment of surrogation emerges in the scene immediately following Suzette's wedding, which, given the musical's preoccupation with Abraham and Selena's relationship, takes a predictably Oedipal turn. The scene positions Selena in a backyard swing that reprises an early moment in the play wherein Young Selena sat and sang her wistful rendition of "Over the Rainbow." In the postelopement scene Selena is dressed in her white bridesmaid dress from Suzette's wedding and swings while her father stands beside her as they reconcile the news of her forbidden act (and the fact that he learned of it on the radio). At one point Selena concedes apologetically to her father, "I know you wanted a big wedding." The scene culminates with Abraham responding with the melodic ballad "If Tomorrow," in which he assures Selena that he would still love her even if she "had never become a star." As Abraham concludes his song a projected image of a wedding portrait of Selena and Pérez emerges above them. Ostensibly the scene depicts a father-daughter reconciliation, yet its staging of loving vows between Selena and Abraham, its order of sequencing immediately following the wedding scene, and Selena's white wedding party costume invariably reinscribe Oedipal overtones found by feminist spectators in the film version of Selena's life.[50]

The cutting of two musical numbers, "My Daughter Wants to Be Just Like Selena" and "Dress Like Selena," reinforced the musical's overdetermined focus on the father-daughter relationship motivating Selena's success.[51] The former song was sung by the mothers of young girls, while the latter accompanied a fashion show sequence that showcased Selena's original designs and the young Latinas seeking to dress like her. The omission of mother-daughter bonding within the space of Selenidad speaks to the ways that Latina mothers and daughters, who composed a substantial portion of Selena's fan base, were everywhere, but nowhere in the staging of many Selena commemorations.[52] The disappearance of the fashion show scene also precluded an interpretation of Selena's entrepreneurial endeavors as aspirational acts that were not tied to patriarchal dreams, but instead facilitated young Latina identification.

And yet, despite *Selena Forever*'s market-driven father-knows-best plotting and promotional projections of Latinas/os as unreliable spectator-citizens, audiences, like most savvy musical spectators, engaged in active and actively resistant ways. At a Sunday matinee in Chicago a middle-aged woman waved a Mexican flag and sang along during Selena's concert scenes, offering a glimpse into the ways that Selenidad provides a space for the assertion of transnational Latina/o citizenship. In response to a scene wherein Selena defies her father's restrictions against her desire to wear her trademark sexually suggestive outfits, a Latina teenager in the audience at a San Antonio performance screamed out, "Go Selena!" This young woman's response signals how the patriarchal plotting that frequently framed Selena's story offered many Latinas a recognizable narrative against which they were emboldened—like Selena—to articulate emerging Latina subjectivities.[53] These Latina engagements with the musical, along with the cut musical numbers, suggest that if we venture beyond the official staging of *Selena Forever* to the balconies and lobbies and other proverbial sideshows, we can gain insights about the subjunctive potentials of Selenidad.

Scenes of the Subjunctive

SCENE I: SELENA, SURVEILLANCE, AND SAVVY CITIZENSHIP

This scene begins in classic epic fashion: in the middle of the action, in the middle of the opening-night performance in San Antonio, in the middle of the musical's crossover plotting, in the middle of the space between the story, just after the curtain has closed for intermission.[54]

In the middle of the balcony, where I am seated along with other Selena fans unable to afford or unwilling to pay for the more expensive tickets, I turn away from the stage to face Francisco Vara-Orta, who is seated next to his mother in the row behind me. Francisco is dressed impeccably for the occasion, his thick black hair slicked back and gleaming. He is wearing a contemporary version of a black and white pinstriped zoot suit; on its lapel he has pinned a black *Hard Rock Cafe* commemorative guitar pendant with Selena's name written across it. His ensemble clearly signifies toward multiple moments in Latina/o history and toward the present moment, wherein mainstream corporate enterprises capitalize on the Latino consumer. To be Latino and to wear a zoot suit is to remember and affiliate with the young, urban, male *pachucos* of the 1940s, who donned the suit as an emblem of resistance. The zoot suit was characterized by its overly wide padded shoulders and excessively draped trousers; its too-too-much style (outlawed by the war effort because it required excessive fabric) commanded attention. Thus for economically disenfranchised pachucos the suit became a way to demand acknowledgment of their presence and to defy normative codes of appropriately tailored fashion.[55]

By affixing the memorial Selena guitar pin onto his zoot suit Francisco memorializes Selena by locating her in an oppositional history, a history of struggle and resistance, that is not, as the musical and its promotional materials asserted, about the attainment of the American Dream. His ensemble also situates *Selena Forever* within Latina/o theater history with its evocation of that other Broadway-bound Latino play, Luis Valdez's *Zoot Suit*.[56] Repositioning Selena thus, Francisco recalls his memories of her: "What drew me to her at first was her *persona*. She was so versatile. She could sing anything; there are seven different styles of music on her last album. It was her persona. It's the same thing with any actor; they can play a drunk or a cowboy or whatever, but that doesn't mean that's who they really are. Selena was the 'Tex-Mex Madonna' and she was also the girl next door. It's the way all of our daughters and mothers are. She was one of the family."

Francisco evokes Selena, or, more precisely, Selena's persona to construct "our . . . family," wherein the women are skilled performers able and, in fact, often required to navigate within the overdetermined sexualized virgin/whore or girl-next-door/Tex-Mex Madonna binary. Here the articulation of latinidad is contingent upon the production of publicly performing, sexualized Latina bodies. But here also Francisco's focus on the notion of persona — "that doesn't mean that's who they really are" — points to the very constructedness of these bodies. His focus on Selena's and our mothers' and daughters' personas acknowledges a space wherein these women can enact a critical mimesis, can perform or repeat these roles with a difference. Moreover, his references to Latina mothers and daughters astutely intervene in the pervasive father-daughter narrative into which the musical and countless other tributes frame Selena's story.

As I talk with Francisco during intermission I am struck by the creative act of his style, by *his* persona. I ask to photograph him for my project, and he graciously agrees. As we begin to make our way outside of the confines of the balcony area, my camera in hand, a middle-aged Latina in a security guard uniform intercepts and detains me. "I need your film, ma'am," she insists. "You're going to have to give me your film." Like any belligerent fan I protest, refuse to let go of my camera, insist that I haven't taken any photographs of the actual production, and put up an ultimately futile fight. But my fight is far less significant, far less meaningful than the fight that ensues around me, as the balcony community comes to my defense, rallying around me, around the undeveloped image. A young Latina behind me stands up, voice insistent: "She didn't take any pictures! She didn't take any pictures!" A middle-aged Latina three rows back approaches me, voice conspiratorial: "If you need a witness, I'll be one. If they take your film, make sure they destroy it right in front of your eyes, because you never know what they're going to do with it." My great-aunt Lucia, seated beside me, begins shouting at the two young Latino cops who have appeared: "Hey, see that flash that just went off down there, in the third row? Why don't you do your job down there?" Francisco rallies, voice authoritative: "If this were the real Selena, she wouldn't care if we did have a camera. She would have posed for us."

Undeniably this battle over the confiscated film is in many ways not unlike others that invariably ensue at theater events and concerts where determined fans defy the "No Cameras Allowed" admonitions. But this particular balcony scene also enacted larger struggles for ownership over Selena's memory, shedding light on the various claims to Latina/o representation—as market segment, citizenry, and artistic product—that traverse Selena's lasting image. Recall Francisco's memories of both the "real" Selena and Selena's "persona"; his investment in both of these is far from contradictory. When he remembers Selena's persona he reveals his awareness of, among other things, the constructed and contingent nature of identity. Hence when, during the struggle over the confiscated film, he asserts, "If this were the real Selena, she wouldn't care if we did have a camera. She would have posed for us," he is not simply nodding to essentialist claims of authenticity. Nor is he claiming to possess this real Selena. Rather, in this particular context—in the balcony of the theater, dressed in his zoot suit—Francisco mourns the loss of Selena as a way of articulating mistrust in any singular, dominant claim of ownership and control over the Latina body. At this moment, when the Latina/o balcony community remembers Selena or instructs me to vigilantly follow the circulation of my film, they are speaking out against the act of surveillance that is part of the process of the marketing of latinidad. In light of the simultaneous celebrations of the Latin Boom and legislation against Latina/o bodies that marked the 1990s, the balcony community's mobilization around the undeveloped film is a critical assertion against what Peggy Phelan calls the "trap of visibility [that] summons surveillance . . . [and] provokes the colonialist/imperial appetite for possession."[57]

But Francisco's memory of Selena also complicates Phelan's observations. By describing the real Selena as one both capable of and indeed skilled at posing (she is, as Francisco observes, all persona), he infuses her with the power to negotiate this trap of the visible. Indeed his comments suggest that the excessive aesthetic of Latina/o "posing" embodied by Selena may in fact work to ward off the imperial appetite for possession. Thus, contrary to the depictions circulating around the production, Francisco's and the other balcony members' defense of my right to the undeveloped film reveals their theater savvy. And within this display of theater savvy is an assertion of Latina/o citizenship; to assert a critical response to the terms of Selena commemoration is to resist Latina/o interpellation by the market or the state or the Latina/o security guards sent to do their bidding. The balcony community's demand for access to Selena constitutes a demand for access to the representational sites wherein Latina/o culture is literally being staged and consumed.

SCENE 2: LATINA/O HISTORIES, LATINA/O FUTURES

This scene begins in the middle of intermission, in the middle of the lobby at a performance in the outskirts of Chicago.

I linger at the concession stand talking with Jerry Ortiz as he sells Selena Barbies to a steady stream of young girls. I ask him why he thinks Selena's story resonates so powerfully with so many Latinas/os, and he replies, "I think it's more than just who she was. I think it's the way with our mothers and daughters."[58] He then proceeds to tell me the story of his own mother's migration from Puerto Rico to New York City:

> My mother is in that book, *From Colonia to Community*. Have you heard of it? . . . She was in her early twenties and came to New York City alone before she got married to my father. I would say she was ahead of her time then and believed in equality of men and women. . . . After the Great Depression, the mayor of New York announced to Puerto Rico that there was a surplus of work to be found in New York. . . . Since there were no translators, they put the Puerto Rican children in slow learning classes or, in many cases, remedial classes, so they really weren't getting educated! Plus, many of the other kids were being sent to be cooks, waiters, janitors—all blue-collar jobs—never sent to be doctors or lawyers.

The book to which Jerry refers is Virginia Sánchez Korrol's now classic study of the history of Puerto Ricans in New York City during the years between the Jones Act (1917) and the early post–Second World War era.[59] Jerry's seamless, unprompted transition from Selena to his mother's journey and then to the midcentury migration and settlement of Puerto Ricans in New York City signals the way that Selenidad acts as a palimpsest onto which Latinas/os write and rewrite their own personal and collective histories. In his narrative shift from the particular story of his mother to an account of collective struggles faced by Puerto Rican laborers during the years following the Second World War Jerry details a history of Puerto Rican labor migration and subsequent political economic positioning in New York City.[60] That his mother serves as the entry point for this history is no surprise given the gendered labor migration patterns that resulted from the targeting of Puerto Rican women as sources of cheap labor for the garment industry in New York.[61] The plight of at least two Puerto Rican women, Maria and Anita, who labored in the New York City garment industry provides the historical context for that other famous musical about Latinos, *West Side Story*.

Jerry deploys Selena to decry past injustices, making a clear connection between her tragedy and the history of tragedies U.S. Latinas/os have faced: "I think it's linked to Selena 'Deborah' because we are all Latinos. No matter the country you are from, we all speak the same language and our cultures are similar. Our struggle to break into this white society has been a very tough one and still is, even today. Selena was real! And very 'Now!'" One of the particular "struggles to break into white society" that Jerry related to me was the story of his own career path. Long before he started selling Selena paraphernalia he had established himself as a musician in a doo-wop band, The Chryslers.[62] Despite his efforts during the 1950s to Americanize his surname to Jerry Darrow, his band, not unlike Abraham Quintanilla's band, was unable to achieve the crossover success he sought. But his hopes continued to live on in his daughter, Onaney Ortiz, whom Jerry informed me was the understudy for the role of Selena in *Selena Forever*.

Jerry's exclamation about Selena's realness may seem at first to be unrelated to the immediately preceding assertion about the challenges Latinas/os face in "white society." But his insistence on Selena's realness and her temporal tie to the present moment actually reveals how Selenidad provides the imaginative space in which to proclaim one's roots, one's "realness" without compromise (as Jerry Darrow, for instance) in the "Now." Selena's tragedy offers a way out of the past struggles, a way to cross over, not in an assimilationist gesture, but in a way that may inaugurate a change of state precisely through the reclamation of Latino roots and at least one Latina mother's routes. For Jerry this change of state is undeniably catalyzed by Selena: "Once we can all, as Latinos, see our relationship to each other, then we can use the economic power of billions of dollars we spend yearly to change many of the stereotypes that still exist out there—and get more of us in Congress and in power. . . . Selena was a spark that opened up many doors. This is a new generation of *Colonia to Comunidad* today!" While Jerry's vision may seem like facile equations of Latina/o power with market power, his explicit linking of Selena with possibilities for Latina/o economic power, representation (as both political power and cultural product), and *comunidad* offers a clear articulation of the ways that the Selena tragedy inaugurates multiple formulations of latinidad. In particular his use of a conditional future tense in conjunction with his reference to Selena as a catalyzing "spark" and his resignification of Sánchez Korrol's title ("community" translated to *comunidad*) actually operate as a political gestus that imagines a collective "memory of the future" for Latinos/as in the coming millennium.

This scene begins offstage but ends onstage, or rather, ends on a screen above the stage, at the end of the show.

Selena Forever does not simply honor Selena as a surrogate for her father's or her community's dreams; like other Selena memorials, the musical generates surrogates as well. Following the ballad sung after Selena's death is announced, the show closes with a video projection of the *Mirador de la Flor* memorial statue in Corpus Christi. The video depicts three hundred young Latina girls laying flowers at the base of the statue of Selena. In the midst of this homage the statue magically comes alive as Annette Hernandez, a model posed and dressed identically to Selena's statue, suddenly breaks her pose and walks down the steps of the memorial. Director Bill Virchis emphasized the importance of this gesture "as a symbol of Selena's spirit."[63] This moment acutely captures the process of surrogation (en)gendered by Selenidad. The video suggests that Selena's spirit lives on through the mass reproduction of young Latina embodiments of Selena. It is through the act of becoming Selena that the future will arrive, as Virchis notes: "The video segment is about passing on the musical and cultural legacy of Selena's work and life to another generation. It's about the youth that will carry on her music. That's why I wanted little children, because that is the future of all of us."[64] In the context of public preoccupation with Latina/o population growth, the appearance of these multiple Selenas at the musical's closing offers a metonymic staging of the future proliferation of Latinas/os across the nation.

SCENE 4: A SURROGATE SPEAKS

This scene takes place in the future, after the show has closed. This scene is a memory.

Onaney Ortiz, an emerging recording artist who was eighteen years old when she understudied for the role of Adult Selena, reflects on why she was compelled to participate in *Selena Forever*:

> I grew up in Puerto Rico surrounded by a musical family—my father is a performer as well. . . . When I was about sixteen or seventeen, I started to hear of Selena. . . . As I was listening to Selena's music, I just kinda started singing along with her and I started to kinda find my

way. . . . My initial influence was through Selena's music. . . . I couldn't imagine my life without being in the play [*Selena Forever*]. . . . By the end of the show — every time — everyone was moved. It affected all of us. In a way, we felt a lot of that pain. It was a really powerful thing. I don't think I'll ever go on a tour like that again. . . . Along the way, I've always included Selena [songs in my repertoire]; without that influence, I may not even be doing this.[65]

Onaney's memory of Selena is inextricably tied to the memory of her own aspirations as an emerging recording artist and performer. Selena's music offered her an auditory guide for cultivating her own singing style and career; "singing along" to Selena's songs did not encourage derivative imitation but helped Onaney "find [her] way." Her self-identification as a Puerto Rican followed immediately by her identification with Selena (a Tejana) signals the ways that Selenidad encourages transnational Latina/o connections. For Onaney the musical provided one such forum for connection wherein Latina/o artists could not only perform, but could mourn together. *Selena Forever* called upon its performers to stage their collective "pain" and to be "moved" in the process. Onaney's closing sentence reveals one of the ways the musical moved her, as she describes how her ongoing performance of Selena in her own musical repertoire is central to her continued development as a Latina performing artist.

SCENE 5: LATINA FEMINIST SUBJUNCTIVES

This scene begins at the end, after the curtain's close on the second act, in the corner of the lobby, at the end of the musical's official premiere.

The lobby is animated by post-show audience chatter and the rattle and chime of cash registers marking the rhythms of *Selena Forever* merchandise sales. Under the canopy of the Southwest Airlines banner Annabelle Medina, a savvy Latina spectator, surveys the scene and proceeds to reflect on mainstream responses to Selena's death: "Unfortunately, when she had that tragedy, they were saying she had raunchy clothes and that she was like Madonna. I don't think she was copying Madonna. That's what they all said. I think that they just didn't want to deal with our culture."[66] Annabelle conveys an incisive awareness of the tension between the hypervisibility of Selena's body and the persistent invisibility of Latina/o communities within U.S. popular culture. She astutely understands popular comparisons of Selena with Madonna, not as celebratory assertions of Selena's successful crossover or as unequivocal acknowledgment of Latinas/os within the national imaginary, but rather as part of a legacy wherein the hypersexualization of Latinas is circulated as a way to consume but not to deal with Latina/o culture. Annabelle's observation points to the possible dangers that arise from deploying Selena to decry larger Latina/o political economic injustices. As her comments make clear, not only are Latinas made visible in ways that can ultimately reenact imperialist constructions of racialized sexuality, but more particularly her sexuality is used to efface the very tragedy of her own and her Latina/o community's plights. Thus, as Annabelle is keenly aware, the repeated comparisons to Madonna strategically evoke Latina sexuality as a means by which to both mark its excessiveness and to contain it.

℘ Selena: A Musical ~~Celebration~~ Surrogation of Life

In the months following the release of the Census 2000 reports confirming that Latinas/os constituted 46.5 percent of the total Los Angeles population and in the midst of Antonio Villaraigosa's first run for mayor of Los Angeles, *Selena: A Musical Celebration of Life* opened in the spring of 2001 for a two-month run at the Doolittle Theater in West Hollywood.[67] The Los Angeles incarnation of the musical maintained the same basic story line as in *Selena Forever*, while paring down the cast and the use of some of its multimedia spectacle. The most notable changes not apparently directly linked to budgetary constraints were the repeated efforts to break the fourth wall. In the opening scene, the "Pueblo" (chorus) entered from the house aisles, and throughout the production girls were plucked from the audience and brought onstage to sing along with Selena.[68] This literal staging of Latina daughters retained the surrogate-generating impulse of the original version of the musical and also theatrically evoked the burgeoning Los Angeles Latina/o population confirmed by the recently released census data.

It was in one of these moments of surrogation that *Selena: A Musical Celebration of Life* actually moved evocatively, as Francisco yearned for, "past her murder." In the show's concluding minutes a young Latina fan named Teresa, portrayed by Agina Alvarez, mourns Selena by performing her, by powerfully reprising Selena's signature song, "Como la Flor." In this reprise the petite Alvarez crosses downstage center and proceeds

33. Onaney Ortiz, recording artist and Selena understudy for *Selena Forever* (2000). Photo by Jerry Ortiz.

to transform the normally bouncy, synthesizer-heavy "Como la Flor" cumbia into an arrestingly still, soulful a cappella ballad. The semiotic shift staged by this closing moment of tribute to Selena—conspicuously without musical accompaniment or a flashy dance number—undeniably foregrounds Alvarez's own vocal skills and leaves audience members moved by both the absence of Selena's body and by the promise of a surrogate, powerfully embodied by Alvarez.[69] The song's plaintive pacing and stripped accompaniment offer a subjunctive soundscape for latinidad at the century's end: latinidad stripped of merchandise tie-ins and father-daughter scenes, propelled by the measured pace of reflection rather than by the cash register's frenzied rhythms. This is how Selenidad should sound: the sound of grief occupied and the sound of Latina/o (vocal) power resounding in the process. In this moment "Como la Flor" emerges as the anthem for Latina arrival, the coming-out song, the bold assertion that the Latina future is now. In this final moment of surrogation the surrogate transcends the original, moves past Selena's murder to a space of self-realization.[70] In this final staging a young Latina's ability to negotiate the visible—and the audible, as Alvarez's vocal skills attest—embodies the musical's assertion that the future for Latinas/os is upon us, that Latinas/os have indeed begun to arrive through the body of Selena. More precisely, young Latina performances of surrogation signal the arrival of an impending change of state following, and indeed enabled by, Selena's tragedy. In this closing moment of surrogation a young Latina performs her grief and, by means of mourning, becomes the future.[71]

The Los Angeles musical's final staging of the subjunctive sounds of latinidad, Francisco's insistence on moving "past her murder," and Jerry's references to his own mother and daughter all configure Selena as both the tragic figure through whom Latinas/os remember their own tragic histories and as the regenerative daughter of our nation, as our issue, securing changes of state in our future. Our motherland has been colonized or left behind; our daughters' potential and, insofar as Selena acts as the surrogate of latinidad, our potential, thus lie in the future. And precisely because Selena not only embodies a daughter of latinidad but successfully (re)produces those daughters, the movement from *"colonia* to *communidad* today" toward a future beyond Census 2000 will be brought about by those young understudies, like Onaney Ortiz, eagerly rehearsing just off-stage (figure 33).

FOUR

Becoming Selena, Becoming Latina

Into the cavities created by loss through death or other forms of departure . . .
survivors attempt to fit satisfactory alternatives. . . . The process requires many
trials and at least as many errors. The fit cannot be exact. The intended sub-
stitute either cannot fulfill expectations, creating a deficit, or actually exceeds
them, creating a surplus.

—Joseph Roach, *Cities of the Dead*

On 7 March 1996 Warner Bros. Studios held a press conference to publi-
cize open-audition casting calls for the much anticipated $20 million biopic
Selena. Gregory Nava, the film's writer and director, along with Abraham
Quintanilla, the film's executive producer, and other studio executives
announced that the production team was looking for two women to become Selena, one to portray Selena as a six- to ten-year-old child and
another to embody Selena as a budding adult in the years just before her
death. They invited young women and girls who were English-proficient
to audition, noting that singing skills were not required for the role but
that dancing ability would be taken into consideration. The auditions
were to be held within the coming weeks in San Antonio, Los Angeles,
Miami, and Chicago—all cities with sizable Latina/o communities. The
studio had even set up a hotline, 1–888–4SELENA, to provide additional
details about the audition sites and requirements.[1]

Over eighty-five thousand calls flooded the hotline. Nearly twenty-four
thousand young women and girls from across the pan-Latina spectrum
participated in the auditions.[2] And despite casting call admonishments
against participants dressing like Selena, thousands of young Latinas arrived at the auditions dressed in sparkling purple pantsuits or black leather

34. Gregory Nava meets young Latinas at the *Selena* auditions (1996). Photo by Genaro Molina. Copyright *Los Angeles Times*. Reprinted with permission.

bustiers, revealing that the practice of becoming Selena was well under way long before this officially sanctioned search for the future Selena was staged (figure 34). At the Miami auditions, for example, "habia jóvenes guatelmatecas, hondureñas, puertoriqueñas, cubanas, una multitud de Selenas con ojos llorosos y sonrisas esperanzas [there were Guatemalan, Honduran, Puerto Rican, Cuban youths, a multitude of Selenas with tearful eyes and hopeful smiles]."[3] The overwhelming response, promoted in a range of English- and Spanish-language print and media outlets, created the largest open casting call in Hollywood history, frequently eliciting comparisons to the Scarlett O'Hara auditions for *Gone With the Wind* and to the phenomenon of Elvis impersonation: "It was a decidedly surreal scene: skinny Selenas, chunky Selenas, Selenas in gold lamé, black lace Selenas, cap-wearing Selenas, dressed-down Selenas. Sort of like an Elvis look-alike convention, but prettier."[4]

In response to this turnout Gregory Nava proclaimed, "There's never been a casting call like this. About 600 boys showed up to be Dennis the Menace. We've had 24,000 Selenas. It shows how deeply she's touched a chord in this nation. . . . This is the story of the American dream. . . . She's a real hero to all of us."[5] Nava summed up the auditions as a welcoming celebration of Latina/o collaboration: "As it turned out, [the auditions] were a beautiful thing to have happened for our community. People felt they were a part of the process because Selena was so important to them."[6] By juxtaposing twenty-four thousand Selenas against six hundred white, archetypal all-American Dennis the Menaces, Nava invokes the proliferation of young Selena aspirants as a symbol of how "we" Latinas/os were emerging as a force to be reckoned with in America. In the equation of Selena's story with the American Dream, in which she is "a real hero to all of us," Selenidad serves as the rhetorical bridge by which "we" Latinas/os become "us" Americans. For Nava the audition process was as an inclusive and, indeed, an assimilative event that celebrated Latina aspirations for the American Dream.[7]

But the "ojos llorosos y sonrisas esperanzas" of the young Latinas described at the Miami auditions tell a different story. The face, as Gloria Anzaldúa writes, is an instructive surface of the body from which Chicana and other Latina feminists can theorize about the resistant embodied practices often adopted by women of color.[8] The multivalent affect captured on the faces of the "multitud de Selenas" who flocked to the auditions points to the capacious expressive space that Selenidad offered young Latinas. For many of these young women and girls, the act of becoming Selena was not simply an exceptional feat undertaken for a special, officially sanctioned occasion, but a quotidian activity that provided a way for them to inhabit and negotiate the fraught terrain of Latina representation in the United States. As a foundational scenario in the staging of Latina identification, becoming Selena was not unlike other identificatory practices that, as Jackie Stacey observes, "involve conscious and unconscious formations of subjectivity."[9] Young Latina efforts to become Selena thus constituted a process not merely of commemoration or star-struck aspiration (as Nava's comments suggest), but of Latina subject formation. To become Selena was to become Latina.

As the sorrowful eyes and expectant smiles of the audition participants suggest, Latinas occupied a paradoxical position throughout the 1990s. While touted as the latest boom of literary voices, the "It" girls of show business, and the (sex) symbols for emerging assertions of latinidad, Latinas suffered most acutely the repercussions of immigration and welfare reform and of economic restructuring resulting from NAFTA that marked the decade.[10] Identification with Selena provided alternative possibilities for Latina subjectivity beyond these representational and material con-

fines, revealing, as Elin Diamond notes, "the radical power of identification to override the constraints of identity."[11] In particular the act of
imitating Selena emerged as a powerfully effective and affective expressive practice whereby many young Latinas negotiated prevailing concepts
of and charted new mappings for Latina identity. This phenomenon is
especially significant given that Latina youths suffered the highest rates
of depression, suicide attempts, substance abuse, and high school drop-
out and reported the lowest levels of self-esteem among adolescent girls
during the decade following Selena's death.[12] Disregarded within social
and economic spheres, many Latinas turned to the cultural landscape of
Selenidad to validate their worlds and their worth.

One of these young Latinas who turned toward—and who turned a
critical eye upon—Selenidad was Claudia Pérez, a Mexican American
cultural critic who participated in the Selena auditions and reported on
the event as a guest correspondent for the nationally syndicated radio
show This American Life.[13] In her report, "1000 Women Become Selena,"
which originally aired on 19 April 1996, Pérez insightfully chronicles her
own participant observations and her interviews with young women and
girls who gathered for the Chicago auditions at Roberto Clemente High
School, located in the predominately Puerto Rican (but rapidly gentrify-
ing) Humboldt Park neighborhood.[14] Pérez describes the scene surrounding the auditions where many young Latinas were engaged in the act of
becoming Selena: "I met all sorts of people at the auditions. Everybody
was really dressed up and looked fabulous. There was Selena music everywhere—TV cameras—girls were fixing their hair and putting their makeup on. People were dancing. At one point, we were talking to these two
girls. They sang us a Selena song, and pretty soon, people we didn't even
know were joining in. Everybody was singing. It was just that kind of
thing."[15]

Despite the insistence that singing was not required for the audition,
the young Latinas that Pérez describes capitalized on the space of the
auditions to collectively practice and flex their vocal skills. This brief description captures how young women and girls who regularly practiced
becoming Selena approached the Selena auditions as a public forum to
showcase how they had already become Selena, not as an opportunity to
suddenly—with official approval—become her. Selenidad thus provided
young Latinas with a cultural script and a repertoire of gestures and at-

titudes for enacting emergent versions of Latina subjectivity within and against the grain of the representational spaces that circumscribe their lives.

Pérez's report instructs us to look beyond the frame and listen behind the scenes of popular representations of Latina celebrity to account for the ways that Latinas have used the space of Selenidad, however delimited by commercial interests, to fashion alternative expressions of Latina desire, style, and community. As her report models, a focus on the process of cultural production and not simply on its final product insightfully foregrounds the political economy of Latina bodies within entertainment industry attempts to represent the Latina body during the 1990s.[16] An attention to the ways that Selenidad carved out a representational space for Latina voices to be heard disrupts the derisive depictions of young women's identification practices that circulate in popular media and foregrounds how young Latinas such as Pérez (in her active roles as interviewer, audition participant, and contributor to the report's final editing process) act as skilled producers and not simply passive consumers of culture.[17] This intervention is crucial in light of the ways that Latinas, identified as the fastest growing segments of the teenage and female markets, have been overdetermined as a burgeoning consumer base even while their economic struggles remain largely unaddressed.[18] Ultimately, to value Latina identification with Selena is to value Latina cultural and critical labor.

℘ Selena's Butt, Selena's Skin

Identification with Selena reaches across a diverse spectrum of Latina racial and national affiliations. This inter-Latina appeal was cultivated in part by Selena's pan-Latina/o musical range and by recording industry efforts to transform her from a regionally marked Tejana artist into an internationally marketable Latina star.[19] But in contrast to homogenizing characterizations of Latinas in popular culture, Latinas did not assume a natural affiliation with Selena largely because of the ways she proudly asserted her regional and working-class affiliations.[20] Even as Selena was emerging as a Latina star, she consistently affirmed her Tejana identity through her Tejana-twang-inflected Spanish, frequent use of fringe and cowboy boots as stylistic accessories, and continued residence in her Corpus Christi neighborhood, characteristics usually derided as too "country," "low-class," or racially marked for cosmopolitan or transnational appeal. As Karina Duran, the makeup artist for *Selena*, observed, "She was so tacky, but she knew it and she loved it."[21] Ultimately it was precisely because of Selena's ability to become a transnational Latina while still maintaining her proudly "tacky" status as a locally identified and working-class Tejana that she achieved such symbolic power among so many Latinas. Her dynamic and dual-nature approach to the processes of becoming Latina provided an unprecedented model for navigating established formulations of Latina identification that often effaced or compromised national, regional, and class allegiances. As such, Selena offered Latinas a compelling strategy for approaching what Nicholas De Genova and Ana Y. Ramos-Zayas call the "fractured and fraught" possibilities for latinidad.[22]

As a critical map with which Latinas navigated some of these fractured inter-Latina/o relations, identification with Selena exposed both the allegiances that foreclose and the affiliations that enable Latina subject formation. Latinas' memories of their experiences as spectators of *Selena* evoked the identifications and disidentifications that animate the circuits of latinidad. In her editorial for the *Syracuse Post-Standard* Cindy Rodriguez writes:

> I sat in the movie theater with my friend, Marilin Martinez, and our Girl Scout Troop, which consists of four pre-teen girls, all Latina. . . . And when Selena's voice filled the theater, the girls sang along: "*Amor prohibido murmuran por las calles porque somos de distintas sociedades.*" ("Forbidden love they murmur on the streets because we're from different societies.") . . . They knew all the songs: the ballads in English, pop-rock tunes in Spanish, the mariachis (traditional Mexican music), and the Tejano songs that won Selena a Grammy. . . . It doesn't matter that none of us has Mexican roots. Ana and Gloryann are Puerto Rican, like Marilin; Iriz and Jandry are half-Cuban, half-Puerto Rican, like me. . . . As the credits rolled, we all sat there quietly, and Selena's voice comforted us.[23]

For Rodriguez and her all-Latina Girl Scout troop, identification with Selena facilitated bonds across generational and national affiliations. The remark "It doesn't matter that none of us has Mexican roots" implicitly references the national boundaries that often fracture latinidad and thereby underscores the significance of cross-Latina affiliation that identification with Selena encouraged. Latina identification emerges here as a performative and not simply a spectatorial mode: the girls not only come together to watch *Selena*, they collectively sing along, moved by Selena to fill the theater with their own voices.[24]

Even as identification with Selena encouraged a momentary inter-Latina connection, disidentification with Selena in the dark hollows of the movie theater also served as a powerful tool for theorizing and enacting Latina subjectivity. Frances Negrón-Muntaner begins her essay "Jennifer's Butt" by describing the originary moment of the essay's creation: her experience of watching *Selena* in a suburban Philadelphia theater along with other Puerto Ricans. In this context Jennifer Lopez's (Puerto Rican) star text and performing body overwhelm Selena's (Tejana) story:

> I went to see the recent Gregory Nava movie *Selena* (1997), in a half-empty suburban theater in Philadelphia with about a dozen other solemn, mostly Puerto Rican families dressed up in their Sunday best. . . . The sight was unusual, even extraordinary, since one rarely sees Phila-Ricans outside of a few segregated neighborhoods. . . . I wondered why *los otros puertorriqueños* had also trekked so far from the streets of *el norte*, where people are more likely to follow La India, Olga Tañón, and Thalía than Selena. . . . Twenty minutes into *Selena*, a queer sense of dread began to overtake me [as] the mimetic pact that generally binds spectator and biopic inexplicably broke down. Regardless of how hard I tried, I did not see Selena. I either saw Jennifer Lopez and Selena, phantasmagorically juxtaposed as if on a glass surface, or *simplemente* Jennifer. . . . From the heavens above me, I heard voices ordering my removal to the lower depths of cultural criticism; away from the American dream, and into the flesh of unjustly denied discursive pleasures. Possessed, I began to write deliriously in the darkness.[25]

Disidentification with Selena turns Negrón-Muntaner toward the "discursive pleasures" of the darkness, where she is moved to explore the contours and histories of Latina racialization. Within this memory of a "queer sense" of *Selena*, the essay becomes performative, enacting Latina subject formation in its attempts to theorize it. To write deliriously in the darkness cast by Selena's spectral body, or, more precisely, by the body of a woman who has become Selena, is to perform Latina "cultural criticism."

Latinas identified with Selena as a means of navigating the very inter-Latina/o tensions fostered within the space of Selenidad. The Warner Bros. biopic made headlines not only because of its history-making audition process, but also because of the controversies surrounding its ultimate casting decisions. Following the announcement that the Nuyorican actress Jennifer Lopez would portray Selena, some Mexican American and Chicana/o communities and organizations, such as the Chicana/o Culture Coalition (Coalición Cultural Chicana), voiced protests and threatened a boycott of the film, arguing that given the ways Selena had proudly asserted her regional and cultural allegiances, a Tejana or Chicana actress should have been chosen for the role.[26] This casting controversy captured the struggles for representation waged between Puerto Ricans and Mexican Americans within the context of U.S. popular and political culture, wherein particular inter-Latina/o distinctions (with regard to citizenship, economic, and racial status) are often effaced by homogenizing official constructions of latinidad. Jennifer Lopez's response to her detractors reveals how Latina identification with Selena worked to circumvent some of these tensions: "I'm all for Latinos playing Latinos, but saying a Puerto Rican couldn't play Selena, a Texas girl, is taking it a bit far. Selena looked like me. She was dark and she was, well, curvy."[27] Lopez identifies with Selena's body to claim a Latina identity—based on shared racialized markings—in an effort to overcome what Jose E. Muñoz calls the incoherence of latinidad.[28] This pan-Latina identification does not rely on facile essentialist claims, but on a pointed critique of the authenticity demands that invariably get played out on Latina bodies. By focusing on the affinities between Selena's body and her own, Lopez deploys the act of Selena identification as a measure for addressing the problematics and potentials of latinidad.

Lopez's comments suggest that wide-ranging Latina identification with Selena arose in large part from the ways Selena's body signified the "dark" and "curvy" (indigenous and African) presence within the Latina racial continuum. Negrón-Muntaner observes, "Despite the fact that Selena was Chicana, an ethnicity not associated in the Caribbean popular imagination with big butts, she was definitely curvy. . . . Selena's butt was, from a Puerto Rican perspective, one of the elements that made her not specifically Chicana, but 'Latina,' and hence more easily embraced as one of our own."[29] Clearly long before the fascination with "Jennifer's butt," Selena's butt was well known among Latinas; moreover, identification with Selena's rear end—and not simply recording industry market-ing—contributed substantially to her metamorphosis into a Latina. Since Selena's status as a Latina is understood as "more easily embraced" by Puerto Rican women than her Chicana status, Selena's body often operated as a bridge that reached across inter-Latina divides. Identification with Selena's body thus took part in transforming both Selena and her diverse array of female fans into Latinas.

Selena's body stood in stark—and dark—contrast to previous portrayals of Latina sexuality in U.S. popular culture. While Selena would not have been classified as dark within the wider Latina/o or Afro-diasporic racial continuum, her decisions not to dye her hair, lighten her makeup palate, or alter her curvaceous body with surgical or sartorial technologies made her considerably darker than other Latina celebrities in U.S. popular culture and in transnational Latin American entertainment outlets such as Univisión. Throughout the twentieth century representations of Latina celebrity were characterized by Dolores Del Rio's "upper-class exoticism" juxtaposed against Lupe Velez's sexually predatory "Mexican Spitfire" in the 1930s and 1940s, Carmen Miranda's excessively adorned body promoting the samba (and the Good Neighbor Policy) in the 1940s, and Rita Moreno's mastery of the mambo accompanied by her assimilationist proclamation "I Want to Live in Amer-ee-ca!" in the 1950s and 1960s.[30] Another notable representation surfaced in the careers of Rita Hayworth and Raquel Welch, who both opted for the total erasure of their Latina identity as a means to secure acceptance as sexual icons. Selena's multifaceted star text, keenly preserved following her untimely death, as a sultry singing siren and a working-class girl next door, as a worldly Latin star and wide-eyed Tejana entrepreneur, as a bicultural Chicana and transnational Latina encouraged many Latinas to inhabit the space of Selenidad as a means of negotiating and moving beyond the established, restrictive parameters of Latina (in)visibility.

Many Latinas laid claim to Selena's body as a means of expressing political or cultural criticism. Claudia Pérez succinctly demonstrated this rhetorical practice when, during my interview with her, she said, "I tell people there's three things that make me mad. One is when you stereotype Mexican people. Can't stand that. And two, when they say Selena had a fake butt. That makes me *real* mad. Or, three, when they pass laws, all these crazy laws against Latino people."[31] Pérez's statement emphasizes the relationships among three phenomena that marked the 1990s:

the struggles over representations of Latina/o identity, the conspicuous celebration—or, more precisely, surveillance—of the performing Latina body (part), and the enactment of the most restrictive immigration legislation in U.S. history. By embedding her sentence concerning Selena's butt within comments about the circulation of stereotypes about Mexican people and legislation against Latino people, Pérez points to ways that constructions of Latina sexuality figured centrally in the creation and maintenance of national nativist projects that shape U.S. political and cultural landscapes.

Like Selena's identity shifts, Pérez's claim to the space of both *mexicanidad* and latinidad reveals the "dual sense of identity" taken up by many Latinas/os within this hostile political climate.[32] Pérez, a first-generation Mexican American, begins by alluding to a national and ethnic self-identification, then highlights how the battles over racial or ethnic authenticity are often enacted on the terrain of the sexualized female body, and finally hints at how and when a counterhegemonic Latina/o subjectivity can emerge. Within the United States, and often in response to the punitive legislative acts Pérez indicts, a Mexican American may momentarily prioritize a political (that is, a Latina/o) affiliation over a national (Mexican) identification as a means of gaining political ground.[33] Through her syntactic shifts Pérez articulates an oppositional latinidad by condemning the regulations of Latina bodies and the policing of American borders "against Latino people" that reproduce and circulate bureaucratic and corporate constructions of Latinas/os. Latinidad emerges not as the strategically homogenizing construct of corporate industries or census measures, but as a momentary alliance based on a shared sense of injury. Her affirmation of a politically oppositional identity conspicuously follows from her reclamation of Selena's butt, revealing her awareness and disdain of the fetishization of Latina bodies and her nuanced understanding of how the racially and sexually marked female body is often deployed as a synecdoche for a subjugated community.

Pérez's indignant protection of Selena's butt indicates how the rear end has become a dominant trope in the racialization of Latina bodies. "A big *culo* [ass]," Negrón-Muntaner writes, "does not only upset hegemonic (white) notions of beauty and good taste, it is a sign for the dark, incomprehensible excess of 'Latino' and other African diaspora cultures."[34] Spanish and U.S. colonialist projects throughout the Americas have historically exerted their force through reliance upon this construction of

Latina (excessive) sexuality and through the violation of Latina bodies.[35] These practices figured prominently in nativist discourse concerning the "threat" of Latina/o immigration and in post-NAFTA constructions of Mexican women wherein the burden of responsibility for violence against female laborers on the border was relocated onto the Mexicana body rather than on the operations of transnational capitalism and state-sanctioned patriarchy.[36] The preoccupation with Latina sexuality as inexhaustible resource and ruinous force continues to frame popular understandings of Latina bodies as laborers, from the entertainment industry to the *maquila* assembly line.

Pérez's comments are suggestive of the ways that Latinas used Selenidad as an identificatory compass for navigating their symbolic and economic positioning in the United States at the turn of the twenty-first century. By including her reclamation of the Latina body (represented here by Selena's butt) in her critique of the political economy of Latinas/os, Pérez foregrounds connections between representations of the Latina body and the obstacles to citizenship and social justice for Latina/o bodies in the United States. Her statement operates as well as a critique of prevailing cultural and legislative practices invested in reinscribing whiteness as normative and of the patriarchal confines within Latina/o communities, wherein Latina sexuality has been traditionally policed.[37] Her comments underscore the ways Selena's body circulated as part of larger struggles over claims to cultural, national, and political identity, while her reclamation of Selena also foregrounds Latina agency in and against these appropriations.

Identification with Selena's body often provided Latinas a way to expose the racism embedded in the double bind of excess and erasure circumscribing representations of Latina sexuality. From the Latina visitors at the Selena Museum who expressed suspicion of the official measurements of the archived purple pantsuit to the young girls who donned their favorite Selena outfit for the auditions, Latinas identified with Selena's body in efforts to craft versions of Latina femininity, sexuality, and style that did not conform to dominant (white) standards for feminine beauty. Sylvia Martinez, editor in chief of *Latina* magazine, spoke about Selena's representational legacy in an article commemorating the five-year anniversary of her death: "She made it OK to be sexy and [to] have more curves than you usually see on magazine covers."[38] In her promotional interviews for *Selena* Jennifer Lopez concurred: "Rita Hayworth (who was actually Rita Cansino) and Raquel Welch could only become stars after they disguised themselves. Selena could be who she was and, as for me, for once, I could be proud of my big bottom. . . . In my movies, I've always had costume people looking at me a little awry and immediately fitting me out with things to hide my bottom. I know it. They didn't say, but I know it. . . . All other movies I've done [besides *Selena*], it always seemed like they're trying to hide [my butt] or they think I look fat. Or I'm not the American tradition of beauty."[39] Lopez positions Selena's body as an affirming corrective to both the kinds and the disguise of representations of Latinas in the entertainment industry's history. Like Pérez, Lopez uses her identification with Selena's "big bottom" to launch an attack on systemic racist practices. Claiming an affinity with Selena's rear end permits the affirmation of a Latina identity that is explicitly inclusive of nonwhite(ning) features, which is significant given the dramatic whitening of Lopez's body in the years immediately following her *Selena* success.

Identification with Selena's complexion, and not simply with the contours of her body, was an important part of the practice by which Latinas revalued the dark side of Latina beauty. In an interview for Lourdes Portillo's 1998 documentary, *Corpus: A Home Movie for Selena*, the filmmaker Renée Tajima-Peña explained, "Selena, I really liked, because she looked *normal*. She was gorgeous, but she had a normal look. She was just beautiful, you know. When I was growing up, I wish I'd had someone like Selena to look up to, someone that looked like me [pointing emphatically at her own face], that looked normal."[40] Tajima-Peña's memory of Selena reinscribes the category of normality as the traditionally undervalued olive-skinned face that both she and Selena share. Identification with Selena thus offers a way to mark whiteness, to expose its construction as normative, thereby intervening in its regulatory regimes.

Many Latinas shared Tajima-Peña's identification with Selena's complexion as a means of proclaiming a (re)vision of their own historically devalued bodies. These affirmations of Selena's dark skin were often suffused with desire. "Female identification," Jackie Stacey writes, "contains forms of desire which include, though not exclusively, homoerotic pleasure."[41] In a scene at a Corpus Christi Tejano radio station depicted in *Corpus: A Home Movie for Selena* a Latina calls into the radio show, asserting, "I wanted to say a little bit about Selena. She was a very beautiful person and, you know, that made me feel great because I'm brown, too, and you know [what] people tend to think [about] these features. I thought she was beautiful and not only that—her skin was so—was so soft and—*brown.*" This particular expression of affinity with Selena's skin captures the erotics of the self-affirming practice of Selena identification. Desire emanates from the final sentence: the admiration of Selena's beauty turns into an expression of longing signaled by the transitional phrase "not only that." The pauses following this phrase not only indicate a momentary immersion in the memory of Selena's skin, but also build momentum toward the erotic reference to the skin's "soft" texture, confirmed only through (imagined) touch, and the final shift in tone from description to sigh, the word "brown" descending in a culmination of desire.

This sense of homoerotic love for Selena served as a declaration of self-love for many young Latinas. Yesenia Santos, a Dominican teenager who participated in the *Selena* auditions held in Miami, asserted, "Mis amigos siempre me decían que me parecía a ella. Pienso que por eso yo la amaba tanto [My friends always used to tell me that I looked like Selena. I think that's why I loved her so much]."[42] Love for Selena is predicated upon her proximity and not her distance from oneself. For many young Latinas, to acknowledge love for Selena is to assert a defiant love for themselves, as Claudia Pérez explained:

> I liked [Selena] because she was *morenita* [dark-skinned], too. . . . Growing up, people used to be, "Aye m'ijo tiene ojos verdes [Oh, my baby has green eyes!]" and they always wanted to have a light-skinned baby, or something, you know? And it made me so happy to know that she was, like, my complexion, and she was beautiful, you know. 'Cause when I was growing up, [my family] they used to tell me, "Stay out [of] the sun, you're gonna get dark[er]." Like saying, like, dark was bad or something, you know? So that made me more, like, "Yeah, you know, I love Selena; she has *my* complexion."

Identification with Selena's complexion not only provided a way to speak out against dominant U.S. representations of feminine ideals but also enabled young Latinas to expose how these racial and gendered hierarchies are internalized by Latina/o communities and are ultimately borne by Latina bodies. To love Selena, then, is to refute the racist discourses that circumscribe young Latina upbringing and to highlight how the dark Latina body is marked and policed by multiple forces.

Like Pérez, other Latinas identified with Selena as an icon of shared struggle against the injuries of gender, race, and class. Lucia Orea Chapa, a Tejana interviewed in Portillo's documentary, recalls her response to Selena's murder: "I was like, 'Not Selena!' I said, 'It can't be!' Selena had gotten so popular. Everybody just loved her to death and the way I felt—I felt like—it had been like—maybe part of—like—as if it happened to me." Chapa's reaction does not reflect simply an escapist fanatical over-identification with a fallen star, but points to how Latinas identify with Selena as a means of facing the realities of their daily lives. To identify with Selena's tragedy is to acknowledge and grieve the shared oppression Latina bodies have suffered as a consequence of the representational and material challenges they regularly confront. Chapa's connection with Selena's tragedy underscores how "it"—not so much Selena's murder as a literal reading of the quote would suggest, but rather the devaluation of the Latina body and the struggle for affirming a Latina sexuality—had "happened" to Chapa and to many other Latinas. Within the pronounced pauses of Chapa's statement is the awakened recognition of this shared sense of injury and the expression of mourning over these injuries that identification with Selena sanctions.

℘ Becoming Selena

Throughout the landscape of Selenidad, young Latinas have frequently performed and dressed like Selena as a means of marking her departure and of asserting their own arrivals. This phenomenon of impersonation has provoked frequent comparisons between Selena and that other American icon, Elvis Presley.[43] Like Elvis impersonations, Latina embodiments of Selena are less often acts of re-creation than of self-creation. Eric Lott argues that "the art of impersonation is built on contradiction. . . . Even as [Elvis impersonators] recognize the uniqueness and special power of Elvis Presley, these performers yearn in often unconscious ways to unseat the master."[44] Similarly the act of becoming Selena registers an unmistakable degree of ambivalence: Latinas become Selena as a means to both revere and replace her. And while this perpetual play of ambivalence certainly resonates with Elvis impersonations, the phenomenon of becoming Selena differs in one significant way: whereas Elvis impersonations, as Lott acknowledges, continue the tradition of effacing the black

35. A young Latina performs Selena. Photo by Anuta Portillo. Photo courtesy of Lourdes Portillo. Reprinted with permission.

sources of Elvis's performances, Selena impersonations provide a space for revealing the dark roots of the American racial imaginary by affirming derided aspects of Latina sexuality and style.

To become Selena is not to flee from the constraints of one's own body or bodily markings, but to more fully inhabit them. Cherríe Moraga noted this distinction after observing several young girls performing Selena at the Tejano Fine Arts Academy (figure 35):

> What's interesting is—it's like Selena gave these girls a way to have Chicana sexuality. . . . You know, they're in their bodies, *totally*. They're doing their little [gestures with her hands, evoking Selena's signature *floreo*-esque wrist turns]. I mean, good dancers, really good dancers. And you know, like, there wasn't any of this typical—particularly at that age with that preteen stuff, you know—no *vergüenza* [shame].

They're like, *in* it, and doing it. . . . They're *being* a sexuality. And these songs, you know, I mean even the ones they sang that weren't Selena songs were all these, like, you know, tortured love songs kinda thing, and all about desire and everything. Their little bodies are doing it, you know.[45]

Selena impersonation allows young Latinas to be, as Moraga says, "in their bodies, *totally*," uncompromised by the limitations imposed on them by parental or institutional surveillance. These expressions of sexuality *sin vergüenza* cannot simply be dismissed as shameful attempts at securing sex symbol status or heterosexual attention. For young Latinas routinely subjected to sexual policing, *"being* a sexuality" is a bold assertion of ownership over one's body. Given their economic dependency on their families, young Latinas become Selena to embody a sexuality that, as Julie Bettie observes in the expressions of sexuality among the working-class Mexican American girls she studies, can "serve to reject teachers' and parents' methods of keeping them childlike."[46]

The practice of becoming Selena afforded many young Latinas a repertoire of critical and choreographic gestures for maneuvering within the systems of surveillance that they faced in their daily lives; however, within the context of the *Selena* auditions, young Latina acts of becoming Selena were at times framed—and sexualized—as a spectacle for voyeuristic pleasure. Claudia Pérez recalled the audition's representational economy: "[At the *Selena* auditions] there was everything. All [kinds of] Latinos. And there were even white girls there and there was a black guy I remember . . . and he had a Selena shirt on. He started telling me about the songs and stuff. He was just watching. He had just come to watch beautiful Latina women, he was telling me. And there were other guys there [watching], too. And Jorge was there from Channel 66. And it was true. All there. They were all beautiful Latina women. All of 'em. You know. From all over."[47] Pérez's comments attend to the Latina bodies called upon to stage the cultural force of latinidad and to the scopophilic frame that surrounds their participation in this process. And yet, while a diverse array of Latinas "from all over" are on display, Pérez's keen observations and her appropriation of the term "beautiful" to describe all of the women present also suggest that the auditions provided a space for Latinas to negotiate this "trap of visibility."[48]

As a commentary recorded for radio broadcast, Pérez's report, "1000

Women Become Selena," troubles this trap of the visible by focusing on the aural terrain of the auditions, showcasing the voices of several young Latinas who practiced becoming Selena. With the skill of a budding ethnographer, Pérez launches her report by thoughtfully interviewing twelve-year-old Jessica Lara, who, with her mother, had undertaken a seven-hour road trip from St. Paul, Minnesota, to participate in the *Selena* auditions. Pérez narrates the recorded interview: "Jessica's a beautiful little girl; she has long black hair and a cinnamon complexion. She's wearing a Selena outfit: knee-length boots, spandex hot pants, and a black padded bustier with gold trimming over the breast. It's Jessica's dream to be like Selena. She wants to be a singer and sing in English and Spanish. She came to the auditions, but not just so she could be a movie star. It's that she wants to feel closer to Selena. . . . I asked Jessica in Spanish how she felt about Selena's death. She started crying. Then I started crying, too. . . . After Selena's death, Jessica and her family went to visit her grave in Corpus Christi, Tejas." The segment then returns to Jessica's voice, recalling the memory of her gravesite pilgrimage: "I was sitting down, and I was, like, hugging the grave . . . and I sang to [Selena]. I think I sang, 'Como la Flor.' I mean, 'cause it reminds me of her." With encouragement and a harmonizing refrain offered from Pérez, Jessica then launches into an improvised rendition of the song: "Como la flor, como la flor / con tanto amor, con tanto amor / me distes tú." Pérez's narration translates over Jessica's soaring vocals: "The words mean, 'Like the flower with much love you gave to me. I'll march on. I know how to lose in love. But, oh my, how it hurts me.'"

Pérez's description highlights how Jessica's identification with Selena captures an expression of an emergent, racially marked Latina sexuality. When detailing Jessica's "Selena outfit" Pérez notes that the gold-trimmed bustier covers "the breast"—not the presexualized chest of girlhood and not yet the developed breasts of womanhood. Pérez's reference to the singular breast acknowledges Jessica's in-between stage of emergent sexuality that is asserted by donning the outfit of a diva whose untimely death crystallized her as the icon of a Latina identity-in-process (rather than one that was fully developed or determined). Jessica harnesses the potential of Selena's embodiment of "becoming" to convey her own emerging nontraditional, nonwhite expression of budding sexuality.[49] Pérez does not judge Jessica's spandex hot pants and gold-trimmed bustier as low-class, age-inappropriate, or pathologically fanatical (a view frequently expressed in press coverage about the auditions) but as what Julie Bettie calls a "symbolic economy of style" through which class and race identifications are declared and negotiated.[50] Given that a large part of Selena's staying power is due to the sense of becoming that she represented—as an imminent "crossover" star, an aspiring clothing designer, a Tejana musician in the process of emerging into a Latina superstar—it is no surprise that young Latinas have used the creative sphere of Selenidad to chart and give voice to the liminal social, economic, and generational roles they occupy.

Pérez's reference to darker physical features and her Spanish-to-English translation of "Como la Flor"'s lyrics highlight the racial and linguistic markings that frame latinidad and suggest how Latinas use Selenidad to resignify these categories. Pérez's introductory affirmation of the traits— black hair and cinnamon skin—shared by Jessica and Selena underscores how Selena's looks legitimated others who share her traditionally undervalued features. Jessica, like Selena, is thus "beautiful" precisely because of these darker physical markings, not in spite of them. In Pérez's closing display of her facility with both English and Spanish she uses the space of Selenidad to counter popular depictions of Latinas as exclusively Spanish-speaking (unassimilated) or exaggeratedly accented-English-speaking (unassimilable) figures in U.S. culture. Pérez's translation of "Como la Flor" riding atop the echoes of Jessica's singing voice transforms the song into a doleful but affirming duet of momentary connection among young Latinas and thereby marks a significant departure from most other public acts of Spanish-to-English translation deployed at the turn of the century to manipulate the Latino vote or the Latino market.

The interview that follows Pérez's opening narration reveals how the act of becoming Selena works as a critically and affectively useful embodied practice among young Latinas. Jessica's memory of hugging Selena's grave and of singing her a love song is suffused with desire and agency, not unlike the girl fans Stacy Wolf describes, whose "longing for the diva captures both identification and desire; it is an intensely homo-erotic affect that is expressed not as about having them [the divas] but about being them."[51] Jessica expresses this identification with and longing for Selena through the performance of mourning: the gravesite visit, the elegy unleashed. And like Viola in *Twelfth Night*, whose response to mourning is to transform herself into the brother she has lost, Jessica mourns Selena by becoming her.[52] For these young women imitation serves as the practice whereby grief is occupied, desire is shaped, and daily life is managed. Mourning literally becomes them; more precisely, mourning Selena through the act of imitation encourages Jessica to become a desiring Latina subject. Jessica's act therefore reveals how young Latinas become Selena, not as a way to lose themselves, but as a means of self-discovery.[53]

This "intensely homoerotic" staging of impersonation subsequently leads to homosocial bonds between and among other young women and girls within the space of Selenidad. Jackie Stacey explains that identificatory practices among female spectators involve the "transformation of the self to become more like the star they admire or to involve others in the recognition of their similarity with the star." As such, these processes are invariably "social practices."[54] This transformational social practice is deftly represented in the interview when Pérez, barely audible but conspicuously unedited, prompts Jessica to sing "Como la Flor" and when Jessica takes up the song's opening refrain. This brief, improvisatory exchange, a re-enactment of a frequently staged scene from Selena's performance history of the song, captures the sharing and consolidation of Latina desire and identification. Just as Selena "passed the mic" to other young women and girls during her live performances of "Como la Flor," offering the song as a vehicle for showcasing a range of Latina skills and aspirations, Pérez and Jessica pass on the song in a gesture of participatory, Latina self-expression. In this context "Como la Flor" is transformed from a bouncy, pop love song into an elegy for Selena and, as with Agina Alvarez in the musical about Selena, into a declaration of emerging Latina (vocal) power. Both Pérez and Jessica easily invoke the song's lyrics and melody, suggesting that sharing in a performance of "Como la Flor" has emerged as a rite of passage for many young women aspiring to become Latina.[55] Sharing the song, the young women become, as Jessica dreams, "like Selena," by becoming Latina through the act of participatory performance.

Moments of Latina connection and community, like that shared by Pérez and Jessica, worked to counter the experience of the audition itself, which, as Pérez describes in her report, proved to be less than inclusive for many Latinas ostensibly invited to be, as Nava asserted, "part of the process": "When you finally get inside to the audition, it's kind of disappointing. It's like it's over before it starts. There were like twenty girls on the stage at a time. They sit you down at these tables, give you this fake smile, hand you a card to fill out, ask you one question, then tell you to stand up and dance. You dance for thirty seconds. Sometimes they don't even play music. When I went up there, . . . [they] didn't bother to look at me. When we were dancing, they only gave you sixty seconds total to make an impression. So what are they looking for?" The segment cuts immediately to Pérez's interview with Nava, in which he answers her question with one word: "Magic." When pushed to elaborate, Nava falters, "Well—I don't know—that special magic that made Selena, that—she was very out-going, an incredible entertainer, very gifted, very beautiful." The editing choice here is instructive: by positioning Pérez's audition description against her interview with Nava, the report demystifies the star discovery narrative that pervaded the open casting call process. In Pérez's account there is certainly nothing magical or inclusive—only fake smiles and swift dismissals—about the experience shared by the young Latinas invited to audition. Once again Pérez attends to the dynamics of hypervisibility and erasure that frame Latina representation; not only does the casting team not appear to be looking for "Selena" or for the magic she ostensibly possessed, but they don't appear to be looking at all.

But Pérez remained undeterred. In the midst of her interview with Nava she narrates over their exchange: "I thought, if he wants magic, I'll give him magic. I told him about Jessica. Of everyone I interviewed, she had the pizzazz. She looked like Selena, she had big dreams like Selena. And she had Selena in her heart." For Pérez, this space of Selenidad, no matter how compromised by Hollywood co-optation, encourages acts of Latina advocacy. Her narration here literally voices over the authority of Nava's evasive references to magic, offering her own definition of a successful *Selena* candidate: someone who possesses Selena's dark features and aspirational values, someone whose pizzazz is predicated on the ways she has already, "in her heart," become Selena. In this act of promotion, Pérez embodies the magic of Selena, the sharing of the spotlight to make way for others like her. To identify with Selena is, ultimately, to identify with and advocate for other Latinas.

In our conversation Pérez elaborated on the details of her audition experience in Chicago, highlighting the racial, gendered, and generational power dynamics that shaped the process:

They gave you a number, or something. They called you up and you went up there. And then you danced—you—they made you—well [they said], "Just dance for me" and you see the girls dancing. And I was sitting down and I was watching the girls, you know, and the guys were not even looking at them. . . . [The casting people] didn't even know who Selena was. Some girl told me, "I didn't know who she was until she died." So that's what got me. It's like you don't get people like that. She was a *guera* [a white girl]. And then when I went up there, I went 'cause my sister was like, "Go! Go! Go! Go! Go!" And I was like, you know, I got to . . . see what's going on here. . . . And um, I went up there and then for sure, he [the casting guy] didn't look at me. And I danced a little bit. Of course, I tried to imitate Selena, but you can't *be* Selena. There's only *one* Selena. And um, you know, I tried and he didn't look. . . . It was just, "Okay, bye, we'll call you." Shheeze call me, yeah right. How's he gonna remember me, you know? . . . Well, I didn't really care. I knew it was a scam. To me it seemed like a scam. . . . Why I did it? Because yeah, I wanted to see what it was about, you know. If they were really scammin.' And I wanted to watch how they watch me.

Pérez registers mistrust in the efficacy of entertainment industry attempts at Latina representation ("but you can't *be* Selena") and in the terms upon which Latinas are let in on the process ("To me it seemed like a scam"). In fact, her hunch about and subsequent investigation of this scam suggest her politically astute belief that the auditions actually reflected the co-optation of Latina practices as a means for increasing publicity and revenues for the film.[56] In her descriptions the political economy of Latinas within this staging of latinidad is made clear: Latino men and corporate executives (Nava, Quintanilla, and Warner Bros.) do the inviting; uninformed *güeros* and *güeras* (the Anglo "girl" who did not know of Selena until after she died and the "guys [who] were not even looking") do the judging; and Latinas perform the labor ("Just dance for me").[57]

While this depersonalized procedure is not unlike any large casting call audition, its staging within the context of latinidad reinscribes invidious inter- and intracultural power dynamics among Latinas/os along the lines of race and gender. Publicly performing Latina bodies — specifically, racially marked Latina bodies — perform the labor in corporate attempts to increase profits and to legitimize this foray into the Latina/o market and in Latino attempts to vie for a piece of the American pie. Yet Pérez's claims also emphasize that the auditions provide a space for at least one Latina to return the gaze. Here also is a place to "watch how they watch me," a place where sisters encourage one another to perform ("Go! Go! Go! Go!"), where fellow audition participants watch after one another. At yet another site of official Selena commemoration (lest we forget the Selena memorial or the musical), Selenidad encourages Latinas to exploit the moments of incomplete surveillance, to assert a Latina subject position in the space where the watchers willfully choose not to see.

Other audition participants shared Pérez's sentiment that "you can't *be* Selena," emphasizing instead that to become Selena is to incorporate her into one's own expression of Latina subjectivity. Pérez closes her report by turning her attention to two young women who offer critical reflections about their participation in the "disappointing" auditions:

> *Pérez*: After a long day, the cars had cleared. Two cousins who flew in from Texas were sitting outside in the cold, eating pizza and waiting for a Chicago family friend to pick them up. They had arrived early in the morning and they didn't get much sleep. They weren't sure when their ride was coming, or where they were going to spend the night. I asked them what they thought of the auditions.
>
> *Young Woman #1*: I dunno, I don't think it went as great as I thought it would be. . . . Because you know, it's like, I don't think the producers were there when, when I got up to, you know, do my stuff. So, I dunno, they [are] look[ing] for something different. . . . They're not looking for a true Selena. They're just looking for appearances. And it's really bad, I mean, they might know who Selena was, but not truly what she meant to us, so. . . .
>
> *Pérez*: They had spent $135 each, saved from baby-sitting to get to Chicago. But they didn't feel bad.
>
> *Young Woman #1*: No, it's fine, because we get [*sic*] to meet a lot of people and stuff. We just came and we knew we were not gonna get picked, you know, but we still came and took a chance because that's the thing that Selena would always say, you know: "You have a thing, you go for it. Don't let nobody put you down. . . . Give whatever you have." And that's what we did. So that's the reason why we came here.
>
> *Pérez*: They just sat there on the bench, waiting. They weren't really dressed for Chicago weather. They wore fishnet pantyhose, real short

shorts, bustiers, and thin leather jackets. You could tell they were really cold. They were anxious for their ride to show up. A couple of weeks later, it was announced that none of the girls from the open auditions were chosen for the Selena part. Not them, not me, not Jessica, nobody.

This exchange troubles Nava's interpretation of the auditions with its focus on the material negotiations (saving baby-sitting money) and the symbolic negotiations (evoking Selena in a way not represented by the audition organizers) undertaken by these Latinas to enable and to assess their participation in the auditions. The experiences of these young women deflate Nava's promises by revealing that working hard and saving money do not guarantee access to the American Dream. The young women reveal their motivations despite their foreknowledge of the setup; they claim they did it because Selena would have wanted it, not because they were invited by Latino men or a major studio. They clearly share Pérez's suspicion that, as she narrates earlier in the episode, *"maybe the auditions were just a publicity stunt."* Participation in the auditions thus provided not simply an opportunity to become American or even part of a cohesive Latina/o community but to assert a Latina subjectivity unrecognized by the inviter or the judges. In this context the assertion "They're not looking for a true Selena" does not signal authenticity but serves as a way to expose and counter the processes by which Latinas are encouraged to participate in the co-optation of Selena.

This is not to deny the allure of the potential financial rewards and recognition offered by the casting call, especially given the economic situation of many Latinas. But notably these incentives were never mentioned by the auditioners during the report or by Pérez during our conversations.[58] In fact the discussions of mobility that surfaced among the participants do not suggest an uncritical yearning for the American Dream, evoked by Nava and by the film's narrative frame, but signal what Lott calls a "trope of triumph" for young Latinas. Lott describes this trend among Elvis impersonators, whose "fantasies about Elvisian excess" and rhetoric of mobility do not signal a longing to enter a higher class but a moment of "self-validation."[59] Likewise, for many Latinas, to move like Selena in performance is also to acknowledge that many of them have been forced to move, like Selena, as a result of economic disparity.[60] To become Selena is to share in and to validate the movements of the Latina laboring body and to move the Latina body in unprecedented directions.⁶¹ In this way identification with Selena was not reducible to "performing like" or "wanting to be" Selena, but operated as a creative embodied practice through which many young Latinas strove momentarily to move beyond the restrictive choreographies of their daily lives. Clearly the auditions provided a culturally sanctioned physical mobility, as revealed by the young women who traveled from Texas and by Pérez, whose intra-Chicago migrations required her to cross local borders from her own predominantly Mexican-populated Little Village neighborhood into Humboldt Park.⁶² Given the historical struggles in Chicago between the Mexicano/a and Puerto Rican communities, this migration signals how the Selena auditions exposed the tensions undergirding latinidad (i.e., intra-Latina/o conflicts) and simultaneously encouraged its creation. But what is perhaps most compelling in Pérez's report is her indictment of the audition's *failure* to crown a successor. Whereas, as Nava would have it, the auditions sought to stage latinidad as a cultural and economic force, this attempt ultimately staged the scenario of the failed Latina crossover, a formulation that framed popular representations of Latinas (and Selena in particular) at the close of the century. This positioning of young Latinas as failed crossovers awaiting entry into the American Dream was, tragically, the only way the auditions acknowledged how these young women and girls had become (like) Selena.

༄ From a Distance, toward Desire

While Claudia Pérez's report foregrounds the savvy young Latinas who, in the face of the audition "scam," attempt to forge a moment of community, the framing of the segment on the radio program *This American Life* in an episode about obsession undercuts the report's representational interventions. Ira Glass, the host of *This American Life*, begins this episode as he always does: "Back for another week documenting life in these United States." The week's title and theme, Glass says, is "From a Distance: Admiring Someone from Afar, Trying to Get Closer to Them." He then chronicles the four acts that the episode will comprise: a young female artist who becomes obsessed with a dead Dutch male artist; Miles Davis's biographer, Quincy Troupe, whose obsession with Davis eventually led to a friendship between the two men; an anonymous man who became obsessed with and began stalking the Snuggles bear featured on fabric softener ads; and one thousand women who attempted to become Selena. Within this context Selena fans are pathologized as obsessive fanatics despite the critically incisive, lucid, and rational responses they conveyed throughout the report. Despite whatever good intentions may have motivated the inclusion of young Latina voices in the soundscape of *This American Life*, the narrative framing works to obscure the creative and critical value of becoming Selena.

From a distance, it appears that within the frame of racialized pathology Latinas are granted space within the borders of this American life. From a distance *This American Life* suggests that Selena and those who would be her have apparently, *por fin*, crossed over. But upon closer scrutiny the episode's frame appears, like the auditions, to offer false promises. Introducing the segment on the Selena auditions, Glass distinguishes it from the others in the episode: "It's one thing to try to get close to someone. It's another thing to try to become them." Set within this frame, the girls' and young women's actions appear as inevitable failures—recall that none were selected to actually become Selena—as futile attempts at crossing over into this American life. The frame and tone of the radio show implies that "it's one thing to try to get close" to a Latina who crossed over into American success—posthumously, no less—but it's pathological to try to become her. One thousand Selenas are thereby transformed into one thousand simulacra, who in the end still wait for their place on the American stage, who remain sitting on the bench, waiting for a ride home, a home that is far from here. In a performative move the show enacts what the auditions promote: the circulation of the Latina failed crossover as the means by which to include Latinas/os within the national imaginary.

Yet the story does not end here, and neither does this episode of *This American Life*. Following the "1000 Women Become Selena" segment, Glass speaks briefly with Pérez. They convey an easy rapport, established, no doubt, as a result of Pérez's participation in a previous episode of the show. For the episode's closing song (differing each week to capture the thematic tenor of the show), Pérez has chosen Selena's rendition of the mariachi song "Tú Solo Tú," which swells behind Glass's and Pérez's voices:

Glass: So, Claudia, so explain why this is the song you wanted us to play on our program after your story about Selena.

Pérez: I like it because she sings it with mariachis. And it's an old song, you know, from Mexico.

Glass: When I think of Selena, I don't think of her as a mariachi singer—

Pérez: Right, you don't. That's why—she didn't sing with mariachis. She was more of a beat-y person, you know, with a lot of beat. And that's why this song, this one and this other song that she sang—everybody sang it when she was—when she left.

Glass: Everybody sang when she left? You mean everybody sang [it] when she died?

Pérez: Yeah, yeah.

Glass: Listen to you. You sound like that girl [Jessica Lara] in your story who's like, "She's not dead, she's just sleeping." The way you just said that.

Pérez: *(laughter)*

Glass: "When she left." She didn't just leave, honey—

Pérez: Well, I don't like saying "death."

The music swells once more, Selena's throaty vocals reverberating across the airwaves. By proclaiming, "I don't like saying 'death,'" Pérez reenacts a gesture from the opening of her report, when she and Jessica passed the torch of Selenidad. In their shared stance of refusing death Pérez and Jessica assert an emergent Latina subjectivity that defies prevailing constructions of Latinas. Pérez refuses the narrative that casts Selena and the Latina subject as a racialized Eurydice whose story begins and ends after her death with a crossing over into another world, where she is promised freedom by a culture which cannot believe she is real until (indeed can assure its own realness only after) it has turned its gaze on her. Selena, and subsequently the girls who become her, are not dead but, as Jessica suggests, "just sleeping." Not a sleeping beauty who awaits the "magic" of an officially appointed, resurrecting prince, but a sleeping giant, *una multitud de Selenas*, the many bodies in the one, beginning to stir.

Pérez intervenes in dominant crossover narratives about Selena and Latinas in general, saying no to death and instead, with her song selection, positioning Selena in an oppositional history. Pérez's choice of Selena's rendition of a mariachi song, a traditional Mexican genre, instead of a hybridized Tejano song "with a lot of beat" may appear at first to be an attempt at staging authenticity, an attempt at simplistically and sentimentally appropriating Selena to perform Mexican-ness as opposed to American-ness. But within the context of the episode, Pérez's evocation of a Mexican *canción* ranchera locates Selena in a particular performance tradition that values voice over voluptuousness. The ranchera is a musical form that foregrounds the vocal skill and the self-conscious, intense emotional affect of its singers and that, like melodrama, directs its over-the-top style steeped in nostalgic longing to topics of social concern.[63] As Olga Nájera-Ramírez notes, female performers and audiences have historically employed the ranchera's self-conscious stylings as a site for engaging in "feminist interventions."[64] Pérez's evocation of Selena's version of a ranchera acts as one such intervention. By positioning Selena within a musical genealogy of powerfully affective singers, Pérez not only critiques the audition's devaluation of Latina voices—recall that no singing skills were required—but also counters dominant crossover rhetoric that constructs Selena as a "Tex-Mex Madonna" pop icon characterized by stylish costumes and dance moves rather than substantive talent.[65] Moreover, since the song Pérez selects does not have "a lot of beat" no one can summon her to dance. This choice not only refuses the failed crossover narrative, but tactically speaks back to the casting personnel who can only say to her, "Just dance for me."

Pérez's choice to close the show with a ranchera does more than simply speak back to the radio producers or the film's casting personnel; it also explicitly carves out a space for grief on her own terms. Like other female consumers of rancheras whom Nájera-Ramírez documents, Pérez uses the ranchera as a powerfully effective and affective means through which to perform grief.[66] The very "excessiveness" of the ranchera's emotional tenor provides an expansive space for the articulation of multiple griefs. Pérez exploits this expansiveness, insisting upon a moment of grieving for more than the loss of Selena. She refuses to say "death" because it cannot encompass the depth and contours of her mourning over a range of injustices: the ignorance about Selena expressed by casting agents, the framing of the radio show, the plight of the thousands of Latinas who were not offered the opportunity to become Selena, and the use of young Latinas by Latino filmmakers and major studios. Pérez's insistence on Selena's rendition of "an old song, you know, from Mexico" signifies a particularly Mexicana emotional register, whereby she momentarily prioritizes an affiliation with mexicanidad over latinidad. By squarely positioning both herself and Selena within Mexicana performance traditions, Pérez recuperates Selena's Mexicana identity, effaced in some Latina appropriations of her. In this way Pérez uses the complex poetics of the ranchera to negotiate the "fraught and fractured" possibilities of Latina identification.

As our interview came to a close I too asked Pérez why she had chosen the song "Tú Solo Tú." She replied, "Because . . . that song she sang more like . . . *con ganas*." To do something *con ganas* is to do so with great desire, gusto, or enthusiasm. To act *con ganas* is to express a self-conscious, unapologetic emotionality. Selena sang "Tú Solo Tú" with *ganas*; like other female ranchera singers before her, she "lived what she sang." That is, she possessed the performative skill to embody—to live—what she sang as she performed, as opposed to singing what she lived. This distinction foregrounds a self-conscious rather than an ontological emotionality expressed by Mexicana ranchera singers. Furthermore Selena sang this song *con ganas* by altering the opening lyrics to "decenter the male perspective embedded in the narrative."[67] Pérez's return to the workings of desire and intense emotion within performance reflects how Selena is invoked and circulated as an actively desiring agent through whom Latinas assert and refashion their own desire. Her comments underscore Emma Pérez's argument that "Selena represents decolonial desire," a desire that emerges "in that in-between space where Chicanas such as Selena exhibited an in-your-face, working-class sexuality and did so with pride, not inhibition."[68]

Claudia Pérez and her fellow auditioners recognize how becoming Selena demonstrates not a pathologically affective Latina/o excess, but a critically generative one. This critically generative excess allows for a space wherein acts *con ganas* can emerge: the resignifying of ranchera lyrics, the refusal to say "death," the clandestine journeys taken by many young Latinas to the Selena auditions. When Pérez protests, "You can't *be* Selena," or when one of the Texas cousins assert, "They're not looking for a true Selena . . . they might know who Selena was, but not truly what she meant to us," these young women are not only indicting entertainment and other corporate industries for failing to acknowledge this distinction, but they are expressing the potent effects of this Latina generative excess. These young Latinas reveal that a worthy surrogate does not simply try to "be Selena," but rather tries to be "what Selena meant to us." For as Pérez suggested, there is "Tú Solo Tú": there is "you, only you," Selena. The worthy Selena surrogate necessarily creates a generative excess of Selena wherein Latina desire can find a home even as the Latina body is consumed and circulated within the market. Thus through their critical articulations and bold migrations, Pérez and the Texas cousins success-fully become (more than) Selena, and in this space of "more than" — of Latina generative excess — these young Latinas "watch how they watch me," watch after one another, refuse the closure of the death narrative, and, if only momentarily, awaken the sleeping giant with formidable *ganas*.

FIVE

"Como la Flor" Reprised: Queer Selenidad

Dissident practices like diva worship function importantly to provide queer subjects with emotional sustenance and tactical knowledges that are quite literally lifesaving, according a safe harbor from which to embark on, and a galaxy of reassuringly brilliant stars by which to navigate, the exciting, indispensable, but ever difficult journey to queer actualization.
— Brett Farmer, "Julie Andrews Made Me Gay"

Bringing back the dead . . . is the ultimate queer act.
— Sharon Holland, *Raising the Dead*

She walks onstage, microphone in hand. She is wearing her trademark outfit: a one-shouldered, fitted red top studded with sparkles and thigh-hugging black spandex pants cut below the navel and flared at the ankle. She is glorious, her black patent-leather stilettos shining, gold hoop earrings swaying as she easily assumes center stage. She is a girl-woman, bronze skin gleaming, a newly minted copper coin eager for exchange. "I love to sing," she says. "I love to sing when I'm sad. I love to sing when I'm happy. I think I was *born* to be a singer. Since I was a little kid, I have had a lot of talents to imitate singers like Selena, Gloria Trevi, Olga Tañon, and others—how they sing and how they dance. I tried to kill myself with pills and by jumping out of a car, and it did not work. I know that God don't want me to die because he has something special for me to do in this world. *I* know it's singing." The bouncy, synthesized opening bars of "Como la Flor" begin to play through the sound system, and she leans into alternating back steps on the cumbia beat as the audience cheers her on. She sings, "Yo sé que tienes un nuevo amor [I know that you have a new love]," and as she starts the second line of the song, "Sin embargo, te deseo lo mejor [Even still, I wish you the best]," a crowd of young girl fans rushes the stage, squealing with delight, clutching their chest and hair in poses of excitement. The girls flank her on the stage as she proceeds, "Si en mí no encontraste felicidad / Tal vez alguien más te la dará [If you did not find happiness in me / Perhaps someone else will give it to you]." With her girl fans caught in the cumbia rhythm alongside her, she slides into the chorus, "Como la flor (Como la flor) / Con tanto amor (con tanto amor) / Me diste tú / Se marchitó / Me marcho hoy / Yo sé perder / Pero ay-ay-ay, cómo me duele / Ay-ay-ay, cómo me duele [Like the flower / With so much love / You gave me / It withered / Today I leave / I know how to lose / But oh, how it hurts me / Oh, how it hurts me]." The fans punctuate the song with their screams of adoration, and she smiles coyly, taking in the acclaim before she launches into the second verse: "Si vieras cómo duele perder tu amor [If you saw how it hurt to lose your love]."

But then she does something unexpected, curious, queer. Instead of singing the second line of the verse as it was written ("Con tu adiós te llevas mi corazón [With your goodbye, you take my heart]"), she repeats the second line of the first verse, "Sin embargo, te deseo lo mejor [Even still, I wish you the best]." The line propels her downstage, where, on the word *deseo*, she reaches for a long-stemmed red rose with her right hand and extends the flower to a woman seated in the audience. The girl fans giggle nervously, knowingly, laughing warmly to affirm the offering. She does not miss a beat. She continues to ride through the remaining verse and repeated chorus, and as she closes with her final "Ay-ay-ay cómo me duele," the audience roars and the girl fans erupt in unrestrained shrieks, hands outstretched with the hope of contact, with requests for autographs. She turns toward them and graciously signs her name, Melissa, and turns one last time to wave to the audience before disappearing backstage. The girl fans run screaming after her, their cries of adulation marking the final sound in the act.[1]

Melissa's staging of "Como la Flor" was one of twenty brief acts in the culminating public performance of original work produced by the participants of Grrl Action, a writing and performance workshop for teenage girls sponsored by the Austin-based theater collective Rude Mechanicals.[2] Within this context Melissa's imitation of Selena, like those embodied by the young women at the *Selena* auditions, operates as an identificatory practice for navigating the material and affective landscapes of emergent Latina subject formation. Melissa (who identifies herself as Puerto Rican later in the show) positions herself within a genealogy of an explicitly pan-Latina pop star pantheon: Gloria Trevi, the scandal-ridden, Mexican pop-rock icon; Olga Tañón, the Puerto Rican performer known for singing Dominican *merengue*; and Selena, the queen of Tejano music. Melissa's reference to her own girlhood practice of imitating these singers signals the process by which young women become Latina through acts of becoming the icons they emulate. She enacts both the aspiration of her own dream to be a singer and the fulfillment of that dream through her staged interaction with the screaming fans who signal and encourage her performance as an accomplished diva. In this way her impersonation does not simply re-create Selena, but stages the process of Selena's iconization. The act is thus a metaperformance of Selenidad. By showcasing the affective sounds and gestures of diva fandom on stage, Melissa's participatory performance underscores Stacy Wolf's argument: "Performance is built into divaness, as is the spectator's emotional labor; fans are necessary for the diva to exist."[3] In particular Melissa's rendition of "Como la Flor" foregrounds the homoerotics of identification with the diva; performing Selena provides a conduit for performing desire, or, as Sarah Myers observes, "Melissa's performance of Selena plays on an even deeper level with the complicated nature of desire—desire to be, to be like, to have, to have sex with, *and* all the complicated spaces between and intersections of such desires."[4]

In her unabashed engagement with the "intersections" of desires, Melissa points toward the queer contours of Selenidad. Her version of Selena's signature song—with its untranslated Spanish expression of same-sex desire, its lyrical alterations, and its depiction of girl fans longing for the Latina diva—stages queer latinidad in both its production and reception modes.[5] Her refusal to translate the song's Spanish lyrics (or to elaborate on her references to Latin/a American pop stars), despite performing for an English-dominant audience, signals her awareness that her assertion of queerness is inseparable from her identification as a Latina. Moreover the untranslated Spanish lyrics sonically establish a moment of queer Latina "counterintimacy" between Melissa and her chosen spectator that uses the public realm of performance to make audible queer desire while explicitly excluding the English-speaking spectators who

share the space.[6] Melissa's untranslated performance reveals how Selenidad functions as a space for what Horacio N. Roque Ramírez calls "queer
sonic *latinaje*," the creation and affirmation of productive queer Latina/o
pleasures and cultural citizenship through the use of sound and movement.[7]

Melissa transforms "Como la Flor" into Homo la Flor, signaling its
status as an anthem for queer Latinas/os. She queers the traditionally im-
plied heterosexual address of the song through the repetition of the line
"Sin embargo, te deseo lo mejor." She clearly knows the correct lyrics to
"Como la Flor"; in the previous evening's performance, in which she did
not offer a flower to one of her spectators, she sang the second verse with
the original lyrics unaltered.[8] Her alteration accompanied by her flower
exchange thus emerges as a conscious expression of queer Latina desire,
wherein queerness is understood as an action rather than an essence.[9]
With her repetition of the word *deseo*, uttered as she reaches for the rose,
Melissa resignifies the verb form "to wish" as its noun form, "desire." She
queers the resigned wish conveyed in the original lyrics of the song, "Even
still, I wish you the best," transforming the lovelorn sigh into an active
expression of emergent queer agency. Her gesture transforms the *flor* in
"Como la Flor" from a metaphor for the withering affections of a former
lover into a symbol of the bold assertion and public exchange of queer
desire. Notably, her fans giggle with approval at such a risky declaration,
offering an instructive response for the spectators offstage to mimic. In
this moment the performance cleverly appropriates the affective terrain of
Selena adoration as the soundscape for marking and legitimating a queer
Latina expressive space. Her performance queers Selenidad: Selena's diva
body is brought back from the dead, to reference Sharon Holland, in the
ultimate queer act. But this staging of "Como la Flor" also reveals Selenidad as a queering agent, as the force that brings Melissa's queerness out,
and, as Melissa's references to her previous suicide attempts suggest, as
the ultimate queer act that brings Melissa back from the dead.

Queer Latinas/os have frequently claimed Selena and Selenidad in
efforts to theorize, practice, and affirm queer latinidad. But what makes
Selena and Selenidad so readily queer(ed)? As chapter 1 illustrated, Selena's
live performances often queered the traditional boundaries of Latin/o
music and dance forms, while the details of her biography and the circumstances of her death have often fit within queer narrative frames. Sub-

sequently Selenidad is frequently interpreted as a legibly queer Latina/o text invoked to structure queer Latina/o self-understandings. But beyond its work as a narrative device, Selenidad also operates as a queering agent within latinidad, as a repertoire of acts or performative practices that consolidate queer Latina/o cultural affiliation. Moreover queer drag performances of Selena refute drag's conventional (white) standards of feminine glamour and thereby frequently serve as disidentificatory practices of belonging within the contexts of latinidad and queer expressive culture.[10] Selenidad activates one such sphere wherein queer Latinas/os productively and imaginatively disidentify with the prevailing heteronormative family structuring of latinidad and with the white racial politics of queer camp culture.

A close look at Selenidad as a queer text, performative mode, and set of performance practices reveals, as Melissa's performance highlights, how Selena's memorial terrain serves as a solid foundation on which queer Latina/o worlds are built.[11] Two of the most prominent queer memorial practices that proliferate within the sphere of Selenidad are Latina lesbian readings of Selena's death scene and queer performances of Selena, from Melissa's emergent queer homage within a girl-empowerment context to drag impersonations enacted at queer venues across the country. Latina lesbians frequently deploy queer readings of Selenidad in efforts to craft feminist critiques of Latino patriarchy, while queer Latina/o drag performers embody Selena as a means of staging survival, realness, and resiliency in the midst of AIDS, racism, and other tragedies. These queer Latina/o cultural practices are evocatively captured in Lourdes Portillo's documentary *Corpus: A Home Movie for Selena* and its companion video, *A Conversation with Academics about Selena*, and in the archives and participant memories of queer organizers and artists at ALLGO: A Statewide Queer People of Color Organization (formerly Austin's Latina/o Gay, Lesbian, Bisexual, and Transgender Association; hence the acronym) based in Austin, Texas.[12] Portillo's films provide illuminating interviews with and footage of queer Latina/o engagements with Selena, and ALLGO community members offer evocative memories of and staged tributes to her. Both realms of queer Latina/o evidence reveal the ways that Selenidad provides an expressive platform for articulating queer Latina/o grief, desire, critical commentary, and working-class Latina/o camp sensibilities.

Not unlike the measurements of her famous purple pantsuit, Selena's diva status was filled out by and overflowed with her fabulously sequined disco fashion, her dolefully expressive singing style tempered by pop star saccharine, and her public struggles with and triumph over Spanish-language acquisition.[13] Selena's persona and performance style thus shared with that of other enshrined divas a delight in self-conscious excess, a frequent staging of perseverance amid suffering, an array of self-created costumes, and a careful negotiation between exquisitely crafted self-image and an embodiment of authenticity. But Selena also brought a specifically *brown* sensibility to divadom. That is, unlike other pop divas, such as Madonna, Selena's fabulousness factor was not predicated on the expropriation of black, brown, or queer expressive practices, but relied instead on the bold assertion of working-class racialized female style without apology and without a distancing, appropriative wink. She derived her diva power from showcasing the dark roots of divadom. Her particular brand of divahood combined and offered homage to a range of racialized and cross-class styles and attitudes: Chicana *rasquache,* Latina *chusmería,* working-class Tejana "tackiness," Dolores del Rio "high-class" glamour, synthesizer-driven polyester pop, Janet Jackson–inspired choreography, voluptuously mature femininity, effervescent girly charm, and softball-playing tomboy grit. The explicitly performative nature of her public and stage personas and the apparent ease with which she moved along their expansive spectrums highlight the queerness of divahood, or the ways that divahood is, as Susan J. Leonardi and Rebecca A. Pope observe, "ever a gender disorder."[14] For Selena the dis-order produced by her divaness did not just reorient heteronormative binaries of gendered and sexual orientation, but also disrupted the white racial—and racist—logic and cosmopolitan classism that undergird conventional constructions of divadom.[15]

Selena's fulsome and emotive vocal quality evoked the *filin,* or deliberately performative singing styles of Latin/a American female bolero and ranchera performers whose melodramatic flair and world-weary resiliency secured their positions as queer Latina/o icons.[16] But unlike many Latina divas who came before her, Selena channeled her throaty, teardrop-in-the-voice musical stylings into an unabashedly crossover-pop casing. The synthetic pop playfulness that framed the soulful qualities of Selena's voice distinguished her as a specifically plebeian diva. She couldn't quite help herself to the shiny plastic accoutrements of pop, but neither did she succumb to its historically whitening effects. She did, after all, perform Tejano-style cumbias, a musical form regarded by dominant U.S. culture and by a range of Latina/o communities as derivative pop schlock with a lower-class country twang. And it was in part due to the ways Selena queered the cumbia that she garnered such a following among a range of queer fans from across the Latina/o spectrum.

Historically the role of the Tejano (and it was invariably a Tejano and not a Tejana) cumbia performer was to "manage" the movements of the dancers through a measured pacing and tempo.[17] Thus Tejano cumbia singers and musicians often maintained a discrete boundary between the orchestrations onstage and the revelry of the dance floor. Selena's live performances, in addition to challenging the entrenched masculinist performance history of the Tejano cumbia, refused such a spatial distinction. Known as much for her dancing skills as for her musical range, she used her choreographic solos during her cumbia performances to lead and to provoke improvised movement among the dancers on and off the stage. By forgoing the conventional heterocoupling of partner dancing, her solo dance moves not only disrupted the traditional female Tejano dance position as follower, but brought the pleasures and kinesthetic negotiations of a queer dance floor ethos to the stage. Selena queered the cumbia by using the musical form to boldly stage a frequently derided sexuality (in this case, working-class Tejana) as a position of power—evidenced in choreographic virtuosity—and as a catalyst for respatializing the gendered and sexual confines of Tejano music.[18]

Selena's *rasquache* sensibilities and *chusma* style also contributed to her queer appeal. *Rasquachismo*, according to Tomás Ybarra-Frausto, refers to the creative sensibility and aesthetic practices of the Chicana/o downtrodden, a resistant stance characterized by an inventive resourcefulness that arises out of material dispossession and bicultural, or *pocha/o*, experiences. More specifically, the term is used both to describe the self-conscious Chicana/o artistic style involving humor, irony, and a "making-do" sensibility and to establish class distinctions by marking a derided "low-class" set of behaviors: "One is never rasquache, it is always someone else, someone of a lower status."[19] Amalia Mesa-Bains elaborates on Ybarra-Frausto's theory by considering Chicana *domesticana*, or "home embellishments, home altar maintenance, healing traditions, and personal feminine pose or style," as imaginative rasquache practices. Like the rasquachismo

Mesa-Bains describes, *chusmería* connotes a gendered, resistant expressive stance through, as Carmelita Tropicana observes, "loud, gross, tacky, and excessive behavior."[20] Chusmería thus shares with rasquachismo a reference to both a resilient-style politics of the working class and a system of classification used by the middle class to deliver, according to José E. Muñoz, "a barely veiled racial slur . . . [or to] connote gender nonconformity, recent immigration status and general lack of 'Americanness.'"[21] Selena's brightly painted acrylic nails, pronounced preferences for Whataburger jalapeño cheeseburgers and Nacho Cheese Doritos, and Spanglish linguistic practices made her undeniably rasquache, while her fringed cow-print self-designed costumes that showcased her audacious Latina curves conveyed her chusma sensibilities.

Selena's rasquache-chusma persona, marked by excessive theatricality and appropriative resourcefulness—a dime-store bra transformed into glittering bustier—highlights the connections between working-class woman-of-color expressive style and queer aesthetics. Chusmas certainly share with queers a devotion to and delight in delicious excess, but as Tropicana and Muñoz convey, chusmas and queers also share a disidentifying relationship to the shame encouraged by the sexist, racist, and homophobic ideologies of dominant culture.[22] Selena discoed and designed and doted on her fans *sin vergüenza*, without shame. She struck a shameless pose in the world, providing a model for boldly inhabiting the dark, fleshy, pop cumbia dancing, Spanglish-speaking Latina/o body. In fact, the "impurity" of Selena's unapologetically code-switching language practices, as Lawrence La Fountain-Stokes observes, can be understood as a potentially queer form of address.[23] In this way Selena's version of divaness encouraged queer Latina/o affiliation and provided a capacious pattern from which to design the contours of queer latinidad.

Like all divas, Selena's public persona, career, and rumored private life "involved negotiations between convention and transgression."[24] For inasmuch as Selena exuded a dutiful daughter and barrio girl innocence, her star text also frequently exceeded such confines. As Emma Pérez and others have noted, Selena's biography has been channeled through an Oedipal narrative in which "the law of the Father is authorized."[25] One consequence of this discursive framing, wherein Selena's fraught relationship with her all-knowing father is foregrounded and her deviation from her father's law or counsel results in her death, is that the conventional marriage plot that frequently structures female star biographies gets sidelined, if not altogether repressed, in Selena's story. That is, the paternalistic emphasis on Selena-as-daughter works to displace a heteroteleological focus on Selena-as-(eventual)-wife. This emphasis is reinforced by the fact that Selena, against her father's wishes, eloped with her band mate Chris Pérez. The elopement is usually positioned as an illicit act of betrayal against the Father that solidifies the Oedipal triangulation scenario among Selena, Abraham, and Chris. And yet her relationships and her de-emphasized "marriage plot" are not exclusively bound by this daughter-father-husband triangulation. More commonly her struggles are attributed to her triangulated relationship with her father and Yolanda Saldívar, her middle-aged female confidante, fan club president, and eventual murderer. In fact, despite the Oedipal force that propels her biography, the relationship that narratively overshadows, and indeed challenges, Selena's bond with her father is her loyalty to Yolanda, who is often depicted as a stereotypical obsessive butch or mannish lesbian figure. It is precisely Selena's oscillation between family convention and these transgressive scenes of "Amor Prohibido" (Forbidden Love) that makes her biography a legibly queer text regularly invoked to affirm queer identification with such forbidden allegiances.

Latina lesbian readings of Selena's biography are often structured around a feminist analysis of her becoming: an adolescent becoming a woman, a musician becoming a clothing designer, a dutiful daughter becoming a defiant adult. In her comments in Portillo's video *A Conversation with Academics about Selena*, the Chicana playwright Cherríe Moraga, observes:

> Where Selena was going is that she was becoming a woman. That's where the feminism, I think, is important . . . because what happens is that she starts to become her own [person]. She's starting her business . . . everything says she was having trouble with her husband and that she was starting these other interests outside of that family circle, so that's what's important [to consider]. . . . It's a very circumscribed world [that Selena lived in]. And Yolanda becomes her confidante. For all intents and purposes, in terms of her career, what she [Selena] was looking at was separation from her father and developing her line of clothes.[26]

For Moraga, Selena's struggles highlight the exploitive constraints of the heterosexual family economy for many successful young Latinas. The break from the family structure—despite patriarchal claims otherwise—does not ensure financial ruin for young Latinas, but instead provides a path toward greater financial success. And within this interpretive framework, the process of "becoming a woman" involves a departure from the "circumscribed world" of the restrictive "family circle" through an alliance with a same-sex confidante. The quest for material freedom and creative control or expression is thus linked to and enabled by the forging of a queer bond.

Latina lesbian interpretations of the Selena-Abraham-Yolanda triangulation frequently serve as a narrative frame through which to expose and condemn the operations of patriarchy. Moraga claims:

> I have called it the Latina *lesbiana tragedia*. . . . [Selena's] a homegirl who got wiped out . . . and she got wiped out by another Chicana. . . . Maybe Yolanda pulled the trigger, but what were all the events that led up to that, you know? And so you're talking about deep, deep, deep patriarchy, you're talking about misogyny, you're talking about a man, you know, a family in which a man is running a little girl's life from the time she was seven years old and *destino* brought her to the point of being wiped out. And so, to me, that little girl's narrative is all of our narratives as Chicanas.

To read Selena's tragedy as a *lesbiana tragedia* is to acknowledge the struggles against patriarchy that Selena shared with *all* Chicanas; to read her queerly is thus to expand and not to delimit her identificatory power. Understanding Selena within a Latina lesbian interpretive frame also troubles the benevolent paternalism that prevails in official Selena narratives and exposes the repressive and violent consequences of such patriarchal investments in control. In her reflections recorded on Portillo's video, the Chicana feminist scholar Yvonne Yarbro-Bejarano concurs: "There is some connection between patriarchy and the repressed lesbian [scenario]. . . . How does Yolanda's narrative hook up with Abraham's? I think there's something there—that Selena is for both of them the object of desire. And perhaps the desire to control—because it is when Selena spins out of Yolanda's control as well as [out of] Abraham's control that she dies." Yarbro-Bejarano positions Yolanda as a repressed lesbian figure not in an effort to further pathologize her (a strategy deployed by Abraham and countless reporters), but to indict the patriarchal and homophobic structures that coerce the repression of queer desires and subsequently promote its destructive results.

Yarbro-Bejarano's recognition of Yolanda as a repressed (butch) lesbian driven to violence and fighting against a man for control over a woman implicitly positions Selena as a femme figure. The emphasis on the slippage from "the desire for" to "the desire to control" suggests the danger assigned to the femme in these scenarios of conflict. "The most troubling figure in this triangle," Lisa Duggan writes, "was the 'normal' woman. . . . She appeared conventionally feminine in identification and embodiment, yet could not be fully known or controlled. She might go either way. She might be seduced by or even choose the lesbian and reveal abnormal desires."[27] Reading Selena as the "conventionally feminine" but ultimately unknowable woman perched on the edge of such competing desires offers a way to express identification with or desire for her as a femme and to acknowledge the femme's power, represented here not only by her potential for performative duplicity but by her potential economic independence. That is, to talk about Selena's potential for financial freedom from her relational confines is also to talk about the potential threat of her desires to "go either way" in the triangulated loyalties that frame her story of "becoming a woman."

Queer readings of Selena configure her not only as a Latina femme, but also as a figure that often provokes gay Latino male identifications. In our interview at ALLGO Lorenzo Herrera y Lozano, the organization's director of arts and community building, proclaimed, "Well, Selena's a drag queen. [According to the mainstream] she had too much ass, she shook it too much, she was too dark. She was an outcast in her family — even though they ate off of her. She didn't fit in." He pauses for a moment in reflection. "She was a gay man!"[28] Selena's stylistic excess and unapologetic racialized markings combined with her struggles against familial control resonate with gay Latino experiences. Herrera y Lozano continued, "Selena was an outcast; she didn't listen to her father and went to that motel [the scene of her murder]." But unlike prevailing narratives of Selena's death, Herrera interprets Selena's refusal to heed her father's warnings as a consequence of her "outcast" status and not simply as a foolish and ultimately self-destructive deviation from the father's counsel. Here a queer identification with Selena suggests that the family structure that would position Selena as an outcast is ultimately implicated in her death. For Herrera and others inclined to read queerly, Selena's defiant gesture and ultimate death is not unlike that of other queer subjects who have historically sought out traditionally criminalized spaces—movie houses, motels, cabarets, discothèques—away from the disapproving purview of their families of origin. Herrera's reference to the motel is no surprise given that Selena's murder is perhaps the most frequently evoked queer scene in her biography. That Selenidad operates so queerly is thus a result not simply of Selena's queerly diva star text, but of the queer circumstances that surround the scene of her death.

Crime Scene Investigation

Date: Friday, 31 March 1995
Location: Days Inn Motel, room 158, Corpus Christi, Texas
Selena leaves home, driving her Chevy pickup truck to the Days Inn Motel, where Yolanda has been staying for the past few days—presumably hiding out from Abraham following his discovery that she has been embezzling money from Selena's fan club and boutique. Selena visited the motel briefly the night before to retrieve financial records from Yolanda and was returning this morning upon discovering that several key documents were missing. When Selena arrives Yolanda tells her that she was raped during a recent business trip to Monterrey, Mexico. Concerned, Selena drives Yolanda to a local hospital for examination, but when the results prove inconclusive Selena grows suspicious and tells Yolanda, "Maybe we should just stay apart for a while so my dad won't get mad." They return to the motel room and an argument ensues after Selena requests the missing financial records. She empties a satchel full of incriminating bank records onto the bed and begins to remove a ring from her finger. The ring, which features a mounted miniature replica of a Fabergé egg, was a gift from Yolanda. As the conflict escalates, Yolanda pulls out a .38 caliber pistol, pointing it at her own head, and then pointing it at Selena. Selena moves toward the door and Yolanda fires, striking Selena in the right shoulder as she tries to flee. Selena runs to the motel's front office—past the pool, the parking lot, a bank of rooms, the restaurant—screaming for help before collapsing in the lobby, all the while "still clutching the egg-shaped ring in her hand." The time is 11:49 a.m. Two motel employees tend to her, asking, "Who shot you?," to which Selena responds, "Yolanda," before paramedics rush her to the hospital. She is pronounced dead at 1:05 p.m.

After shooting Selena, Yolanda runs through the motel parking lot, pistol in hand, and locks herself in the cab of her pickup truck. She remains there for nearly ten hours in a standoff with police. The hours are marked by her threats of suicide and her exclamations: "I loved her. I didn't mean to kill her. . . . Her father hates me. Her father is responsible for this. He made me shoot her. . . . Her father came between us." Just before 9:30 p.m. she surrenders, and the crowd that has gathered at the scene erupts into cheers as the police take her away. At midnight she issues a statement to police in which she confesses to shooting Selena and claims, "Her father had told her that the papers I had brought from Monterrey were wrong and that her father had said that I was a lesbian."[29]

This death scene features a striking slippage between the financial record and the record of lesbian desire, or the evidence of financial duplicity and the evidence of sexual transgression. Predictably, official accounts of the scene often exploit this elision between purported lesbian identification and economic betrayal and murder as a means of proving or reinforcing Yolanda's criminality. This final encounter between the two women, replete with noirish confrontation and exaggerated drama, is often characterized as the tragic consequence of a good girl who fell in with bad company and ended up in the wrong place at the wrong time. The tragedy, so the logic of such an account goes, was that Selena, in her youthful naïveté, did not obey the Law of the Father and suffered the devastating consequences.

But the scenario played out here also conspicuously follows the script of other iconic death scenes. In many ways the scene of Selena's murder resembles the murder scenes of hate crimes against transgender and other non-gender-conforming youth of color wherein the victims are blamed for their tragic fate because they dared to trust the wrong companion or trespass into illicit spaces. More commonly the queer implications of the (thwarted) desire, triangulated accusations, and failed attempts to secure a same-sex bond through claims of male violation or coercion that permeate the scene are also understood within a lesbian love triangle trope. In *A Conversation with Academics about Selena* the film critic B. Ruby Rich observes:

> When I first heard this narrative—you know, that [Selena's] killed in the motel with another woman with a ring—I thought, "This is the classic lesbian narrative." . . . In a way, you could say that what "proves"—despite knowing or not knowing anything about Yolanda—what "proves" that she was a lesbian was that she murdered a woman. . . . A huge percentage—I think it was something like 40 or 60 per-

cent—of the women on death row are lesbians or were accused of being lesbians at their trials. So I think the fact that this comes out around [Yolanda's] trial is really significant.

The "classic lesbian narrative" to which Rich is referring is the influential cultural narrative of the lesbian love murder story that "portray[ed] romance between women as dangerous, insane, and violent, [and thereby] worked to depoliticize, trivialize, and marginalize the aspirations of women for political equality, economic autonomy, and alternative domesticities." Lisa Duggan explores the emergence and cultural function of this narrative during the late nineteenth century and early twentieth, identifying "four crucial elements that characterize the lesbian love murder—a masculine/feminine contrast between the central female couple, a plan to elope, an erotic triangle, and a murder."[30] Selena's murder scene—with its mannish and femme central characters (who drive pickup trucks, no less), prominent ring (with its suggestion of engagement and its mounted egg, a clichéd symbol of womanhood), suspicious location (a budget motel just off the highway), hysterical postmurder rantings implicating the male figure in the love triangle, and explicit accusation of the murderer as a lesbian—easily adheres to the lesbian murder trope. The narrative inclusion of a conspicuous communal body of cheering spectators who applaud Yolanda's apprehension by the police also stages the trope's cultural function of containment of the lesbian threat to the polity.

But not all who interpret Selena's death scene within the "classic lesbian narrative" deploy the script as a cautionary tale against same-sex female desire or as a means of "proving" Yolanda's deviance. Cherríe Moraga notes:

> [Yolanda] takes this ring out—it's such like a lover['s narrative]. . . . It'd be different if she were a "real" lesbian—a practicing, "out" lesbian. . . . Repression is the point [here]. If Yolanda had relationships with other women and all that and she had had a friendship with a straight woman—*pos, 'sta bien* [well, it's all right], no big deal. . . . But the thing is that she was not an "out" lesbian. For all intents and purposes, if you look at the scenario of her life, she is the perfect profile of a repressed lesbian. So then that's where everything gets perverted. So my [interest in] the scenario with Yolanda and Selena is that one of the reasons [Yolanda] had that gun and everything went crazy and the ring got

thrown on the bed and Selena dies with the ring in her hand, I mean, *por favor* [please], she dies with the lover's ring in her hand. They were not [actual] lovers, OK? So it's like . . . "Who pulled the trigger?" Greed in terms of the father created a narrative that would eventually lead to this very tragic destiny for Selena. In terms of Yolanda, it was sexual repression, it was the repression of sexuality for Chicanas and homophobia that led to her scenario. I feel like she's a victim of homophobia.

Moraga's interpretation of Selena's death scene exposes and implicates the patriarchal confines that structure latinidad, or, more specifically, Chicano culture. Here the father's economic malfeasance (capitalizing on his daughter's success) and not Yolanda's is blamed ("pulled the trigger"). Moraga not only provocatively foregrounds Yolanda's own victimization but reveals the links between her tragedy and Selena's: Yolanda's victimization as a result of homophobia and sexual repression ultimately has dire consequences for *all* Chicanas. The pronoun referent in the comment "she's a victim of homophobia" can thereby be understood to refer to both Selena and Yolanda. Moraga's version of the murder thus acts as a cautionary tale directed at patriarchal power warning that repressed female or lesbian desire, and not the expression of it, will invariably provoke violence against patriarchy's favored (and income-producing) daughters.

While Moraga identifies Selena's death scene as a "Latina lesbiana tragedia" that serves to implicate patriarchy, other Chicana lesbians productively disidentify with the tragic narrative that frames the Selena-Yolanda story. In our conversations about Selena, T. Jackie Cuevas, a member of ALLGO and a writer based in Austin, recalled:

I came out the same week of Selena's death, in a way, because of it. You know, there were all these rumors circulating about Selena and Yolanda — well, in the queer community, they weren't considered rumors, they were just treated as fact — and while, on the one hand, the rumors gave the butches that loved Selena and the femmes that emulated her style a sense of validation, I also knew that I didn't want to identify with Selena's script. I didn't want to live like that — a life lived in rumor — living a life as that *tía* [aunt] people talked about who lived with her "roommate" — or going to family birthday parties with my girlfriend but never being able to hold hands or anything. And also, even though I identified with Selena as another Tejana from Corpus,

knew that in Selena's story, I couldn't be Selena. First of all, because
m butcher than butch, and also because I can't sing! But I also knew
at I didn't want to wind up like the other woman, the crazy lesbian
murderer, the woman going crazy and giving queers a bad name. I
didn't want to identify with that script. In Corpus there just aren't that
many scripts for how to live a fulfilling queer life. It's sad. So I decided
to come out to myself and to my family and friends and live my life
openly and proudly as a butch Tejana dyke.[31]

Here Selena's death serves as a foundational scenario in a Tejana lesbian
coming-out narrative. But whereas Cuevas found affinity with and desire
for Selena as a fellow Corpus Christi Tejana and a femme figure, she dis-
identified with the tragic "script" of Selena's death. This act of disidentification with Selena's tragedy ultimately served to propel Cuevas to craft
an alternative and "fulfilling queer life" wherein she could live "proudly
as a butch Tejana dyke" beyond the circumscribed scripts of rumor and
repressed desires.

Cuevas's comments also foreground the ways that Selenidad, like the
memorial landscape of any bona fide diva, is traversed by the tracks of
"rumor, innuendo, and myth."[32] Like endless miles of railroad steel connecting the far corners of a country, gossip and wild speculation have provided the means by which various communities have forged connections
and unofficial routes of remembrance across Selena's memorial terrain.
In fact, the general tenor of Selenidad is marked by the dishy delight in
speculation about Selena's body (Did she have liposuction in Mexico?),
career plans (Did she want to give up her music career to pursue fashion design?), and relationships (Was her marriage on the rocks? Was she
seeking creative freedom from fatherly constraints? Did she share a queer
bond with her murderer?). It is precisely this vast network of rumor and
gossip that is central to Selenidad's queerness. "The contexts of queer
world making," as Lauren Berlant and Michael Warner argue, "depend
on parasitic and fugitive elaboration through gossip, dance clubs, soft-
ball leagues."[33] Rumor has long been a crucial locus of meaning making
and identity production among members of queer counterpublic spheres.
The discursive realms of rumor and gossip thus serve as reliable codes of
queer engagement with Selenidad.

Given the ease with which such gossip travels, these forms of "fugitive elaboration" predictably provoke anxieties among those invested in

more official memories of Selena. A convincing indicator of the persuasive effects and subsequent threat of the queer rumors that fuel Selenidad surfaces in a full-page, bilingual, eight-item list, "The Truth about the Rumors," that was published in the March/April 2000 special issue of *Estylo* magazine commemorating the fifth anniversary of Selena's death. This anonymously authored list begins with the observation, "Selena's death launched a web of rumors, innuendo, and just plain lies." It strives to offer "the lowdown on some of what was said" by enumerating the most widespread rumors about Selena, which it counters with "facts." Half of the rumors on the list revolve around Selena's purported relationships—with her plastic surgeon, her father, her husband, and her former fan club president and murderer. The claim that was most forcefully denied was the rumor (number five on the list) that "Yolanda and Selena had a lesbian relationship." Unlike the other seven rumors that were refuted with straightforward claims delivered in a journalistic tone, this rumor elicited an exasperated exclamation: "(Ohhhh please!) Major Falsehood. **Fact**: The person Yolanda hated the most was Selena's father who was the one who caught her stealing. Consequently, she is given to saying things that she knows will be most hurtful to Abraham Quintanilla. Yolanda has never been able to prove or corroborate any of her accusations concerning the Quintanillas."[34] Such an emphatic denouncement of the rumored relationship does not so much offer the convincing truth about Selena's sexual orientation as it attests to the power and perceived threat of the lesbian (sub)text that frames queer interpretations of Selena and Selenidad. What is perhaps most interesting and, indeed, quite queer about this claim is the fact that it does not actually refute the rumor, but instead posits the triangulation narrative (among two women and a man) that is a common feature in the lesbian murder trope. This explicit engagement with the "rumors, innuendo, and just plain lies" about Selena speaks to the unlikely destinations reached by the narrative tracks that veer queerly off-course through Selena's memorial landscape. That is, the list, with its continued circulation of and detailed response to these rumors, provides evidence of and, albeit unwittingly, contributes to Selenidad's pervasively queer rhetorical mode. Ultimately, as Cuevas's insights suggest, Selenidad insists that we take these rumors seriously, that we ask in a rather queer way, What is the truth about the rumors? or, more precisely, What truths are revealed in rumor? Cuevas's coming-out story provides compelling evidence that, in fact, the rumors that surround Selena's life and death do not so much reveal truths about Selena as uncover important truths for and about the queer Latina/o communities that evoke her memory.

Selena's death not only induces lesbian readings but also contributes to her position as a queer Latina/o camp icon. In his catalogue of the reasons Selena is enshrined as a queen of Latina/o camp, Herrera succinctly remarked, "There's the dead factor," astutely recalling camp's "necrophilic economy," or, more precisely, "camp's obsession with flesh, death and decay."[35] But queer Latina/o fascination with Selena's death differs in one striking way from camp's usual preoccupation with the decaying female body. Caryl Flinn observes, "Human icons [that] body camp brings into its fold are often deeply involved with death—a fleshy, grotesque, decaying death that is imposed onto some bodies more than others." This obsession has led ultimately to what Flinn refers to as the "aging diva phenomenon" or the "grotesquefication of the female body."[36] While the process of performing Selena may involve grotesquefication, it is important to note that her body and the impersonations of her portray a youthfulness, a ripening that is full of promise rather than decay. Selena's body is not the alcohol-soaked aging diva body of Judy Garland or even La Lupe, nor the excessively altered body of Cher. Rather, Selena's too-too-soon death, her unsullied body intact, seals her forever in that moment before concessions to recording industry demands for lighter hair and a smaller ass had to be made, before the resignation to decay. Herrera speaks evocatively of this sense of promise that Selena's body holds out for him as a queer subject intent on survival: "When I connected most with her was after I was diagnosed with HIV. When that magazine published pictures of her autopsy and she didn't look dead. She still looked so beautiful, with her hair pulled back. She had bullets in her but she just looked unconscious. She seemed immortal. And that's how I felt: the bullets were in me, but I wasn't dead." Here, then, is the youthful body struck down by death too soon. But here also is the "immortal" body, undecayed by bullet or virus. Not only does Selena's death offer a platform for grieving loss and for implicating the homophobia of latinidad, but, as Melissa's performance of "Como la Flor" made clear, Selena's dead body is capable of prompting a queer resurrection, of bringing Herrera back from the dead.

She walks onstage, microphone in hand. She is wearing a trademark out-fit: a white, buttoned-down blouse tied above the navel and fitted black pants with a silver-studded belt. She is glorious, her red acrylic nails shin-ing, silver hoop earrings swaying as she easily assumes center stage. She is the idea of a woman, bronze skin gleaming under layers of makeup, face framed by a cascading black wig, costume filled out to generous propor-tions with strategically placed padding. She is freshly minted, a burnished copper coin eager for exchange. The bouncy, synthesized opening bars of "Como la Flor" play through the sound system, and she raises her left arm, twirling her wrist in a *floreo* gesture as the audience cheers her on. She leans into alternating back steps on the cumbia beat as she encour-ages the audience to join her, "Todo el mundo [The whole world]," before she launches into the lyrics: "Yo sé que tienes un nuevo amor [I know that you have a new love]." She claps as she sings, extends her arms toward the audience, inviting their participation, so that by the time she reaches the song's most famous refrain, "Pero ay-ay-ay, cómo me duele / Ay-ay-ay, cómo me duele [But oh, how it hurts me / Oh, how it hurts me]," the spectators encircling her are singing along. The name embroidered across her blouse in sinuous black script is "Selena," but the caption that flashes across the screen in Portillo's documentary recording the performance provides the performer's own (stage) name: Malissa Mychaels.[37]

After the opening cadenza of Mychaels's version of "Como la Flor" Por-tillo's camera cuts to an audience shot that captures Lucia Orea Chapa, a Selena fan interviewed earlier in the documentary (and discussed in chapter 4), clapping approvingly as she sits among a group of multigen-erational, male and female Latina/o spectators. The camera returns to Mychaels, and as she launches into the first verse of the song her per-formance is framed by a voice-over spoken by Franco Ruiz Mondini, a San Antonio–based Latino visual artist, who reflects, "You would never see drag queens speaking in Spanish. You would never hear them joking around in Spanish. All of that was a world that was invisible, and was not talked about, did not exist, was kept in the closet. Maybe your sexu-ality wasn't in the closet anymore, but still, your basic roots were still in the closet. And Selena had a very, very big part of it—where people were just like, 'I am someone. This area I come from, I can be just as glamorous as anyone else.'" The camera editing and voice-over narration of Portillo's film frames Mychaels's performance of "Como la Flor" at a Corpus Christi venue as a scene of queer Latina/o coming out, wherein one's "basic [racialized] roots" could be proudly announced outside of the proverbial closet. The camera's focus on Chapa, an older female spectator watching approvingly in ways evocative of a supportive Latina maternal figure, visually conveys a moment of Latina/o familial acceptance of one of its queer children. This staged approval is especially notable given the well-publicized opposition to the inclusion of Selena drag performances that Portillo faced from Selena's father during and after the film's release.[38] As Ruiz Mondini's comments make clear, Selena drag provides an affirming practice for making queer Latina/o identifications visible to both larger queer communities and to Latina/o communities of origin. This brief scene suggests that the code-switching linguistic playfulness (evidenced in Spanish-language joking) marking the sexual and gendered code-switching of Selena drag facilitates the consolidation of a specifically Latina/o camp sensibility that disidentifies with conventional drag's racialized and classed standards of glamour.

Malissa Mychaels's performance is one among many Selena drag tributes that proliferate across the stages of Selenidad: "Since her death in 1995, the Queen of Tejano has crossed over to the Queen of Camp. . . . On drag show stages from L.A. to Miami, Selena is in the spotlight with oft-mimed superstars Barbra Streisand, Liza Minnelli, Cher, Diana Ross and Bette Midler."[39] Along with Selena drag acts performed at queer nightclubs and drag contests sponsored by queer college organizations, entire evenings dedicated to Selena impersonation and homage have been staged to mark or announce Latino queer presence across the country. Within these contexts the act of becoming Selena operates as an indispensable cultural practice that serves to consolidate queer Latina/o communities and performance sensibilities. One of these events, Como la Flor: A Tribute to *la inolvidable diosa tejana* Selena (Like a Flower: A Tribute to the Unforgettable Texas-Mexican Goddess Selena), was organized by ALLGO in April 2002 in an effort to provide "at once a celebration of a powerful and affirming cultural icon for the Latina/o community and an innovative HIV/AIDS education opportunity targeted to communities who have historically not had access to this information" (figure 36).[40]

On the evening of 20 April 2002 hundreds of community members gathered at ALLGO's Tillery Street Theatre, located in a predominantly working-class black and Latina/o neighborhood on Austin's east side.

Austin Latina Latino Lesbian, Gay, Bisexual and Transgender Organization

Como la Flor

Saturday, April 20, 2002
9:00 p.m.
701 Tillery Street
Austin, Tejas

Featuring

- Emcee Kelly Kline
- The outstanding performances by some of Tejas' finest female impersonators honoring nuestra consentida... la super Selena!
- Altar & Art exhibit
- Cena ~ recepción ~ ambiente to remember ~ honor & be muy excited!

FMI contact ALLGO:
512.472.2001 ● allgoinc@aol.com
www.allgo.org

Funding for Como la Flor provided in part by the City of Austin under the auspices of the Austin Arts Commission, Texas Commission on the Arts and Community Support.

36. Como la Flor promotional flyer. Collection of the author.

Since its inception in 1985 ALLGO has gained national recognition for its creative approach to community building, queer empowerment, and HIV education among communities of color. The April 2002 event, funded in large part by the Texas Commission on the Arts and the Austin Arts Commission, was the product of joint efforts among three of ALLGO's programming areas (as they were constituted at that time): Informe-VIDA, an HIV/AIDS case management and prevention education effort; ALMA, a community-building program; and Viva Arte, Viva Cultura!, a queer Latina/o cultural arts project. The planning of the tribute included a call for submissions of Selena-inspired artworks that addressed themes such as "Selena's role and significance in breaking stereotypes and 'crossing over'" and "Selena's relation to the transgender and 'drag' community" and an invitation to LGBT (lesbian, gay, bisexual, transgender) service agencies from across Texas to nominate female impersonators to perform as representatives of their communities.[41] Letters of invitation to participate announced, "ALLGO proudly presents this evening of female impersonation, altar exhibits and spoken word in honor of one of queer Latinidad's most celebrated icons—Selena Quintanilla Perez. . . . Como la flor reflects our commitment to recognizing and supporting the artistic contributions and *tradiciones* of all members of our lgbt *familia*."⁴² The ALLGO organizers agreed to pay the performers a modest artistic fee of $200 for performing one Selena song and another song of the artist's choosing, requested that the collaborating agencies "assist their representatives in travel, food, and lodging costs," and pledged continued support for the career aspirations and creative development of participating artists: "Whether this take the form of Letters of Support [that] ALLGO submits for an artist's [future] grant application or financial support to attend a pageant, we believe in mutually respectful, mutually beneficial artistic collaborations."⁴³

The event, which began with bilingual AIDS educational forums in the afternoon and culminated with a Selena Drag Show, also included a dinner, visual art reception, dance, silent auction, and Selena Barbie doll raffle. The Austin-area queer celebrity and "Selena illusionist" Kelly Kline acted as emcee for the evening (figure 37). Five other Texas-area performers—Erica Andrews, Diamond, Paloma, Vanessa Raye, and Melissa West—joined Kline with their own renditions of Selena songs, including Andrews's version of "Como la Flor" and "Cada Vez" performed in a poet's shirt and black jacket resembling Selena's outfit featured on the *Amor Prohibido* album cover (figures 38 and 39). The audience at Como la Flor was among the most diverse that ALLGO had drawn in its nearly seventeen-year history: intergenerational families, working- and middle-class black and Latina/o lesbians, children, grandmothers, gay men, and transgender performers all shared the space (figure 40).

In addition to the standard inclusion of event schedule, performer bios, and local advertisements, the twenty-page program included welcoming comments from Joe Jiménez, ALLGO's program and fiscal coordinator: "Como la Flor brings diverse members of our community together to affirm the value of our lives and to use such an opportunity to share information about health, wellness, and HIV/AIDS treatment."⁴⁴ The program also featured a poem by Lorenzo Herrera y Lozano, "Virgen morena de tacones altos" (Dark Virgin of High Heels), that closed with the phrase "como la flor/ en ti buscando, en tu imagen/ maneras para sobrevivir [like the flower / in you searching, in your image / ways to survive]." A statement from Dennis Medina, curator of the evening's artist showcase, reflected on the meaning and function of Selena memories for queer Latinas/os:

37. Kelly Kline and Como la Flor spectator, 20 April 2002. Photo courtesy of ALLGO.

38. Diamond performs Selena at Como la Flor, 20 April 2002. Photo courtesy of ALLGO.

39. Erica Andrews performs "Amor Prohibido" at Como la Flor, 20 April 2002. Photo courtesy of ALLGO.

40. Diamond and young Como la Flor spectator, 20 April 2002. Photo courtesy of ALLGO.

Do you remember where you were when Selena died? I was attending an academic conference in Washington, D.C. . . . I remembered a colleague from Brownsville who also was attending the conference. . . . Later, he would tell me that he heard the maids in the conference hotel discussing Selena's murder. We experienced an indescribable feeling of belonging partly to the world of academia, partly to the world of the housekeeping staff. We were both students, exploring the space that we would one day occupy as "professionals." We were "crossing over," but we weren't going to leave anyone behind. We were Selena. The place that we are from also has been hard to describe in words: *la frontera* . . . the borderlands . . . *nepantla* [a Nahuatl word that translates roughly as "place in the middle"]. It is a physical place, yes, but also a mental state, with boundaries that pervade and shift depending on your location. Sometimes clear, other times hazy and elusive. Remembering Selena also reminds me of my best friend Joe. He died in 1991 of complications related to AIDS. . . . Memory is a nepantla place—neither here nor there, not now or then—a crossroads between spaces. . . . Remembering Selena is much like remembering my friend. We remember Selena and ourselves, too. . . . I am grateful to Selena for leaving us with a beautiful memory and a medium through which we may choose to remember our lives and our loves, our identities, our cultures and our "cross-over" dreams.

By the evening's end Como la Flor participants had collectively remembered Selena by sharing song, dance, visual art, food, and AIDS prevention and treatment information.

Not unlike Melissa's Grrl Action performance and Malissa Mychaels's drag act, ALLGO's event resignifies "Como la Flor" as a slogan for an affirming queer Latina/o space. Specifically the event evokes Selena and her signature song to mark and to playfully evince queer Latina/o camp, evidenced in the bilingual and hyperbolic title and the tongue-in-cheek Selena Barbie doll raffle combined with the sincere homage expressed in the drag performances. The diverse cross section of Latina/o participants also suggests that remembering Selena serves as a means of bridging what are frequently divided Latina/o community and familial lines and of engaging in the queer Latina/o cultural practice of "making *familia* from scratch."[45] As Medina's statement makes clear, the collective act of mourning Selena also operates as a bridge for accessing one's own "crossover dreams" by offering a way to achieve realness, to access professional aspirations within a white, privileged world while remaining connected to the Latina/o laboring class (i.e., the maids in the hotel). Selena's tragedy also works here as a recognizable narrative frame through which to mourn the ravishes of AIDS among the queer Latina/o community, which, the Como la Flor promotional materials report, suffers among the highest and most disregarded HIV/AIDS casualties. Moreover Selenidad serves as a catalyst for theorizing the *nepantla*, or middle, space or borderlands of memory—indebted, of course, to Chicana feminists such as Gloria Anzaldúa and Pat Mora, who have written evocatively about these concepts.[46] In fact, within Medina's rhetorical shifts between memories of Selena and memories of other losses and Herrera's emphasis on Sele-nidad as "a way to survive," the program notes enact the *nepantla* space of queer Latina/o memory, suspended within the realms of both sorrow and renewal.

Como la Flor's emcee and show director, Kelly Kline, joined ALLGO's organizational efforts because of her long-standing identification with Selena. In our interview Kline introduced herself with an attentiveness to and a refusal of the binary categories that circumscribe gendered and racialized identities: "Kelly Estrella is my legal name. Kelly Kline is my stage name. So it's two different people. . . . People ask me, what are you? Man, woman? And I say, 'I'm Kelly.'"[47] A working-class trans-gender Latina who was born in Mexico City and raised along the border in Brownsville, Texas, Kline moved to Austin in her early twenties: "Be-cause my parents didn't agree with my lifestyle." She recalled how her performances of Selena contributed to her early success as an "illusionist" in the Austin drag scene:

> So when I started performing, I became literally an overnight success in Texas because I was the only person who was not afraid of doing Latin music. And that's where Selena helped me. . . . When I moved over here, people [thought] "Oh, we don't care about Spanish music, it's just not in, it's not happening, it's not popular." Well, at that time Selena was still alive and she was doing amazingly well and people liked my performance and immediately I became seriously like an [she snaps for emphasis] overnight success. And everybody knows me as . . . they call me "Miss Telemundo" or "Miss Televisa" because I dress very Latina, I feel Latina, I like to look Latina. I don't go around bleaching my hair and, you know, stuff like that. I speak Spanish in my micro-phone and so people — you know, other Latinos — like that.

Kline's engagement with Selena, especially when cast in relief against her conspicuously non-Latina stage (sur)name, resonates with the observa-tions made by Franco Ruiz Mondini in Portillo's documentary, revealing that embodying Selena provides a way for Kline and her Latino specta-tors, who affirmingly rename her "Miss Telemundo," to "come out of the [Latina/o] closet" and to disidentify with what José E. Muñoz refers to as "drag's prescriptive mandate to enact femininity through often white standards of glamour."[48]

Kline continued to register this critique as she described what distinguishes Selena from the other "characters" she performs: "You know I do everything from Marilyn Monroe, Liza Minnelli, Judy Garland, Ann-Margret, you name it. And I do the look and I look like them with the music and the costumes, but whenever I get into Selena, it's just a different energy. The people dance with me, they wanna dance with me. People come on stage and literally treat me like I'm a celebrity. . . . For [performing] Selena . . . it's not about being glamorous; it's about just being you." Kline's comments make clear the (white) racialized dimensions of feminine glamour mapped by drag and point to the ways that embodying Selena intervenes in such constructions. For Kline it is not that Selena is equated with nonglamour; Kline inhabits Selena as a means of achieving realness within a working-class black and Latina/o drag performance tradition of being (or feeling) real. Understood within this context, realness operates as both enactment of authenticity and convincingly staged (class or social) passing. Joshua Gamson observes, "To be real is to be authentic, down-to-earth, not fronting. To feel real is to let out something you recognize as your genuine self. . . . Yet, to some people . . . to be 'real' is to pass in a social role that has been denied you. . . . To feel real, in this sense, is to make the costume into your skin, or bring the fantasy self into actual being. . . . Perhaps in the end, realness simply means refusing to be denied, being exactly who you feel yourself to be, occupying your space with all your might."[49]

Kline's reflections about the ways that Selena drag allows her to be both glamorous and simply herself suggest that performing Selena encourages queer Latinas/os to embody the contradictory poles of realness as both genuine self and seamless social passing. A Selena illusionist can thus aspire to the superstar delights inaccessible in daily life while simultaneously affirming a genuine brown and glittery self. Kline's assertion that being Selena is "about being you" serves as an example of the ways that Selena drag enables queer Latinas/os a means by which to "bring the fantasy self into actual being." Moreover impersonating Selena establishes a markedly different relationship between the drag performer and the spectator: here the distancing wink of camp (that invariably reinscribes its spectator as white and masculine) is troubled by the shared dancing onstage, where "it's just about being [affirmed for being] you." Unlike other impersonations, becoming Selena actually allows Kline to become, as she says, a "celebrity." Like Melissa's performance at Grrl Action, queer Selena drag invariably induces the staging of fan labor so central in the formation and sustenance of the celebrated diva.

While Kline also noted that she sometimes performs other contemporary Latina celebrities such as Thalia and Paulina Rubio, she made a clear distinction between them and Selena: "You see I consider [Selena], like, to be more . . . for lack of a better explanation, in Mexico, you're either upper class or lower class. I consider them to be more upper [class]. Selena was for everyone. She started from here and worked her way up here. Some of the other people are not the same way. Maybe Thalia — because she came from a lot of poverty, but Thalia's a little more, you know" — [she sticks her nose up in the air to indicate snobbery]. Kline not only translates Selena's self-fashioning as an accessible and successful working girl who "worked her way up" into a cross-gender and sexual availability ("Selena was for everybody"), but also deploys such a positioning to intervene in the bourgeois affiliations traditionally assumed by drag. The aspiration to "be real" when performing Selena, a superstar who retained and even flaunted a working-class aesthetic in her self-image, counters the tragic, deluded aspirational narratives into which Latina/o and African American drag queens have been historically channeled (most famously evidenced in Jenny Livingston's *Paris Is Burning*).[50] Clearly Selena impersonation is not about a self-loathing that motivates pitiful aspirations to white wealth, but instead offers a model for class mobility predicated on the affirmation of working-class, racialized glamour.

References to and praise of Selena's particular brand of barrio girl glamour marked by its conspicuous lack of pretense pervaded Kline's and Herrera's memories of Selena. Herrera noted, "Selena was the closest we had to being authentic. I don't know if it was conscious or not. She was Tejana. She wasn't trying to be Mexican. She was who she was. Thalia made so many concessions. Even Shakira dyed her hair." Kline echoed his assertion:

> Something about being humble always attracts me to a person. It makes me just like a magnet to them. And that was one thing that led me to Selena because I've always, I mean, admired people for their talents and their beauty, but when I saw an interview [with] Selena, she was like, "Naw dude!" You know, her baseball cap was kinda crooked [when she played softball] and the way she was laughing and the way

she was talking. I've never seen anyone who was so successful be-
have or act like that. [She wasn't] too busy trying to be "Miss"—you
know—"I'm Miss Prim and Proper, Miss"—what's the word—"Miss
Debutante." She was being herself and since then I got hooked. . . .
[With Jennifer Lopez, well . . .] I dislike Jennifer Lopez very much. I
really feel, if she hadn't done Selena, she wouldn't be where she's at
right now. . . . And I don't think she's humble [about it].

In some ways Herrera's and Kline's fixation on Selena's lack of artifice
contributes to the burden of authenticity that most racialized women are
forced to bear. This emphasis on authenticity and humility is not, however, reducible to facile essentialist claims, but emerges here as a critical
vocabulary for exposing the racialized and classed markings of drag. What
is striking about these comments is that within the realm of camp impersonation, where the premiums placed on pose and artifice are traditionally high, Selena's value is based upon her "humble" demeanor (the an-
tithesis, one could argue, of campiness and bitchiness), her refusal of diva
status (with her crooked cap and loud laugh), and her explicit positioning
against the oft-embraced white camp icon "the debutant." Selena's "humility" or "authentic" Latina style is deployed to redefine drag's narrow
definitions of glamour—to claim some of the Kelly Estrella beneath the
Kelly Kline. The positioning of Selena against the high-society debutante
serves to mark the disidentifying aesthetics of a queer Latina/o camp sensibility that incorporates and resignifies notions of humility and authenticity as codes for distinguishing queer Latina/o realness from the (white)
racialized and classed conventions of traditional drag practices.

Queer Selena impersonation thus operates as a means by which to
grieve, survive, educate, and camp it up—Latina/o style. To embody her
is to embody the disease-free, ripening body that still delights, proclaims,
and produces a queer Latina/o subject. In fact, despite, as Herrera proclaims, "the dead factor" contributing to Selena's camp popularity, queer
Latina/o performances of Selena fiercely embrace her liveness, her distance from death and not her proximity to it, as an anecdote from Como
la Flor's curator, Dennis Medina, suggests: "There is a (true) story about
an Anglo drag queen portraying Selena at the San Antonio show bar 'The
Saint.' The drag queen came out of a coffin to begin the number. The
predominately Latino/a audience did not react well at all. They threw
napkins and other stuff and booed the performer off the stage. I don't

know if the audience was reacting to the racial dynamic (an Anglo inter-loper) or if they thought the coffin was too 'campy' and disrespectful, or both."[51] This legendary event is also captured and criticized in a poem by one of Como la Flor's organizers, Joe Jiménez. The poem "Selena out of a Coffin" and the legendary story it depicts has circulated widely among the ALLGO *familia*:

> Girl, what were you thinking?
> Popping out of a coffin wearing the purple
> rodeo outfit—that was your talent?
> Girl, that was sabotage.
> Candles lighting up the stage like the Astrodome
> and everybody watching:
> which one of your friends *no te dijieron* [didn't tell you], girl,
> what a mess you'd be making,
> what a mockery,
> what a miserable memory. . . .
>
> They threw pennies at you, balled-up paper
> napkins. Booed and hissed you.
> Not out of the coffin.
> Not at this pageant. . . .
> No, she didn't!
> Yes, girl, I hear that every time I tell the
> story.[52]

The performance described by Medina and Jiménez in many ways em-bodies the classic, exemplary camp scene: the garish parody of the dead, excessively adorned diva, risen from the grave for one last aria. And yet the napkin-throwing, hissing, and incredulous "No, she didn't!" responses among queer Latina/o audiences highlight the performer's failure to ac-knowledge that to be real in Selena impersonation means re-creating her not within traditional narratives of the dead or decaying (white) divas, but within the ongoing narrative of the living, of, as Herrera remarked, "the immortal." The terms and the aims of Selena drag and its distinctions from white camp are made clear: to perform Selena is to enact an affinity with her and not to stage conventional drag's sneering distance from its object of impersonation.[53]

These accounts also offer a glimpse of the unsettling effect that Latina/o spectatorship has on the ways that camp traditionally positions its spectators within an unmarked whiteness. In a world where the point generally is that everything is up for grabs (recall camp's necrophilic tendencies), Selena memories are guarded tenaciously. Selena belongs to some and not to others not simply because of essentialist investments in Latina/o identity, but because the embodiments of her possess the potential to disturb drag's racialized and classed inscriptions. To lay claim to Selena impersonation is, ultimately, to assert Latina/o queer presence and survival amid the ravages of suffering—at the hands of racism, poverty, or AIDS—that often mark queer Latina/o lives.

Queer identification with Selena provided a path not only for coming out, but for coming home. Emma Pérez writes, "In many ways, the power of [Selena's] seduction, her sensuality consciously performed, not only allowed my own lesbian gaze to be replenished, but, equally important, it allowed me to come home. I came home to Tex-Mex music when Selena reinscribed macho rancheras. Third space feminist perspective permitted me to hear a woman's agency in songs that are usually performed by men and in which women are only objects. When Selena sang, she was no victim."[54] Selenidad offers queer Latinas/os a route of return from lives lived in what Manuel Guzmán and others refer to as "sexile" from their families or communities of origin.[55]

In her interview about Como la Flor, Ixchel Rosal, ALLGO's former artistic director and house manager for the event, recalled, "The event was tremendous. Many memorable moments. You know, everyone was there. Grandmothers, children, plus the queer community. What moved me, was noticing how Selena, or the idea of Selena, brought all those elements of community together. She transcended so much. She embodied possibility for [us], and everyone (regardless of sexual identity) was allowed to participate."[56] Rosal's emphasis on the "elements of community" brought together by queer Selena commemoration conveys an understanding of the ways that, as Horacio N. Roque Ramírez asserts, "'home' . . . is never a given for queer Latinas and Latinos. . . . Whether kicked out or slowly pushed out, we do not take home for granted."[56] Rosal's attention to the sense of "possibility" embodied by Selena resonates with Medina's assertion that Selena acts as a medium through which to enact queer Latina/o "crossover dreams." Rosal's insights expand Medina's claims to suggest that Selenidad offers the possibility not only of fulfilling dreams of successful crossovers within drag performance realms or within chosen career paths, but of crossing over or back into communities long left. For those who have considered (and attempted) suicide, for those forced to leave their families in Brownsville, for those surrounded by the death and decay of lovers and friends, Selenidad enables — if only for a moment — a sense of belonging to communities of the living.

"Pero, ay-ay-ay, cómo me duele"

Finally, I have suggested that the ghost is alive, so to speak. We are in relation to it and it has designs on us such that we must reckon with it graciously, attempting to offer it a hospitable memory out of a concern for justice. Out of a concern for justice would be the only reason one would bother.
—Avery F. Gordon, *Ghostly Matters*

For its Thursday night prime-time slot on 7 April 2005, Univisión broadcast what would become the highest rated and most watched Spanish-language show in television history: *Selena ¡Vive!* (Selena Lives!).[1] The three-hour tribute concert brought together many of the biggest names in Latin music to perform for a sold-out crowd of fifty thousand fans at Reliant Stadium in Houston in honor of the tenth anniversary of Selena's death. Throughout the evening well-known performers from across Latin/o America, including Thalia, Gloria Estefan, the Barrio Boyzz, Ana Gabriel, La India, Alejandro Guzmán, Paulina Rubio, and Olga Tañon, sang Selena songs and shared their memories of the fallen star. The show culminated with a moving performance that has since achieved legendary status and frequent YouTube play. The act begins with a video of Selena introducing "Como la Flor" as the closing song in her final concert at the Houston Astrodome in February 1995. As she speaks, a fifty-five-member children's choir dressed in jeans and white T-shirts takes to the Reliant Stadium stage, along with all of the performers who had participated in the concert that evening. On the video screen Selena sings the opening cadenza of the song, and in the well-known pause before she delivers her first "Pero, ay-ay-ay, cómo me duele [But, oh-oh-oh, how it hurts me]," the crowd at the tribute concert fills the stadium with cheers of anticipation and reverence as they wave white roses above their heads. Throughout the song the camera cuts to Selena's parents seated in the front row as they solemnly watch the events unfold. After Selena finishes the song's opening refrain in the Astrodome footage, the performers onstage — backed by the children's choir and joined by the audience members — echo the line "Pero, ay-ay-ay, cómo me duele / Pero, ay-ay-ay, cómo me duele." When Selena launches into the first verse, everyone falls silent again, swaying and clapping to the cumbia rhythm, before responding to her call: "Como la flor (Como la flor) / Con tanto amor (con tanto amor) / Me diste tú / Se marchitó / Me marcho hoy / Yo sé perder / Pero, ay-ay-ay, cómo me duele / Ay-ay-ay, cómo me duele [Like the flower / With so much love / You gave me / It withered / Today I leave / I know how to lose / But, oh, how it hurts me / Oh, how it hurts me]."

Selena closes the song with a *despedida* (farewell) in her trademark *pocha* Spanish: "¡Houston, Tejas! ¡A todos nuestros hermanos en Mejico! Queremos dar muchisimas gracias a todos ustedes para hacer esta noche posible [sic]. Quebramos [sic] el record — hoy esta noche. ¡Dan un fuerte aplauso! Mil abrazos y mil besotes a cada uno de ustedes. Cuidensen muchísimo y nos vemos muy pronto. Hasta luego. ¡Ciao! [Houston, Texas! To all of our brothers and sisters in Mexico! We want to thank all of you who made tonight possible. We broke the (attendance) record — this very night. Give yourselves a huge applause. A thousand hugs and kisses to each and every one of you. Take good care of yourselves, and we'll see you soon. Until later. Goodbye!]." The *Selena ¡Vive!* participants join together for one last "Ay-ay-ay, cómo me duele," their voices lifted from sorrowful lament into resounding anthem.

Three weeks before the tribute concert a crowd of Latina/o spectators gathered together to sing along to a different anthem. On Sunday afternoon, 20 March 2005, the New York Mets hosted the Los Angeles Dodgers in a spring training game at Tradition Field in Port St. Lucie, Florida. After waiting out several rain delays, Onaney Ortiz, the aspiring young Puerto Rican recording artist who was an understudy in the touring musical *Selena Forever* (and who shared her memories of the experience in chapter 3), took to the field to lead the predominantly Latina/o crowd in singing the national anthem. Onaney was enlisted to perform at the ballpark on this day to celebrate Family Day Latin Festival, a scholarship fundraiser sponsored by the Latin Chamber of Commerce of the

Treasure Coast. (Two dollars from each six-dollar ticket would benefit the Latin Chamber Scholarship Fund.) In addition to Onaney's rousing performance of the "Star Spangled Banner," the festival featured player lineups announcing the Mets' newly acquired free agents, the Dominican pitcher Pedro Martinez and the Puerto Rican center fielder Carlos Beltran, delivered in both Spanish and English. Immediately following the game the terrace adjoining the stadium was transformed into an outdoor festival, with food stands selling Puerto Rican *empanadas*, Colombian *arepas*, and Mexican-style sausages. The sold-out crowd danced to salsa music performed by a thirteen-piece orchestra and sang along with Onaney once again, this time as she performed a number of Selena's well-known hits, including "Amor Prohibido" and "Como la Flor," in a moving hour-long tribute to honor the tenth anniversary of Selena's passing. After the event Onaney was reported saying, "The Latino community is really growing in the area and it's a great thing to show our unity."[2]

A year and a half after Univisión's and Onaney's tribute concerts Selenidad made an appearance on *Ugly Betty*, the U.S. version of the internationally popular Colombian *telenovela Yo soy Betty, la fea* (I Am Betty, the Ugly One). In the episode "Queens for a Day" Betty gets her hair and nails done in a Queens beauty parlor while, in contrasting intercut scenes, an executive from the magazine where she works receives a beauty treatment from a high-end hairdresser in Manhattan. Following their respective makeovers, an establishing shot serves to distinguish the working-class Latina/o neighborhood in Queens where Betty lives from the midtown Manhattan high-fashion district where she works. The establishing shot is actually a montage of images from a crowded street: a young Latina in a leopard-print jacket, a man in sunglasses carrying a piñata, men in hard hats repairing the street on which an NYPD police car is parked, a *botanica* (herbal pharmacy) storefront, and a lingering glimpse of a mural depicting an image of Selena from the cover of her *Amor Prohibido* album. The camera cuts from the Selena mural to a synecdochic shot of Betty's feet walking triumphantly down a city street in red patent-leather peep-toe platforms as nondiegetic music plays the opening lyrics of Wyclef Jean and Shakira's popular duet, "Hips Don't Lie": "I never really knew that she could dance like this / She makes a man want to speak Spanish."[3]

These scenarios reveal that in the opening decade of the twenty-first century Selenidad continues to provide an organizing anthem for latinidad, a performative realm for articulating Latina/o citizenship, and a visual icon for marking Latina/o geographies and budding Latina sexuality. But Selenidad operates not only as an identifiable referent invoked to encourage us to cheer on young Latina protagonists as they pursue their dreams. For inasmuch as Selenidad and the commemorations of famous dead Latinas like Frida Kahlo and Evita Perón deflected attention from other dead Latina bodies during the close of the twentieth century, Selenidad also offers us the opportunity to honor the dead, to speak their names, to retrieve, as Toni Morrison writes, "the unspeakable things unspoken" in U.S. Latina history.[4]

Selenidad invokes the ghosts whose presence must be spoken, whose suspension within the realms of silence must be broken. Selena has in recent years been the ghost whose presence haunts me — my shadow self, my yet-to-be-fulfilled dream for myself — a fellow Tejana performer who was my age and who was, like me, raised in a south Texas, working-class Tejano family. She is the one who ultimately could not cross this far, but she is also the critically generative force that creates room for more, who conjures thousands of Latina bodies, storming the gates of history. Selenidad unfolds itself as the drawbridge over which I cross into a future filled with promise and over which I cross back, to retrieve other dead Latina bodies.

To remember Selena is thus to walk bravely, as Señoras Norma Andrade and Ramona Morales (whose journeys were briefly chronicled in the introduction) walked through the doors of the Organization of American States, demanding justice for their murdered daughters along the U.S.-Mexico border. To remember Selena is to walk bravely as Theseus walked through the labyrinth, with every step moving nearer and nearer to the beast's lair.

Selenidad draws us through the maze of a collective Latina memory. We remember her, and with every turn we remember other dead Latina bodies: Gloria de la Cruz (1978–1996) of Oxnard, California, who auditioned for *Selena* and was murdered, her body found in a Los Angeles dumpster; Delilah Corrales (1982–2005), a transgender Latina from Yuma, Arizona, stabbed, severely beaten, and drowned in the Colorado River; Hilda Uguna (1979–1998) of Sleepy Hollow, New York, stabbed to death by her abusive husband after having been denied an emergency court order for protection from a White Plains court; Gloria Anzaldúa (1942–2004), Chicana lesbian feminist activist, writer, and visionary. Around every corner, another body.

Like Ariadne's unwound thread that led Theseus back from his struggle with the minotaur, the names of the dead unfurl themselves before us: Arlene Diaz (1974–2002), a transgender Latina from El Paso, Texas, shot and killed in a hate crime; one "unidentified Hispanic woman" found in a park in Queens, New York (1998) and another in a pickup truck in San Antonio, Texas (1998). The names mark the path of our return: Bella Evangelista (1978–2003), a transgender Latina victim of a hate crime shot to death in Washington, D.C.; Olivia Hernandez (1974–1998) and Maria Perales (1978–1998), undocumented Mexicanas whose nude bodies were found strangled and dumped in a public area in Dallas; Jessica Mercado (1979–2003), a transgender Latina from New Haven, Connecticut, stabbed and set on fire.

Selenidad instructs us to speak the names of the dead so that we may move through and beyond the corridors of sorrow that have marked U.S. Latina/o lives. To move through Selenidad is to be reminded that memory is, as poet Marjorie Agosín evocatively describes:

an imprecise canvas . . . which expands
to become a table where
everyone writes what she wants
or does not want to remember:
a blade of smooth wood where we can invent
maps of our most cherished possessions,
memory . . . transforming itself
into a necklace of words
strung between the captive stones
that cannot say anything.[5]

Agosín's shifting metaphors capture memory's resistance to definitive categorization; even within the lean corridor of a single stanza memory will not hold still: a canvas, a table, a blade, a necklace of words. Memory is the shape-shifting storehouse crowded with countless inscriptions, words like jewels laced together, treasure maps that plot the remains sunk in our deepest interior. But memory is also the space sustained by lacunae, by that which we strive not to remember, by that which "cannot say anything." The effect of the poem is the revelation that memory acquires its power precisely through its ontology as a mutable force in both senses of the word: memory adapts and memory silences. But memory is also, as Selenidad shows us, the necklace of words unfastened that leads us back, like Ariadne's thread, from within the treacherous chambers of grief and loss through which we move.

Selenidad grants us the language to "speak the unspeakable," to mourn the accretion of losses in a nation that, as Anne Cheng notes, is "at ease with the discourse of grievance but terribly ill at ease in the face of grief."[6] Mourning Selena returns us to the story of Theseus, who, upon his return, forgot to hoist the white sail of victory. Instead he sailed toward Athens with his black sail raised, causing his father, who watched from the shore, to throw himself into the sea in anguish, believing his son to be dead. Theseus held onto his grief until he reached the shore and then set about rebuilding the nation. During this moment, following the anti-immigration legislation of the 1990s, the horrors of September 11, the levees and the lives broken in New Orleans, the unsolved murders of young Latinas along the U.S.-Mexico border, the disproportionate recruitment and deaths of working-class black and Latina/o soldiers in Iraq, Selenidad offers us a space to legislate our grief. This elegy is a testament to the powerful ways that Selenidad suggests, as Peggy Phelan writes, "the possibility that something substantial can be made from the outline left after the body has disappeared."[7] Remembering Selena provides both the evidence and the methods by which we can ensure that the Latina body remains palpably re-membered among us.

Notes

Introduction

1 Field notes from visits conducted in January 2001 and December 2005.

2 For more on Jennifer Lopez as Selena, see Negrón-Muntaner, "Jennifer's Butt"; Aparicio, "Jennifer as Selena."

3 This fact is especially impressive given that more than a third of the works up for auction at Christie's failed to meet their minimums. Belejack and Plagens, "Frida on Our Minds"; "Iowa Gets $1.5-million from Sale of Painting," *Chronicle of Higher Education*, 29 May 1991, A2.

4 S. Miller, "Selling Evita to the Masses," 92.

5 Ellen Bernstein, "The Selena Look," *Corpus Christi Caller-Times*, 20 November 1997; Mary Gottschalk, "Selena Lives On in Clothing Line," *Houston Chronicle*, 25 June 1998, Fashion sec., 1; Lisa Lenoir, "A Dash of Spice: Selena Legacy Hits High Note in Clothing Line," *Chicago Sun-Times*, 20 May 1998, 29.

6 Nathan, "Travels with Evita"; Judd Tully, "'Self-portrait' Sets Kahlo Record," *Washington Post*, 18 May 1995, C6.

7 Hewitt, Harmes, and Stewart, "Before Her Time," 49; Armando Villafranca, "Second Tragedy Stuns Corpus Christi; Selena Buried with Red Rose in Her Hands," *Houston Chronicle*, 4 April 1995, A1.

8 Patoski, "The Queen Is Dead," 110.

9 "Hoping for Stardom: 3,000 Selena Look-Alikes Turn Out for Casting Call," *Phoenix Gazette*, 18 March 1996, A2; "Wanted: Actress for Selena Role," *Houston Chronicle*, 8 March 1996, 1; Elena De la Cruz, "En busca de Selena," *La Opinión*, 15 March 1996, 1D; Lydia Martin, "2,000 Try Out to Play Slain Tejano Singer," *Miami Herald*, 18 March 1996, A1.

10 See Connerton, *How Societies Remember*, on the ways memory is "sedimented" in bodily practices; Lipsitz, *Time Passages*, on the role of popular culture in the making of collective memory; Roach, *Cities of the Dead*, on the links between

performance and memory; Sturken, *Tangled Memories*, on cultural memory and national identity.

11 Roach, *Cities of the Dead*, 33.

12 Sturken, *Tangled Memories*, 3, 44.

13 One of the first scholarly treatments of Selena to appear in print was "Santa Selena" written by the Latin/o American scholar Ilan Stavans. Stavans offers a cursory and cavalier analysis of the process of Selena's iconization wherein he reinscribes the border as a racialized site of pathologized fans who uncritically worship Selena as "a patron saint." For astute explorations of Selena and the commercialization of Latino culture, see Coronado, "Selena's Good Buy"; Jim Mendiola, "Selena and Me," *Frontera Magazine*, http://www.fronteramag.com/issue5/Selena/index.htm.

14 Rodman, *Elvis after Elvis*, 19.

15 Raymond Williams defines structure of feeling as "the specifically affective elements of consciousness and relationships: not feeling against thought, but thought as felt and feeling as thought." Like performance and memory, a structure of feeling is ultimately, as Williams observes, "a social experience which is still *in process.*" *Marxism and Literature*, 132, emphasis in original.

16 Following Foucault, Marita Sturken refers to these charged circuits as "technologies of memory" (*Tangled Memories*, 9, 258). David L. Eng and David Kazanjian understand these symbols of loss as melancholic objects capable of expressing multiple losses at once and thus possessing "a certain palimpsest-like quality" ("Introduction: Mourning Remains," 5). Eng and Kazanjian seek to de-pathologize Freudian notions of melancholia, and instead understand it as "a continuous engagement with loss and its remains [that] generates sites for memory and history, for the rewriting of the past as well as the reimagining of the future" (4). For more on the role of melancholia as a generative identificatory and activist mechanism for queer communities of color, see Muñoz, *Disidentifications*, 57–74.

17 Roach writes, "Celebrity, performing in constitutional office even in death, holds open a space in collective memory while the process of surrogation nominates and eventually crowns successors" (*Cities of the Dead*, 76). Sharon Holland also writes about the "serviceability" of dead bodies in nationalist projects and among marginalized communities within the nation struggling to articulate emergent subjectivities (*Raising the Dead*, 9). Holland writes, "The ability of the emerging nation to speak hinges on its correct use of the 'dead' in the service of its creation. Here the dead are the most intimate 'enemy' of the changing and growing nation. Should they rise and speak for themselves, the state would lose all right to their borrowed and/or stolen language" (28). Her work also explores the ways that "embracing the subjectivity of death allows marginalized peoples to speak about the unspoken — to name the places *within* and *without* their cultural milieu" (4–5).

18 Bronfen, *Over Her Dead Body*.

19 For an analysis of Frida's emergence as an icon in the United States, see Molina Guzmán and Valdivia, "Brain, Brow, Booty." For analyses of Evita's afterlife, see Diaz, "Making the Myth of *Evita Perón*"; Taylor, *The Archive and the Repertoire*, 133–60.

20 Several Latina/o scholars have addressed the cultural significances of female "Latin" stars such as Dolores del Rio, Lupe Velez, and Carmen Miranda. See Beltrán, "The First 'Latin Invasion'"; López, "Are All Latins from Manhattan?"; Baez, "From Hollywood and Back"; Rodriguez, *Latin Looks* and *Heroes, Lovers, and Others*; Sandoval-Sanchez, *José Can You See?*, 21–61.

21 Peña, *Música Tejana*, 14.

22 For more on Selena's biography, see Patoski, *Selena*; Vargas, "Bidi Bidi Bom Bom."

23 During the 1980s the term "Tejano" emerged as a distinct and recognized subgenre in the recording industry. Deborah Vargas notes that Tejano music was transformed and embraced by what she refers to as a "unique 'Tejano generation' located somewhere between the post-Chicano civil rights era and the emerging pan-Hispanic identity formation of the mid-1980s" ("*Cruzando Frontejas*," 226).

24 As Deborah Vargas documents, several remarkably talented and resilient female performers managed to achieve recognition and sustain careers within the male-dominated and machismo-saturated Tejano music industry. These Tejana artists included Lydia Mendoza, Ventura Alonzo, Rita Vidaurri, Eva Garza, Chelo Silva, Beatriz Llamas, Rosita Fernandez, Laura Canales, Patsy Torres, Eva Ybarra, Elsa García, and Shelly Lares. Vargas's dissertation, "*Las Tracaleras*," constructs a long-overdue genealogy of these female performers in the history of Tejano music.

25 My analysis of Selena's star text is informed by Richard Dyer's landmark studies of celebrity. See *Stars* (London: British Film Institute, 1979) and *Heavenly Bodies: Film Stars and Society* (New York: St. Martin's Press, 1986).

26 See Willis and Gonzalez, "Reconceptualizing Gender," 9–16.

27 Johnny Canales, quoted in Rick Mitchell, "Selena," *Houston Chronicle*, 21 May 1995, Magazine sec., 6. It is important to note that the narratives that exalted Selena's wholesome family values often elided the fact that she was a Jehovah's Witness. This elision undoubtedly corresponds to the fact that one's status as a Jehovah's Witness does not fit easily within dominant constructions of Latina/o authenticity.

28 This double-edged sexuality discourse is nothing new in the historical representations of women of color. While Selena's biographer, Joe Nick Patoski, interprets Selena's complex persona within the confines of the virgin/whore or good-girl-from-the-barrio/hypersexy-international-superstar dialectic, several scholars have attempted more nuanced analyses. Notably, Emma Pérez

posits that Selena represented "decolonial desire" by affirming a Chicana feminist sexuality (*The Decolonial Imaginary*, 102). José E. Limón argues that Selena's "good girl narrative" ultimately served to control the "dark possibilities" of her sexualized image (*American Encounters*, 183).

29 Joseph Roach argues, "Performers are routinely pressed into service as effigies, their bodies alternately adored and despised but always offered up on the altar of surrogacy. . . . [An effigy is] a cultural trend in which the body of an actor serves as a medium . . . in the secular rituals through which a modernized society communicates with its past" (*Cities of the Dead*, 39–40, 78). In a similar fashion, Gilbert Rodman, borrowing from Stuart Hall, describes Elvis as a "point of articulation," or a specific cultural site "that serves as the major conduit by which two or more *other* phenomena come to be articulated to one another" (*Elvis after Elvis*, 27).

30 Stavans, "Santa Selena," 181.

31 For a discussion of the ways that Elvis worship produces whiteness by effacing the African American sources of Elvis's music and style, see Roach, *Cities of the Dead*; Lott, "All the King's Men," 192–227.

32 David Hinckley, "Stern Heats Up Mexican Tempers," *Daily News*, 6 April 1995, 102; Arraras, *Selena's Secret*, 24.

33 Hinckley, "Stern Heats Up Mexican Tempers," 102. In response to the threatened boycotts, several national retail chains, including Sears, McDonalds, Quaker Oats, and Slick 50 Products, vowed to refuse advertising during Stern's show. John Makeig, "Still after Stern for Selena," *Houston Chronicle*, 10 April 1995, A1. See also Jerry Crowe, "Advertisers React to Stern's Comments Radio," *Los Angeles Times*, 13 April 1995, F2.

34 In his discussion about Princess Diana in "Exemplary Differences," Johnson notes that the conscious decision to "not mourn" Diana is as equally fraught with politicized implications as the decision to mourn the princess.

35 It is important to note that Stern issued his statement just twenty-four hours before Senator Alfonse D'Amato (R-NY) parodied Judge Lance Ito on Don Imus's nationally syndicated morning radio show. Critical of Judge Ito's handling of the O. J. Simpson trial, D'Amato launched into a fake Japanese accent, despite the fact that Ito does not speak with one, proclaiming, "Judge Ito will never let it end. Judge Ito loves the limelight. He is making a disgrace of the judicial system, little Judge Ito." See Lois Romano, "The Reliable Source," *Washington Post*, 6 April 1995, final ed., B03. Considered alongside D'Amato's performance of yellow face, Stern's performance of "not mourning" Selena underscores the ways Selena's discursive body was often evoked as a means through which to police the Latina/o body politic.

36 I borrow the term "new nativism" from Perea, *Immigrants Out*, and Sánchez, "Face the Nation."

37 Colino, "The Fallout from Proposition 187"; Davis, "The Social Origins of the

Referendum"; Escobedo, "Propositions 187 and 227"; Martin, "Proposition 187 in California"; Prado, "'English for the Children.'"

38 Nevins, *Operation Gatekeeper*, 62, 195. Nevins describes "territorial denial" as a "'prevention through deterrence' strategy that attempts to thwart migrants from entering the United States (as opposed to the old strategy of apprehending migrants after they cross) through the forward deployment of Border Patrol agents and increased use of surveillance technologies and support infrastructure" (2).

39 Nevins, *Operation Gatekeeper*, 78. For more on Light up the Border and the counterdemonstrations staged against them, see Davidson, "The Mexican Border War"; Seth Mydans, "As Sun Sets, Tempers Rise at Border," *New York Times*, 22 June 1990, A12; Katharine Webster, "A New Iron Curtain," *San Francisco Chronicle*, 8 December 1991, This World sec., 8/21.

40 http://www.homestead.com/SelenaRemembered/TexasSenateResolution .html.

41 "State Honors Selena," *Houston Chronicle*, 14 April 1995, A30.

42 Hewitt, Harmes, and Stewart. "Before Her Time," 49.

43 Jones, "Inside People," 2.

44 Jones, "Inside People," 2.

45 Dávila, *Latinos Inc.*, 4.

46 Maria Elena Cepeda addresses the decontextualized and dehistoricized construction of Latina/o performers as crossover acts in "'Columbus Effect(s).'"

47 In an interview with Manuel Peña, the Arista Records executive Cameron Randle notes, "'Crossover' is pretty much one concept . . . which is to crossover from a more obscure genre, a more confined genre of music, into a mainstream awareness or consciousness" (Peña, *Música Tejana*, 195).

48 Scholars of popular music such as George Lipsitz and Reebee Garofalo have written persuasively about the ideological repercussions of the musical crossover narrative. See Garofalo, *Rockin' Out*; Lipsitz, *Dangerous Crossroads*. Garofalo observes that the crossover categorization's "identification of music with race, which has tended to exclude African American artists and others from certain marketing structures in the music industry, makes the task of unearthing an accurate history of U.S. popular music quite difficult and encourages serious underestimates of the degree of cross-cultural collaboration that has taken place" (11–12).

49 For an incisive commentary on Selena and the crossover narrative, see Vargas, "*Cruzando Frontejas*."

50 Jones, "Inside People," 2.

51 Quoted in Hector D. Cantú, "Selena's Death Got Attention of Market," *Houston Chronicle*, 28 March 1999, 1. The article begins with the pronouncement, "Tejano pop music singer Selena died [on March 31]. Looking back, March 31 also marks the day, many observers believe, that U.S. Latino pop culture

was born." For additional commentary on the economic phenomenon that ensued after Selena's death, see Cantu, "Cashing In on Selena."

52 Quoted in Adriana Torrez, "Selena's Death Put Latinos in New Light," *San Diego Union-Tribune*, 4 April 2000, Lifestyle sec., E3.

53 Taylor, "Opening Remarks," 6, emphasis in original.

54 Oboler, *Ethnic Labels*.

55 Padilla, *Latino Ethnic Consciousness*, 13; Flores and Yudice, "Living Borders," 58.

56 Agustín Laó-Montes, "Mambo Montage: The Latinization of New York City," in *Mambo Montage: The Latinization of New York*, ed. Arlene Davila and Agustín Laó-Montes (New York: Columbia University Press, 2001), 17, emphasis in original.

57 Dávila, *Latinos Inc.*, 2; G. Pérez, "Puertorriqueñas Rencorosas." See also De Genova and Ramos-Zayas, "Latino Rehearsals."

58 Román, "Latino Performance and Identity," 151.

59 Negrón-Muntaner, "Jennifer's Butt," 184.

60 Muñoz, "Feeling Brown," 67, 68.

61 Rivera-Servera, "Choreographies of Resistance," 274, 286.

62 Selena continued to make endorsements for the company until her death. In fact, largely due to their desire to capitalize upon the growing Latina/o market, Coca-Cola renewed Selena's contract after 1992, the year in which it dropped celebrities from its ad campaigns. Patoski, *Selena*, 162–63.

63 By definition, the category of Latin music requires that at least 50 percent of an album's tracks must be in Spanish. The promotion of this music occurs largely in Spanish-language media, underscoring that Latinas/os are primarily defined by language. Cepeda, "*Mucho loco* for Ricky Martin."

64 The sophisticated video for "Buenos Amigos," Selena's 1991 duet with the Honduran pop singer Alvaro Torres, introduced Selena to audiences on the East and West Coasts and helped the ballad reach number one on the Billboard Latin tracks chart. Selena followed this with a guest appearance on the video for "Donde Quiera Que Estés," wherein she sang and danced in hip-hop formation against an urban backdrop with the Nuyorican boy band Barrio Boyzz. Freddy Correa, one of the members of Barrio Boyzz, went on to tour with Selena as one of her backup singers and dancers.

65 In his biography of Selena, Joe Nick Patoski frequently falls prey to the colonialist fascination with Selena's body: "Her lips had filled out voluptuously; so had her breasts and hips. Her rear was 'the kind you could place a beer glass on without spilling the foam,' as one admiring disc jockey put it. She was the total Latina" (*Selena*, 115).

66 Aparicio, "Jennifer as Selena," 97.

67 The first annual Latin Grammys took place on 30 September 2000 in the midst of public criticism expressed by Gilberto Moreno, general manager

of Fonovisa, the California-based Latin music label known for releasing regional Mexican recordings. Moreno accused the Latin Academy of Recording Arts and Sciences, the producers of the Latin Grammys, of ignoring
Mexican regional and Mexican American artists — as nominees for major
awards and as performers for the telecast — in favor of artists affiliated with
Sony and with the Cuban American producer and Sony executive Emilio
Estefan. Moreno's comments, initially printed in the Spanish-language
newspaper *La Opinión* and reported on in major papers across the country,
reflected larger sentiments among many Mexican Americans that despite
their demographic status as the majority group among Latinas/os, they continue to be absent or underrepresented in English- and Spanish-language
media outlets. These conflicts belie the inter-Latino tensions that arise along
lines of race, class, and region within the United States. For more on the
controversy, see Blanca Arroyo, "Una falta de respeto total," *La Opinión*,
1 September 2000, 9C; Blanca Arroyo, "Arde Troya! Pepe Aguilar y muchos
nominados no aceptarian el premio; 'Es una fiesta de Sony y Emilio Estefan,'" *La Opinión*, 29 August 2000, 1B; Mireya Navarro, "Latin Grammys'
Border Skirmish; New Awards Face Complaints about Slighting a Mexican
Genre," *New York Times*, 30 September 2000, E1. The second annual Latin
Grammys was also rife with controversy, as Cuban exiles in Miami, where
the awards were originally scheduled, protested the showcasing of Cuban
performers from the island. In an effort to avoid a major disturbance, organizers moved the event to Los Angeles and rescheduled it for 11 September
2001. Given the national crisis that occurred that day, the Latin Grammys
were again postponed and the televised coverage was canceled. See Ramiro
Burr, "Sanz, Juanes Top Latin Grammys; TV Coverage Was Canceled Due
to Attacks," *San Antonio Express-News*, 31 October 2001, A2; Dana Canedy,
"Discord over Miami's Bid for Latin Grammys," *New York Times*, 30 March
2001, A14.

68 In an interview with the ethnomusicologist Manuel Peña, Cameron Randle,
an executive at Arista Records, makes this point clear: "We just came back
from the *Billboard Magazine* Latin conference in Miami. And you go down and
get a sobering reminder of Tejano's place within the Latino family, musically.
It's still treated essentially as a blue-collar, secondary genre of music that is
confined to a geographical area" (Peña, *Música Tejana*, 196).

69 De Genova and Ramos-Zayas, "Latino Rehearsals," 45.

70 Fusco, "Artist's Statement." http://www.thing.net/~cocofusco/subpages/
performances/performancepage/ subpages/betteryetwhendead.html.

71 Richard Schechner argues that performance is "always subject to revision" because it is never performed by the same performer in the same way or for the
same audience in the same moment. Thus performance is "never for the first
time . . . [but instead] for the second to the nth time" and thereby always and

already repetition with a (critical) difference (*Between Theatre and Anthropology*, 36). Drawing from Schechner's (as well as Victor Turner's and Richard Bauman's) definitions of performance, Joseph Roach understands performance as surrogation: "Performance . . . stands in for an elusive entity that it is not but that it must vainly aspire both to embody and replace" (*Cities of the Dead*, 3). Elin Diamond echoes these assertions with her claim that performance embeds features of previous, now absent performances while also producing new experiences that are only partially dependent upon these previous histories, and as such offers "a permeable understanding of history and change" (introduction, 1–2). Diamond's view of performance as "both a doing and a thing done" resonates with Margaret Thompson Drewel's insistence that performance "privileges process, the temporally or processurally constructed nature of human realities" ("The State of Research," 1). That is, precisely because performance is not simply the product of a historical moment but also simultaneously renders visible the processes of history making (because it is always, as Drewel writes, "repetition and revision"), performance provides a uniquely indispensable archive, or as Diana Taylor astutely notes throughout *The Archive and the Repertoire*, a repertoire, for examining the complex ways individuals negotiate their entanglements within the matrices of history, culture, and power.

72 Taylor, *The Archive and the Repertoire*, 15.
73 See Conquergood, "Rethinking Ethnography."
74 Haraway, *Simians*, 196.
75 Phelan, *Unmarked*, 146.
76 Taylor, *The Archive and the Repertoire*, 143.
77 Anzaldúa and Moraga, *This Bridge Called My Back*.
78 For feminist scholarship about the Juárez murders, see Gaspar de Alba, "The Maquiladora Murders"; Monarrez, "Serial Sexual Femicide"; Fregoso, "Voices without Echo"; Livingston, "Murder in Juárez"; E. Pérez, "So Far from God"; Wright, "The Dialectics of Still Life." For artistic works that address the murders, see Gaspar de Alba, *Desert Blood*; Coco Fusco, *The Incredible Disappearing Woman*, performance, 2003; *Señorita Extraviada*, dir. Lourdes Portillo, 76 min., Women Make Movies, New York, 2001.

1. Soundtracks of Selenidad

1 Aparicio, "Jennifer as Selena," 93.
2 Rivera-Servera, "Choreographies of Resistance," 274. Rivera-Servera's understanding of latinidad as an affective mode follows José E. Muñoz's writings on Latina/o affect. See Muñoz, "Feeling Brown."

3 For more on the dual temporality of performance, see Carlson, *The Haunted Stage*; Diamond, introduction, 1–14; Taylor, *The Archive and the Repertoire*.

4 Dolan, *Utopia in Performance*, 5, 6, 20, 169. Dolan argues that through the "soaring sense of hope, possibility, and desire that imbues utopian performatives . . . we can encounter our inarticulate longings toward a future that, through utopian performatives, might still remain *mute*, but can on some deeper level be *felt*" (8, 164, emphasis in original). Thus utopian performatives "aren't iterations of what *is*, but transformative doings of what *if*. This kind of hope represents an opening up, rather than a closing down, of consciousness of the past and the future in the present" (141, emphasis in original). Following Raymond Williams's theories about structures of feelings, Dolan's concept of utopian performatives also resonates with José E. Muñoz's notion of disidentificatory performance that "offers a utopian blueprint for a possible future while, at the same time, staging a new political formation in the present" (Muñoz, *Disidentifications*, 200).

5 Kun, *Audiotopia*, 21, 17. Kun writes that audiotopias offer listeners and musicians the maps that "point to the possible, not the impossible . . . [that] lead us not to another world, but back to coping with this one" (23).

6 *Selena Live—The Last Concert*. 55 min. Image Entertainment, 2003, DVD.

7 The songs that compose Selena's "Disco Medley" include "I Will Survive," "Funky Town," "Last Dance," "The Hustle," and "On the Radio."

8 Both Deborah Vargas and the film scholar Chuck Kleinhans argue that Nava deploys this concert scene to position Selena's story within an American assimilationist narrative. See Vargas, "Bidi Bidi Bom Bom"; Kleinhaus, "¡Siempre Selena!"

9 Deborah Vargas challenges the music crossover narrative through which Selena's career has been discursively channeled by positing an alternative conceptual mapping that she calls "cruzando frontejas" (crossing Texas-Mexico; "*Cruzando Frontejas*," 226). For other scholarly critiques of the crossover narrative that frames Selena's career, see Kleinhans, "¡Siempre Selena!"; Limón, *American Encounters*, 169–70.

10 Aparicio, "Jennifer as Selena," 97.

11 Peña, *Música Tejana*, 206.

12 I have drawn my information of the history of disco from the following sources: Peter Braunstein, "The Last Days of Gay Disco," *Village Voice*, 30 June 1998, 54–55, 58; Dyer, "In Defence of Disco"; Echols, *Shaky Ground*; Hughes, "In the Empire of the Beat"; Kooijman, "Turn the Beat Around"; Krasnow, "Fear and Loathing"; Lawrence, "'I Want to See All My Friends'"; Lawrence, *Love Saves the Day*.

13 Kooijman, "Turn the Beat Around," 258.

14 Dyer, "In Defense of Disco," 152–53. Krasnow notes, "Disco's insistent pri-

macy on the beat . . . reaffirmed the centrality of dance in popular music" ("Fear and Loathing," 40).

15 Alice Echols notes, "Some listeners thought [disco] sounded 'white,' a perception fueled by the number of white artists who jumped on the disco bandwagon in 1979. In fact, disco's popularity with pop listeners owed a great deal to the way it mainstreamed blackness by rendering artists' color incidental, almost irrelevant. Disco's apparent racelessness allowed it to cross over with the white pop audience" (*Shaky Ground*, 164–65). For more on the history of discophobia, see Krasnow, "Fear and Loathing."

16 Jose E. Limón also makes this observation about the concert setting in *American Encounters*, 169–70.

17 For more on the language of and "linguistic terror" against the inhabitants of the U.S.-Mexico borderlands, see Anzaldúa, *Borderlands*.

18 In his biography, *The Fabulous Sylvester*, Joshua Gamson theorizes the concept of queer fabulousness as part of the disco aesthetic: "Fabulousness has a *je ne sais quoi*, like other indefinable things—beauty, love, star quality, good television. You know it mostly by encountering it. Most forms of excess are fabulous, at least when they are admired, and especially when they exceed or defy expectations. . . . As a personal attribute, fabulousness involves extravagance (which others sometimes interpret as showiness) and extreme committed self-possession (which others often mistake for haughtiness). . . . Sequins don't hurt. The sea parts for fabulous" (38).

19 Krasnow, "Fear and Loathing," 44.

20 Allen R. Myerson, "A Tejano Singer Sets Out to Bridge Music and Nations," *New York Times*, 1 January 1996, 45.

21 The Tejano *bailes de negocios* ("business dances" or "taxi dances"), popular during the 1920s and 1930s, were held at cantinas where male dancers would purchase tokens (*fichas*) in exchange for a dance with a female partner. The female dancers at the bailes de negocios were associated with and often relied upon prostitution as a means of earning income, especially during the Depression era, when poor rural families frequently brought their daughters to the dances to earn extra income for the family. See Peña, *Música Tejana*, 89–90. José E. Limón provides an ethnographic study of the gender politics and cultural poetics of conjunto dance halls in *Dancing with the Devil*.

22 Many argue that during the early 1980s Patsy Torres was the first Tejana artist to move beyond the stationary singing styles of Silva and Mendoza. See Vargas, "Las Tracaleras."

23 Lawrence "'I Want to See My Friends,'" 153.

24 Lawrence "'I Want to See My Friends,'" 153.

25 Cusick, "On a Lesbian Relationship."

26 Lawrence, "'I Want to See My Friends,'" 148, 149, 150.

27 Peña, *Música Tejana*, 197.

28 For more on the history of Tejano music, see Peña, *Música Tejana*; for a discussion of the dance styles of Nuyoricans at the Palladium, see Hutchinson, "Mambo on the 2."

29 Dyer, "In Defense of Disco," 157.

30 My thanks to Jackie Cuevas for calling my attention to the Tejana style of Selena's bell bottom design.

31 Ramírez, "Crimes of Fashion," 3.

32 See Kooijman, "Turn the Beat Around," 260; Echols, *Shaky Ground*, 180–81.

33 My thanks to Deborah Vargas for sharing this insight at the Tejano Music Symposium in Austin, Texas, 21 April 2006.

34 The Tejano *orquesta* groups popular during the civil rights era such as Little Joe y La Familia and Sunny and the Sunliners drew from pan-Latino and Afrodiasporic musical influences. For example, Little Joe was raised in an African American neighborhood in the east Texas town of Temple, where he encountered the influences of blues and jazz in addition to the traditional Tejano music played in his own home. He initially modeled his image in part after James Brown, but following his encounters with the ideologies of *latinismo* in California, he changed his look and sound to be more Chicanocentric. See Peña, *Música Tejana*, 166.

35 *Recordando a Selena*, Univisión, 30 April 2005.

36 Negrón-Muntaner, "Jennifer's Butt," 185.

37 Stavans, "Santa Selena," 181.

38 For more on the utopic potential of disco, see Dyer, "In Defence of Disco," 155–56.

39 Krasnow, "Fear and Loathing," 41. Hughes also notes that "the prolongation of [disco's] own continuity is its only end" ("In the Empire of the Beat," 149).

40 This attention to live performance does not discount the very real and embodied ways that technological innovations have ensured that Selena's beat goes on. In particular, the marketing and consumption of Selena karaoke on eBay and other outlets contribute to the ongoing circulation of Selena's live performances. The item "Disco Medley I Selena," for example, encourages a reenactment of Selena's Astrodome concert version of the song by preserving her deviations from and mistakes with the original lyrics of "I Will Survive." My thanks to Deborah Vargas for calling my attention to this.

41 A large part of *Amor Prohibido*'s appeal to a range of Latina/o listeners was its mixed repertoire of sounds that represented the culmination of Selena and her band's creative efforts to combine traditional Tejano forms with other Latin/o and African American sounds and instrumentation. The album included the title track, a pop cumbia with a descending keyboard hook; "Techno Cumbia," a cumbia updated with vocal samplings, second-line drumming from New Orleans, and horn charts from Caribbean soca; "No Me Queda Más," a traditional romantic bolero; "Tus Deprecios," an accordion-driven conjunto; "Bidi

Bidi Bom Bom," a Spanish-language pop melody; and "Fotos y Recuerdos," an inspired, Spanish-language cover of The Pretenders' 1980s new wave classic, "Back on the Chain Gang." The title track from *Amor Prohibido* unseated Gloria Estefan's critically and popularly acclaimed single "Mi Tierra" from its reign at the top of Billboard's Latin International chart after the record had spent forty-eight weeks at number one. This symbolic triumph over Estefan on the Billboard charts significantly recharts traditional mappings of the Latin Music Boom that posit its origins and output with Gloria and Emilio Estefan's Miami-based Sony affiliate Crescent Moon Studios and, in particular, with Ricky Martin's (one of the Estefan-produced crossover artists) 1999 Grammy performance of "Livin' la Vida Loca." See Cepeda, "*Mucho loco* for Ricky Martin," for a discussion of mainstream chronologies of the Latin Music Boom.

42 The first Tejano artist to win a Grammy was Flaco Jimenez, who, in 1986, garnered an award for a remake of his father's song, "Ay Te Dejo en San Antonio."

43 Popular acceptance and success in Mexico was crucial in the promotion of Selena's career because within the performative economy of the music business crossover maneuvering from a regionalized Mexican American genre (Tejano) into the larger Mexican American or U.S. Latino market ironically first required a migration across the border. In the logic of the recording industry Tejano artists like Selena had to acquire commercial success in Mexico as a means of proving their potential to reach pan-Latino U.S. audiences and of assuring an eventual ranking on Billboard's Mexican regional (Mexican American) and Latin charts.

Not unlike many third-generation, working-class Tejanos, Selena was not entirely proficient in Spanish. In fact, early on in her career she was unable to conduct interviews with the Spanish-language media without an interpreter and was often derided for it. Moreover, Selena's *morena* features further entrenched her affiliation with the working class, as Larry Rohter reported: "South of the border, too, there was resistance at first, to what Selena represented. In the upper-class neighborhoods of Mexico City, she was at first derided as *naco*, an ethnic and class slur meaning coarse or vulgar, because of her mestizo or mixed European and Indian features, which were a marked contrast to those of the typically fair-skinned and light-haired soap opera stars." Larry Rohter, "A Legend Grows, and So Does an Industry," *New York Times*, 12 January 1997, H39. It was thus necessary for Selena to cross over linguistic and class borders in addition to musical and cultural ones.

At the Monterrey press conference Selena deftly compensated for her language shortcomings through the shrewd negotiation of her performing body, momentarily intervening in the prevailing Mexican stereotype of Tejanos as inauthentic, low-class Mexicans cut off from their cultural roots. In an improvised performance of Mexican middle-class authenticity, she graciously greeted each of the reporters as they arrived with a welcoming phrase and a hug, an act considered proper manners for a young middle-class Mexican woman greeting elders or people of respect. This display of middle-class Mexican decorum and courtesy (that many Americanized, third-generation Tejanas may often fail to perform) tactically overshadowed her language deficiencies, countered her *naca* image in Mexico, and effectively won over the wary reporters, who expressed their adoration of her in their subsequent coverage of the event (Patoski, *Selena*, 124).

44 Historically, the term *pocha/o* was deployed as a derisive epithet to describe Mexican Americans who did not possess fluency in Spanish or were thought, in general, to be too Americanized. The term has been appropriated by recent generations of Chicanas/os as an assertion of bicultural pride. See, for example, the work produced on www.pocho.com.

45 See Aparicio, *Listening to Salsa*, for an analysis of salsa lyrics.

46 Quoted in Peña, *Música Tejana*, 197.

47 Aparicio, "Jennifer as Selena," 97.

48 Quoted in Rick Mitchell, "Selena," *Houston Chronicle*, 21 May 1995, Magazine sec., 6.

49 Vargas, "Bidi Bidi Bom Bom," 123.

50 Personal video of Selena in concert, Rosedale Park, 1992, in collection of author.

51 I borrow the concept "affective investments" from Grossberg, "Is There a Fan in the House?" Vanessa Knights offers an insightful application of the concept in her discussion of affective investments that listeners make within the *boleros* performed by female *boleristas* in "Tears and Screams," 87.

52 Barthes, "The Grain of the Voice," 188.

53 Quoted in Rohter, "A Legend Grows," H39.

54 For a feminist analysis of rancheras and their reception, see Nájera-Ramírez, "Unruly Passions."

55 In her queer analysis of Chavela Vargas and La Lupe, Vanessa Knights describes *filin* ("feeling") as "an explicitly emotional or expressive style of singing achieved through various techniques . . . [that include] its gestural performance style incorporating silences and pauses for dramatic effect" ("Tears and Screams," 87). For more on La Lupe and Chavela Vargas, see Aparicio, "La Lupe"; Aparicio and Valentín-Escobar, "Memorializing La Lupe and Lavoe"; Yarbro-Bejarano, "Crossing the Border."

56 Lorca, "Play and Theory of the Duende," 55.

57 For more on diva singers and queer spectatorship, see Koestenbaum, *The Queen's Throat*; Leonardi and Pope, *The Diva's Mouth*.

58 Hughes, "In the Empire of the Beat," 156, 148, 156.

2. Colonial Past, Tejano Present

1 The term "Anglo" is a technically imprecise term interchangeable with the category "white." I deploy it here because it is the term used in Corpus Christi to refer to the communities generally understood to be racialized as white.

2 McWilliams, *North from Mexico*. For more recent scholarship that explores the makings of civic identity and history in the U.S. Southwest, see Deverell, *Whitewashed Adobe*; Gutiérrez, "Significant to Whom?"; Kropp, "Citizens of the Past?"; McClung, *Landscapes of Desire*; Montgomery, *The Spanish Redemption*, 97–104; Wilson, *The Myth of Santa Fe*.

3 Deverell, *Whitewashed Adobe*, 7–8. In his work on Santa Fe civic identity, Chris Wilson also observes this phenomenon: "Initiated to promote tourism, [the myth of Santa Fe] has also provided a sense of coherence and continuity to a region in the midst of social and economic transformation. Central to this myth is the rhetoric of tricultural harmony; that is harmony among Native Americans, Hispanics, and Anglo-Americans. Despite this rhetoric of social tolerance, and despite the unifying image provided by ubiquitous adobe-colored stucco, the myth of Santa Fe obscures long-standing cultural and class frictions" (*The Myth of Santa Fe*, 8).

4 Roach, *Cities of the Dead*. Roach builds on the philosopher and historian Pierre Nora's distinction between "places of memory" (*lieux de memoire*) and "environments of memory" (*milieux de memoire*). Nora associates milieux de memoire with preindustrial peasant communities, claiming that the onset of modernity has replaced these "spontaneous" environments of memory with artificial sites or places of memory such as cemeteries, museums, archives, monuments, and festivals ("Between Memory and History," 289). Roach troubles Nora's modernist nostalgia for lost peasant culture's (static) milieux de memoire by arguing that such historical gestures have not actually been entirely eroded by the technologies of modernity because the spontaneous gestures of milieux de memoire, always enacted by self-conscious dynamic agents, were in fact never "retained" without also being simultaneously reinvented. For Roach, memory, like performance, is always repetition with revision and as such can emerge in seemingly unlikely gestures or locales.

5 Wilson, *The Myth of Santa Fe*, 313.

6 For more on the gendered labor required for civic maintenance, see Jackson, *Lines of Activity*.

7 For this section's subtitle, see Lessoff, "A Texas City," 329.

8 Singer, "Texas Shipwreck," 78.

9 Acuña, *Occupied America*; Montejano, *Anglos and Mexicans*.

10 Acuña, *Occupied America*, 49; Montejano, *Anglos and Mexicans*, 34, 39.

11 Foley, "Mexicans, Mechanization."

12 Cynthia E. Orozco, "Nuecestown Raid of 1875," *Handbook of Texas Online*, http://www.tsha.utexas.edu/handbook/online/articles/view/NN/jcnnt.html.

13 Lessoff, "A Texas City," 313. Prior to this, large ships were unable to bring cargo all the way into the bay; thus the construction of the deep-water port helped promote commerce and trade.

14 Christopher Long, "Corpus Christi, Texas," *Handbook of Texas Online*, http://www.tsha.utexas.edu/ handbook/online/articles/view/CC/hdc3.html. The population rose from 10,522 to 27, 741.

15 Lessoff, "A Texas City," 305.

16 Gordon, "The Implementation of Desegregation."

17 Corpus Christi Chamber of Commerce, "Demographics, 2002."

18 According to the 2000 Census findings, the total Latina/o population was composed of the following: 64 percent Mexican American, 4.6 percent Puerto Rican, 1.8 percent Cuban, 35 percent other. The census also reported that two-thirds of Corpus Christi's entire population earned less than $30,000 annually. U.S. Census, "Report," 2000, http://census.tamu.edu/data/census/2000/demoprof/msa/mstab-64.txt.

19 Montejano, *Anglos and Mexicans*, 299. In this way post-1960s Corpus Christi shared with the rest of south Texas what José E. Limón characterizes as "a period of *mexicano* working-class postmodernism," whereby many Tejanas/os experienced postmodern late capitalism not as a ludic multiplicity of shifting identities but as a devastating psychic and material "depthlessness" and "double negation" of identity brought about by economic restructuring and schooling that displaced Spanish-language skills without adequate instruction of middle-class English skills necessary for greater economic mobility (*Dancing with the Devil*, 112).

20 As a result, by end of 1998 the number of Border Patrol agents had doubled since 1993. Jim O'Connell, "South Texas to Get More Border Agents," *Corpus Christi Caller-Times Online*, 21 October 1999, http://www.caller2.com/1999/october/21/today/local-ne/1953.html.

21 Mary Lee Grant, "Local Hispanics Fear Immigration Backlash," *Corpus Christi Caller-Times*, 22 October 1999, A1.

22 Frank Bonilla, a Corpus Christi attorney, charged that the measure was "a continuation of a very regressive movement we are presently experiencing in the southwest. [The new policy] is just going to be a litmus test based on how you are dressed and how good your English is." Quoted in Grant, "Local Hispanics," A1.

23 Mary Lee Grant, "Enforcement of Immigration Policy Varies between Counties," *Corpus Christi Caller-Times*, 24 October 1999, A1. In the same article, Nestor Rodriguez, director of the Center of Immigration Studies at the University of Houston, concurs that the policy further transforms the south Texas border region into "a police state."

24 Glaston Ford, "Truan: NAFTA Has Little Impact on City," *Corpus Christi Caller-Times Online*, 11 February 1998, http://www.caller2.com/busarch/bus3512.html.

25 "Corpus Christi's Lack of Growth," editorial, *Corpus Christi Caller-Times Online*, 24 October 2000, http://www.caller2.com/2000/october/24/today/editoria/7365.html. The writer reports recent census findings that show flat economic growth throughout the 1990s, noting that even while Corpus Christi grew about 10 percent (just above the national average) the city's growth paled in comparison with the growth of other south Texas cities (Laredo, 45 percent; McAllen, 39.5 percent; Brownsville-Harlingen, 26 percent).

26 Tom Whitehurst Jr., "City Loses to Valley at Leapfrog," *Corpus Christi Caller-Times*, 23 April 2000, D1.

27 In cities throughout the U.S. Southwest, as a result of the legacy of colonization, Mexican American aspiration has often been linked to an asserted affiliation with Spanish (i.e., European) as opposed to Mexican roots.

28 Lessoff, "A Texas City."

29 Lessoff, "Public Sculpture," 320.

30 Lessoff, "Public Sculpture," 320.

31 In its initial evaluation of the monument, the Municipal Arts Council board criticized the sculpture's "static" composition. Lessoff, "Public Sculpture," 213.

32 James Pinkerton, "Troubled Waters," *Houston Chronicle*, 2 April 2000, State sec., 1; James T. Yenckel, "Replicas of Columbus's Ships Sailing to U.S.," *Chicago Sun-Times*, 19 January 1992, Travel sec., 9; Singer, "Texas Shipwreck," 78.

33 Quoted in Singer, "Texas Shipwreck," 78. Lessoff also notes that the ships were an "example of how Corpus Christians of both major ethnic groups reach[ed] beyond the modern city to Texas myth and romance for meaningful history . . . yet the notion that first drove the campaign to acquire the ships—that they provide Corpus Christi 'a particularly dramatic link to its own heritage'—remains largely unproven" ("A Texas City," 318).

34 It was at this time that the association also convinced the Smithsonian to lend its exhibit Seeds of Change to Corpus Christi's Museum of Science and History. Singer, "Texas Shipwreck," 78.

35 Tom Whitehurst Jr., "Columbus Ships May Go Back," *Corpus Christi Caller-Times*, 11 October 1999, A1; John Tedesco, "Paying Their Freight," *San Antonio Express-News*, 9 May 2001, 1B.

36 Tara Copp, "Durrill Slaps Lien on Ships," *Corpus Christi Caller-Times*, 13 January 2000, A1; Whitehurst, "Columbus Ships," A1.

37 "A Texas Welcome for Columbus's Ships," *New York Times*, 14 June 1993, A10. Quote from Christina Lamb and James Langton, "First Fleet Comes to Grief in Texas," *Sunday Telegraph*, 4 February 2001, 34. Mark Singer also notes that the "clear subtext of the quincentenary celebration was that, for a change,

Anglo and Hispanic Corpus Christi would jointly embrace the city's cultural patrimony. The visit of the Columbus ships offered an ideal symbol" ("Texas Shipwreck," 78).

38 Durrill continued, "Texas has a history of discarding history, of saying we can build it bigger and better and newer. I thought the whole story needed to be told. Spain changed the face of the world. They brutalized people? Yeah, but hell, everybody brutalized people. They triggered the exodus from the European nations to the Americas. Religion, farming, the whole shooting match of what occurred. That's the story." Quoted in Singer, "Texas Shipwreck," 78.

39 Singer, "Texas Shipwreck," 78.

40 "Columbus Ships Damaged," *New York Times*, 13 April 1994, B9; George F. W. Telfer, "Barge Accident Damages Columbus Replicas," *Journal of Commerce*, 18 April 1994, 7B.

41 Tara Copp, "Fleet Repair Funds Paid Down Debt," *Corpus Christi Caller-Times*, 24 February 2000, A1; Tara Copp, "Fleet Priorities Questioned," *Corpus Christi Caller-Times*, 24 April 2000, A1; Dee Jacques Moynihan, "Columbus Fleet Docked in Corpus for 50 Years," *Houston Chronicle*, 31 March 1996, Texas Magazine sec., 4; John Tedesco, "Riding Out the Storm," *San Antonio Express-News*, 3B; Pamela LeBlanc, "Sad Times for Columbus Ships," *Austin American-Statesman*, 1 May 2005, Travel sec., D4.

42 Syd Kearney, "Corpus Halting Tours of Its Columbus Fleet," *Houston Chronicle*, 14 November 1999, Travel sec., 2; Tara Copp, "Battle over Ships Continues," *Corpus Christi Caller-Times*, 18 January 2000, B1. Norman Wallace, chairman of the CFA, decried the ships' demise: "What killed the ships is the cost of the concrete slab. If it weren't there, the ships would still be open." Quoted in Copp, "Fleet Repair," A1. A local group of volunteer sailors who cared for the ships formed Las Carabelas de Colon Historical Foundation in response to the CFA's mismanagement and demanded an investigation of CFA activities, the ships' removal from the museum, and an apology to Spain. Tara Copp, "Sailors Hope to Help Salvage the Fleet," *Corpus Christi Caller-Times*, 27 March 2000, B1.

43 Quoted in Singer, "Texas Shipwreck," 78.

44 Singer, "Texas Shipwreck," 78.

45 Tedesco, "Riding Out the Storm," 3B.

46 Quoted in Venessa Santos, "Reopening May Be in the Near Future for the Columbus Ships," *Corpus Christi Caller-Times*, 21 July 2000, B1. See also Tedesco, "Riding Out the Storm," 3B; Tedesco, "Paying Their Freight," 1B.

47 Benjamin West, letters to the editor, *Corpus Christi Caller-Times*, 16 May 2001, Editorial sec., A9.

48 Amanda Nelson, "CVB Rolls Out Fun New Logo," *Corpus Christi Caller-Times*, 26 August 2004, B8. In another report in the paper's business section, Jeff

Frahm noted that the "seemingly snake-bit Columbus replica ships" had been a major factor in preventing the city from emerging from its economic "doldrums." Jeff Frahm, "City Notes Significant Point in Its Progress," *Corpus Christi Caller-Times*, 18 April 2005, D8.

49 Brandi Dean, "Clouds Clear for Columbus Ships," *Corpus Christi Caller-Times*, 1 March 2006, A1.

50 "Slow Leak Found in Nina after Month of Repair Work," *Corpus Christi Caller-Times*, 28 July 2002, B8; Jesse Bogan, "Replica Ships Cost Real Cash," *San Antonio Express*-News, 2 August 2002, 1B.

51 Sue Ann Presley, "A Singer's Life after Death," *Washington Post*, 21 March 1997, B1.

52 Meoldy Galvan, quoted in Veronica Flores, "Neighbors Saw Role Model in Girl from Molina," *San Antonio Express-News*, 2 April 1995, B1.

53 Dabby Noyola, quote in Flores, "Neighbors Saw Role Model," B1. West Oso High School is located on Corpus Christi's west side and is composed primarily of working-class Mexican Americans. Yvonne Peña, one of Selena's neighbors, echoed Noyola's remarks: "She [Selena] said she wasn't moving for a long time because she loved the barrio, especially the kids. She liked them climbing on the fence and screaming her name." Quoted in Flores, "Neighbors Saw Role Model," B1.

54 Hewitt, Harmes, and Stewart, "Before Her Time," 48–53.

55 Gretchen Beaconsfield of the Corpus Christi Chamber of Commerce explained the city's reasoning for this decision: "It was a necessity, because of demand: more than 700 visitors each weekday, and 1500 on weekends. . . . It's not what we want to be known for, because it's such a tragedy, but the city has had to be very sensitive to the family and to the many visitors who want to know about her life." Quoted in Kathleen Kenna, "Saint Selena Bigger in Death Than in Life," *Toronto Star*, 13 April 1997, D1.

56 The Tejano music scholar Manuel Peña concurred with Carillo: "To call for such emulation or hero worshipping is hard for some Anglos to understand, when they see them, perhaps, as just another Mexican." Quoted in Ellen Bernstein, "The Loss to Hispanics Is Difficult for Anglos to Understand, Academics Say," *Corpus Christi Caller-Times Online, Selena Tribute*, 31 March 1996, http://www.coastalbendhealth.com/selena/sextra7.htm.

57 Bernstein, "The Loss to Hispanics."

58 Local reports noted, "Selena already shows signs in death of becoming a major focal point for visitors to Corpus Christi. Without the benefit of billboards or brochures, local cab drivers meet tourist demand for private tours of Selena sites." Ellen Bernstein, "Selena Could Become a Local Tourism Draw," *Corpus Christi Caller-Times Online, Selena Tribute*, 16 April 1997, http://www.coastalbendhealth.com/selena/se1107.htm.

59 Quoted in Bernstein, "Selena Could Become."

60 Lessoff, "Public Sculpture," 190.

61 Bernstein, "The Loss to Hispanics"; Rosemary Barnes, "Plans for Selena Memorials," *Corpus Christi Caller-Times Online, Selena Tribute*, 31 March 1996, http://www.coastalbendhealth.com/selena/sextra6.htm.

62 Brandesky argued that the poor response to the radio promotion indicated that even Selena's fans weren't interested in memorials to the late singer. This equation of the lack of funds with a lack of interest ignores the fact that many of Selena's fans are from working-class and economically disadvantaged communities with little or no expendable income. Barnes, "Plans for Selena Memorials."

63 Quoted in Nicole D. Pérez, "Selena Lives On: Selena Statue Unveiling Brings Tears, Joys," *Corpus Christi Caller-Times*, 26 May 1997.

64 Paige Ross, "Children's Mural Pays Tribute to Selena," *Corpus Christi Caller-Times*, 5 October 1997.

65 For more on the Vietnam Veterans Memorial, see Marita Sturken, *Tangled Memories*.

66 Nick Jimenez, "Disrespect for Selena's Memory," *Corpus Christi Caller-Times*, 23 July 2000, Editorial sec., A11.

67 A report in the local paper noted, "The continued writing on the memorial — including the carving of 'Ray G + Thelma G' into the statue's bronze chest — has bothered Selena's family." Michael Hines, "Barrier for Selena Statue OK'd," *Corpus Christi Caller-Times*, 20 July 2000, A1. The *Abilene Reporter-News* also reported on "the steady stream of visitors who leave behind signatures and, in some cases, gang signs." Diane La Monte, "Fans' Tributes: Honor or Graffiti?," *Abilene Reporter-News Online*, 22 July 1998, http://www.texnews.com/1998/texas/selena0722.html.

68 All preceding quotes in this paragraph drawn from La Monte, "Fans' Tributes."

69 Quoted in Sara Lee Fernandez, "'Friendly' Barrier May Be in Works to Protect Selena from Graffiti," *Corpus Christi Caller-Times*, 2 June 2000, B1.

70 Jimenez, "Disrespect for Selena's Memory," A11.

71 "No Way to Honor Selena," editorial, *Corpus Christi Caller-Times*, 11 June 2000.

72 Jimenez, "Disrespect for Selena's Memory," A11.

73 Quoted in Hines, "Barrier for Selena Statue OK'd," A1.

74 Guy H. Lawrence, "Railings are Installed to Protect Selena Memorial," *Corpus Christi Caller-Times*, 26 Sept 2000, A1.

75 La Monte, "Fans' Tributes."

76 Letter to the editor, *Corpus Christi Caller-Times*, 31 July 2000, Editorial sec., A8.

77 Quoted in Hines, "Barrier for Selena Statue OK'd," A1.

78 Limón observes that these acts "are forms of a continuing, if repressed, war

with a late-capitalist urbanized Anglo culture of postmodernity. Through these forms, [working-class Tejanas/os] articulate . . . a critical difference of consciousness in antagonistic contradistinction to this now dominant culture" (*Dancing with the Devil*, 116–17).

79 Muñoz, "Feeling Brown," 70. In his discussion of citizenship as the performance of affect, Muñoz writes, "Standard models of US citizenship are based on a national affect. . . . From the vantage point of [the official] national affect code, Latina/o affect appears over the top and excessive."

80 Ana Castillo also evokes the Iphigenia analogy in her obituary for Selena in "Selena Aside."

81 Grosz, *Volatile Bodies*, 23.

82 For more on the trap of visibility for minoritarian communities, see Phelan, *Unmarked*, 6.

3. *Selena Forever*

1 *Estylo*, March/April 2000, 26–27.

2 Field notes, 23 March 2000.

3 Roach, *Cities of the Dead*, 80, 38–39.

4 Fabre, "African American Commemorative Celebrations," 72–73, emphasis in the original.

5 For studies that address the interplay among race, sexuality, and pleasure in musicals, see Clum, *Something for the Boys*; D. A. Miller, *A Place for Us*; Most, "'You've Got to Be Carefully Taught'"; Sandoval-Sanchez, *José Can you See?*; Wolf, *A Problem Like Maria*; Wolf, "'We'll Always Be Bosom Buddies.'"

6 Ellen Bernstein, "Selena's Tragic Story Is Subject of Musical," *Houston Chronicle*, 18 October 1999, 3.

7 Most, *Making Americans*.

8 This approach to the ways the promotion, staging, and spectatorship of the musical contributed to the consolidation of latinidad constitutes a methodological response to Jill Dolan's call for a "model of exchange between theatre and other fields and disciplines, rather than one in which the performative evacuates theatre studies" (*Geographies of Learning*, 67). Dolan argues for a retention of theater studies as a disciplinary home while calling for the productive disruption of its apparent coherence through the inclusion of people and geographies it has historically excluded. She observes, "Theories of the performative . . . creatively borrow from concepts in theatre studies to make their claim for the constructed nature of subjectivity, suggesting that social subjects perform themselves in negotiation with the delimiting cultural conventions of the geography within which they move. But as much as performativity seems to capture the academic imagination, and as much as

performance captures the political field, theatrical performances, as located, historical sites for interventionist work in social identity constructions, are rarely considered across the disciplines, methods, and politics that borrow its terms" (65). As one possible methodological approach, she proposes exploring theater studies as "an ethnography, while avoiding the imperialist gesture of the anthropologist's gaze" (85). My work takes up this call.

9 Personal interview, 23 July 2001.

10 See Anzaldúa, *The Borderlands*. Deborah Vargas, in *"Cruzando Frontejas,"* discusses how Selena's public struggles with and eventual mastery over the Spanish language provided many Latinas/os with a crucially affirming emblem of triumph over "linguistic terrorism."

11 Roach, *Cities of the Dead*, 33. In the edited volume *Mourning Diana*, Adrian Kear and Deborah Lynn Steinberg also note that the classical tragic model "provides an exposition of the performative structures of mourning. That is, the public performance of grief brings about the community it appears to represent precisely by invoking the ghosts of the past. The theatre of mourning, then, provides a key stage for the performative construction of the contemporary through the dramatic rearticulation of the past" ("Ghost Writing," 6).

12 Roach, *Cities of the Dead*, 35.

13 Public discussions about the challenges that the Latina/o population (in particular, undocumented workers) posed to an accurate census count invariably involved conversations about the "problem" of Latina/o citizenship. See Fred Alvarez, "Region's Farm Workers Urged to Stand Up, Be Counted," *Los Angeles Times*, 8 March 2000, 12; Mary Mogan Edwards, "Strategy Helping Latinos Overcome Fear of the Form Census 2000," *Columbus Dispatch*, 9 April 2000, 1F.

14 Given that low-income communities are often denied access to technologies such as computers and the Internet, this website can also be understood as a sign of a growing Latina/o middle class attempting to assert its presence and as a preview of increased Latina/o participation in a necessarily changing mainstream.

15 Quoted in Burr, *"Selena Forever* Premiere," 89.

16 The official website of the U.S. Census Bureau provides information about the Road Tour and other outreach measures implemented as part of the Census 2000: http://www.census.gov/dmd/www/advroadtour.html and http://www.census.gov/dmd/www/americanindian/partners.htm. For reports on the 2000 Census promotional process and projections about the Latina/o population, see Rick Badie, "Latinos Get Extra Attention from the Census 'Road Tour,'" *Atlanta Journal-Constitution*, 31 March 2000, 1; Leticia Garcia-Irigoyen, "Fondos para centros de informacion sobre el censo," *La Opinión*, 3 February 2000, 1B; Eric Miller, "Hispanic Group Uses Humor to Try to Spur Census Returns," *Tampa Tribune*, 10 April 2000, 6; Indraneel Sur, "Latino

Entertainers to Aid Census Drive," *Los Angeles Times*, 1 April 2000, 3; E. J. Tamara, "El autobus del censo: Al comenzar a llegar los cuestionarios del Censo 2000," *La Opinión*, 13 March 2000, 1B.

17 Latinos made up 97 percent of all census respondents who marked the "Other Race" option. For discussions about the ways that Latinas/os were reshaping the national discourse on race and ethnicity, see Morales and Rodríguez, "Latinos and the 'Other Race' Option"; Patrisia Gonzales and Roberto Rodriguez, "When the Census Stops Making Sense," *San Diego Union-Tribune*, 15 April 2001, G-3. In their astute letter to the editor in response to Orlando Patterson's assumptions about Latina/o claims to whiteness, Miriam Jimenez Roman and Gina Pérez succinctly note, "'Hispanic' is a demographic category, and the grouping does not constitute a race. Still, the sociological fact — and one fraught with meaning — is that it is a demographic category that is treated as an expression of race." "A Category, Not a Race," *New York Times*, 15 May 2001, 24.

18 "Identity Shift? Latino Trends May Signal a Different Kind of Assimilation," *Houston Chronicle*, 23 September 2001, 2. Sixty percent of Latinos reported Mexican ancestry on the census; the second highest group after that indicated "Other" for national origin. In response to these statistics the *Houston Chronicle* report observed, "Instead of relying on national origin, language, cuisine or religion as cultural markers, these Latinos would tend to draw on their sense of shared experience as a minority in the United States. Put another way, ethnicity rather than national origin may be taking over as a self-identifying factor" (2).

19 Tom McGarrity, the president of network sales for Univisión, remarked, "It's almost as if our industry hired the Census Bureau to do our public relations. Companies can't overlook the Hispanic market now." Quoted in Eduardo Porter, "For Hispanic Marketers, Census Says It All," *Wall Street Journal*, 24 April 2001, B8. Representative Gonzalez quoted in Santiago Tavara, "Census Hispanic Community Remains a Sleeping Giant," EFE *News Service*, 9 May 2001. The article also reported similar comments from Juan Figuero, the president of Puerto Rican Legal Defense and Education: "Latinos don't just want to be recognized for their buying power . . . we want to be considered when political decisions are made." See also Roberto Suro, "It Will Take Time for the Population Boom to Translate," *Washington Post*, 26 June 2005, B1.

20 Cynthia Tucker, "Latino Growth a Wake-Up Call for Black Folks," *Atlanta Journal-Constitution*, 18 March 2001, 10B. Juan Gonzalez also asserted, "The new census figures make clear how big a part of America's future Hispanics have become." Juan Gonzalez, "Latinos Now Major Players," *New York Daily News*, 9 March 2001, 17. Many of the reports on the census projections and findings about Latinas/os as the future were pervaded by a conspicuously anti-black rhetorical framing that pit Latinos against African Americans or

compared the two communities in efforts to imply that Latinas/os were better (off) than blacks. These public discussions attempted to mitigate mainstream anxieties about an imminent minority-majority nation by projecting an intrinsic tension between the nation's two largest minority groups. For example, an article in the *New Orleans Times-Picayune* proclaimed, "At stake is the right to be America's No. 1 minority. It is a symbolic distinction with real-world consequences for each group's respective claim for public resources, concern and attention. There are only so many Ford Foundation grants, 'Nightline' town meetings and doctoral dissertations to go around, and the consideration of Latino America cannot help but come at least a little bit at the expense of black America, which must increasingly surrender its unique claim as the alpha and omega of the race experience in America." Jonathan Tilove, "Census More Than Black and White: African-Americans Vying with Hispanics for No. 1 Status," *New Orleans Times-Picayune*, 8 March 2001, 1. It is in this context that Cynthia Tucker expressed her concerns: "If African-Americans are to continue progressing toward the nation's economic mainstream, we need to start looking forward, too. The heyday of black civil rights is over. It's time to let it go" (10B). Tucker's article does not necessarily prove an actual and inherent divide between Latinas/os and blacks but in fact provides evidence of the effects of the circulating discourse that deployed census results to reinforce notions of access to resources within a zero-sum frame.

21 *Selena Forever* press release.

22 Census data reported a staggering 58 percent population growth among Latinos in the decade since the 1990 census. Lynette Clemetson, "Latino Populations Growth Is Widespread, Study Says," *New York Times*, 31 July 2002, A14.

23 In San Antonio, the city that hosted the premiere of *Selena Forever*, Latinos emerged as nearly 60 percent of the total population. Eric Schmitt, "Census Shows Big Gain for Mexican-Americans," *New York Times*, 10 May 2001, 28; Sherry Sylvester, "Hispanics Move Up to Numero Uno," *San Antonio Express-News*, 23 May 2001, 1A.

24 Leonel Sanchez, "Diverse, Yet Distinct: Latinos, Population Young and Growing," *San Diego Union-Tribune*, 1 April 2001, A1. The median age of Latinas/os was 25.9, compared to 35.3 for the overall population. Georgia Pabst, "Census Data Show Impact for Latinos, but Future Work Force Continues to Struggle," *Milwaukee Journal Sentinel*, 16 July 2001; 6A.

25 *Selena Forever* press release.

26 Wolf, *A Problem Like Maria*, 93. Merman's no-nonsense stage persona, as Wolf writes, made "the Broadway musical available to all Americans" in large part because of its construction within working-class terms: "A presumption of her averageness with respect to class serves at once to render her publicly accessible and to make her rise to stardom seem extraordinary, deserved, and also possible for others" (100).

27 Quoted in Wolf, *A Problem Like Maria*, 100. Wolf describes the belting voice's racialized markings: "'The belting voice is a voice of strength, demanding that the woman sing high in her chest voice, that she support the sound to hit the note seemingly just out of reach. It is a voice that evokes darkness in tone and timbre, a 'colored' voice" (102).

28 The producers Jerry Frankel, Michael Vega, Tom Quinn, and Forbes Chandlish had among them financed previously successful Broadway productions that included *Jekyll and Hyde*, *The Wiz*, *Death of a Salesman*, and *Charlie Brown*. Edward Gallardo, the librettist, is the Puerto Rican playwright best known for his play, *Simpson Street*, which depicted a Nuyorican family's struggles in the Bronx. *Selena Forever* marked the fourteenth musical that the Cuban-born composer Fernando Rivas had scored. The director, William Alejandro ("Bill") Virchis, had previously directed the Los Angeles production of that other iconic Latino play, Luis Valdez's *Zoot Suit*.

29 Méndez, "Selena *por siempre*."

30 Ellen Bernstein, "Staging Selena—*Selena Forever* Performers Prepare for Opening Night," *Corpus Christi Caller-Times*, 12 March 2000, H1.

31 The *Corpus Christi Caller-Times* observed, "Upon entering the lobby, the audience was greeted with a merchandise display rivaling that of a Disney production, complete with Selena T-shirts, hats and dolls." Ricardo Baca, "Crowds Enjoy Preview of *Selena Forever*," *Corpus Christi Caller-Times*, 22 March 2000, A2.

32 Deborah Martin, "Outfits Based on Selena's Design Sketches," *San Antonio Express-News*, 21 March 2000, 2D.

33 In his review in the *Dallas Morning News* Mario Tarradell concurred that, ironically, the music in the musical did not adequately encompass the range of Selena's talents: "[The show's flaws] could be forgiven if *Selena Forever* presented a more comprehensive overview of the icon's greatest gift—her music. But for the most part, cumbias are all we get. No attention is given to Selena's talent for interpreting heart-wrenching rancheras, snappy polkas or classic disco. Those styles were replaced by Broadway-bound showstoppers." Mario Tarradell, "Strained Salute: Legend Gets Lost in *Selena Forever*," *Dallas Morning News*, 31 March 2000.

34 Kelley Shannon, "Musical about Tejano Singer Heads to Next Texas City," *Associated Press State and Local Wire*, 27 March 2000.

35 Alisa Valdes-Rodriguez, "An Eternal Star Shines 'Forever,'" *Los Angeles Times*, 25 March 2000, F1.

36 Ricardo Baca, "Forever a Local Legend," *Corpus Christi Caller-Times*, 31 March 2000, E12.

37 Nina Garin, "When 'Forever' Isn't," *San Diego Union-Tribune*, 23 May 2000, E1.

38 An interview published in the *Los Angeles Times* illustrates: "'Latinos are new to the theater,' Robert Treviño [who arranged sponsors for the tour] said,

echoing comments made at the musical's premiere in San Antonio by its director, William Alejandro Virchis, and producer Tom Quinn. 'They come at the last minute.'" Alisa Valdes-Rodriguez, "L.A. Run of Stage Musical *Selena Forever* is Canceled," *Los Angeles Times*, 9 May 2000, 1. Treviño continued to deploy this characterization in an interview printed in *Billboard*: "Maybe Latinos did not understand the concept." Quoted in Burr, "'Selena' Show's Producers Sue HOB, 40. In another interview that appeared in the *San Diego Union-Tribune*, the director Bill Virchis commented, "Latinos are more of a walk-up buying market. The same tactics used for *Cats* won't work for this audience. We had discussions everyday about how we were going to reach this market. This tour is sort of like Johnny Appleseed, you have to build an audience, it's an expensive thing. But the reward was that many of these people had never been in a theater before." Garin, "When 'Forever' Isn't," E1.

39 Surprisingly, only one Spanish-language newspaper reported on the musical's woes, briefly noting, "La visita [californiana] fue cancelada por falta de acuerdo entre promotores y productores [The musical's California visit was canceled due to disagreements between the show's promoters and producers]." "Suspenden gira de obra Musical *Selena Forever*," *El Mundo* (Oakland), 6 July 2000, 6. This conspicuous absence of commentary likely reflects a lack of promotional outreach to Latina/o-sponsored enterprises rather than a lack of Latina/o community interest in Selena.

40 Dávila, *Latinos, Inc.*, 4.

41 Personal interview, 20 September 2005.

42 Quoted in Garin, "When 'Forever' Isn't," E1.

43 Valdes-Rodriguez, "L.A. Run of Stage Musical," F1.

44 A report in the *Los Angeles Times* noted, "Selena has assumed a symbolic importance greater than most commercial productions in Los Angeles, for it is the first production at the Doolittle since the Ricardo Montalban Nosotros Foundation bought the theater last year with the intent of converting it into a Latino-oriented performing arts center." Don Shirley, "*Selena* Producers Upbeat Despite Losses," *Los Angeles Times*, 13 June 2001, F1.

45 Quoted in Shirley, "*Selena* Producers Upbeat," F1.

46 Quoted in Shirley, "*Selena* Producers Upbeat," F1. The report continued: "Only about $60,000 was left for advertising for the production, which was originally slated to run two months. By contrast, several local theatre marketers said the rule of thumb is to spend at least 10% of the potential gross on advertising — which in the case of 'Selena,' would amount to $32,000 a week."

47 Shirley, "*Selena* Producers Upbeat," F1.

48 Arlene Dávila writes about the ways that marketing was "constitutive of U.S. Latinidad" during the 1990s (*Latinos Inc.*, 3).

49 Selena had landed a contract with Coca-Cola early in her career and continued to make endorsements for the company until her death.

50 Emma Pérez offers a feminist psychoanalytic reading of the Oedipal narrative that pervades the biopic *Selena*, in *The Decolonial Imaginary*, 114–21.

51 The songs were included on the final program printing and were performed at the preview performance I attended but were cut by opening night.

52 Long before the *Wicked* craze, in which mothers and daughters attended the musical as an event of mother-daughter and girl-power bonding, *Selena Forever* and other Selena memorials drew large numbers of Latina mothers and daughters who shared a love for Selena before and after her death. An interview printed in the *San Diego Union-Tribune* reveals one instance of this: "'This is our first time to the theatre,' says [Rosie] Jimenez, who has brought her daughter, Jasmine and her mother, Leonor Ramirez, to the performance. 'We're here to remember Selena.'" Garin, "When 'Forever' Isn't," EI.

53 Chapter 4 explores young Latina identification with Selena in greater detail.

54 In this section I refer to respondents by their first name in an effort to position them as dramatic protagonists and to convey the sense of intimacy and community fostered among participants at the musical.

55 For more on the zoot suit as an emblem of resistance, see Daniels, "Los Angeles Zoot"; Mazón, *The Zoot-Suit Riots*; Noriega, "Fashion Crimes."

56 The legacy of *Zoot Suit* haunted the production in one other way: Daniel Valdez, who portrayed Selena's father, had starred in the original production of *Zoot Suit*.

57 Phelan, *Unmarked*, 6.

58 Personal interview, 23 April 2000.

59 Sánchez Korrol, *From Colonia to Community*. The book was first published in 1983 and updated and reprinted in 1994.

60 Jerry's comment about the mayor of New York is a reference to Mayor Robert F. Wagner Jr. and his call for cheap Puerto Rican labor during the 1950s, which occurred in tandem with Operation Bootstrap, the economic development program implemented by the U.S. government and corporations during the late 1940s. One of the consequences of Operation Bootstrap was that Puerto Rican migrants became an important source of cheap labor in New York. During this time petrochemical and pharmaceutical corporations shifted industrial operations to areas outside the mainland United States, prompting the now common trend of outsourcing. U.S. policy makers, motivated by the Malthusian notion that Puerto Rico was overpopulated, deployed two major means of population control: coordinated out-migration and forced sterilization. For more on the economic repercussions of Operation Bootstrap, see Dietz, *Economic History of Puerto Rico*. For more on the sterilization of Puerto Rican women during this period, see the documentary film *La Operación*, dir. Anna Maria Garcia, 1982.

61 The exploitation of female labor has emerged as an emblem for the deploy-

ment of Puerto Rican labor at this time. See Ortiz, *Puerto Rican Women and Work*.

62 Four years following his involvement in *Selena Forever* Jerry went on to join the Florida-based doo-wop group Sha-Boom. Personal interview, 20 September 2005.

63 Quoted in Deborah Martinez, "Selena Video Attracts Dozens of Little Girls," *Corpus Christi Caller-Times*, 6 March 2000, A1.

64 Quoted in Paige Ross, "Wanted: Girls to Carry Roses for Selena," *Corpus Christi Caller-Times*, 3 March 2000.

65 Personal interview, 2 October 2005.

66 Personal interview, 23 March 2000.

67 Los Angeles County led all counties nationwide in total Latino population (4.2 million); East L.A. reported the highest percentage (96.8) of Latino residents in any neighborhood in the country. Bill Hillburg, "County Is U.S. Latino Capital," *Los Angeles Daily News*, 10 May 2001, N1.

68 The chorus was replaced by a single narrator, the Accordion Man, a figure reminiscent of El Pachuco in *Zoot Suit* and Che in *Evita*. Nearly all of the changes in the show were the result of budget constraints.

69 Following the performance Alvarez made a brief appearance in the lobby, where she was engulfed by audience members bestowing praise and admiration for her performance skill and powerful stage presence. Interestingly, none of her admirers praised her for her ability "to sound like Selena," but, rather, for her *unique* vocal skills. For example, one audience member effused, "Your version of 'Como la Flor' was the best part of the show!" Another noted, "It was like the role [of Selena] gave her [Alvarez] a way to really come into her own." Field notes, 4 May 2001.

70 Two of the reviews published in the *Los Angeles Times* also comment upon the surprising and powerful "transcendence" of the show's closing moments. Michael Phillips writes, "In an often plodding show's final minutes, something bizarre happens: it finds itself. . . . Spotlighted along with her white rose, an ardent young fan (wonderful Agina Alverez) gives 'Como la Flor' her all, before the curtain call." Michael Phillips, "Storytelling Takes Back Seat to Music in Dreamy *Selena*," *Los Angeles Times*, 24 April 2001, F1. Julio Martinez remarks, "Also deserving mention [is] diminutive Agina Alvarez, who offers a transcendent, show-closing, a cappella reprise of 'Como La Flor.'" Julio Martinez, "Selena Returns in Patchy New Musical," *Los Angeles Times*, 24 April 2001, F1.

71 While this moment can also be understood as staging a new Latina body caught up in the beginnings of commodification and in the appropriation of latinidad, this does not foreclose the possibility that it also provides a space for the expression of emergent aspirations for what latinidad could be.

4. Becoming Selena

1 "Wanted: Actress for Selena Role," *Houston Chronicle*, 8 March 1996, 1.

2 Estimated numbers for the audition turnout: 8,000 in San Antonio, 10,000 in Los Angeles, 3,000 in Miami, 3,000 in Chicago. "Hoping for Stardom: 3,000 Selena Look-Alikes Turn Out for Casting Call," *Phoenix Gazette*, 18 March 1996, A2; Elena De la Cruz, "En busca de Selena," *La Opinión*, 15 March 1996, 1D; Lydia Martin, "2,000 Try Out to Play Slain Tejano Singer," *Miami Herald*, 18 March 1996, A1.

3 Lydia Martin, "Aspiran las chicas de Miami," *El Nuevo Herald*, 18 March 1996, 1A.

4 Melissa Fletcher Stoeltje, "Searching for the Perfect Selena," *Houston Chronicle*, 18 March 1996, 1.

5 Quoted in Dave Hoekstra, "Thousands Vie for Role as Tejano Star," *Chicago Sun Times*, 28 March 1996, Late Sports Final ed., 31.

6 Quoted in Robert Dominguez, "Biopic Tryouts Had to Be Selena to Be Believed," *New York Daily News*, 22 March 1996, 49.

7 Other promotional events tied to the film reinforced constructions of Latinas/os within marketplace values. For example, the Bank One Corporation spent more than $1 million on a series of marketing tie-ins with the movie and issued a line of checks and check cards imprinted with Selena's image. Stuart Elliott, "Bank One Uses Promotional Tie-ins to a Movie about Selena to Reach Out to the Hispanic Market," *New York Times*, 21 March 1997, D6.

8 Anzaldúa writes, "Among Chicanas/*méxicanas*, *haciendo caras*, 'making faces,' means to put on a face, express feelings by distorting the face—frowning, grimacing, looking sad, glum or disapproving. For me, *haciendo caras* has the added connotation of making *gestos subversivos*, political subversive gestures, the piercing look that questions or challenges, the look that says, 'Don't walk all over me,' the one that says, 'Get out of my face.' 'Face' is the surface of the body that is the most noticeably inscribed by social structures, marked with instructions on how to be *mujer*, *macho*, working class, Chicana." "*Haciendo caras, una entrada*," In *Making Face, Making Soul = Haciendo Caras*, xv.

9 Stacey, *Star Gazing*, 29.

10 Cepeda, "Shakira"; Holmlund, *Impossible Bodies*, 109–22; Marchevsky, *Not Working*; Valdivia, *A Latina*.

11 Diamond, *Unmaking Mimesis*, 126. Jackie Stacey also writes about the ways that identification involves "the production of desired identities, rather than simply the confirmation of existing ones" (*Star Gazing*, 172).

12 Cloe Cabrera, "Latina Teens Help Each Other Deal with Problem Issues," *Tampa Tribune*, 20 July 2000, Final ed., 4; Choi, "Ethic Differences"; Kent Davis-Packard, "Era of Prosperity Largely Skips Latino Teens," *Christian Science Monitor*, 8 August 2000, 3; Maria Elena Fernández, "Cultural Conflict:

Latina Teens Caught between Two Worlds, Are Often Depressed," *Los Angeles Times*, 13 December 1999, B3. By the close of the century Latina teenagers suffered the highest health risks among adolescent girls, but were targeted by the fewest treatment services. Asquith, "Researching Latinas in Crisis."

13 Claudia Pérez was an eighteen-year-old high school senior when she served as guest correspondent on *This American Life*. This report marked the second project she undertook with the radio show; her first assignment was for the episode "New Year" that aired on 3 January 1996. She became aware of and involved with the radio show through her participation in the outreach organization Street-Level Youth Media. Personal interview, 8 May 1999. Street-Level regularly collaborates with a number of arts and media organizations in Chicago in an effort to "educate Chicago's inner-city youth in media arts and emerging technologies for use in self-expression, communication and social change" (http://www.artdiscovery.org/Street-Level-Youth-Media.html).

14 For more on gentrification in Humboldt Park, see G. Pérez, *The Near Northwest Side Story*; reports released by Chicago's Puerto Rican Cultural Center, http://www.prcc-chgo.org/prcc_confronting_gentrification.htm.

15 C. Pérez, "1000 Women Become Selena." This and all subsequent excerpts from the radio report are my own transcriptions of the audio recording of the episode.

16 Like Pérez, I am concerned with Latina spectatorship and participation in the making of *Selena*, and not with an analysis of the film itself. As an official narrative of Selena's life (sanctioned by her father and backed by a major studio), the film predictably channels Selena's career within an assimilationist crossover frame. The film was released nationally on 21 March 1997 and roundly derided by feminist critics for the ways that the American Dream triumph narrative glossed over the material struggles faced by aspiring musical artists like Selena. The biopic's most obvious omission, as the film scholar Rosa Linda Fregoso observes, was attention to Selena's fan phenomenon. For astute readings of the film, see Fregoso, introduction to *Lourdes Portillo*, 15–21; Kleinhaus, "¡Siempre Selena!"; E. Pérez, *The Decolonial Imaginary*, 116–25.

17 For more on girl fandom and female youth culture, see Ehrenreich, Hess, and Jacobs, "Beatlemania"; Mazzarella, *Girl Wide Web*; McRobbie, *Feminism and Youth Culture*; Scheiner, *Signifying Female Adolescence*; Wald, "'I Want It That Way'"; Wolf, "*Wicked* Divas." For girls as producers of media culture, see Kearney, *Girls Make Media*. For Latina identificatory practices, see Aparicio, *Listening to Salsa*; Nájera-Ramírez, "Unruly Passions."

18 Cobo, "Latin Biz"; Teresa Puente, "Culture Clash Complicates Latina Teen Years," *Chicago Tribune*, 28 February 1999, A1.

19 For latinidad as a marketing technology, see Dávila, *Latinos Inc.*; Negrón-Muntaner, "Jennifer's Butt."

20 For more on inter-Latina relations and disidentifications, see G. Pérez, "Puertorriqueñas Rencorosas."

21 Larry Rohter, "A Legend Grows and So Does an Industry," *New York Times*, 12 January 1997, H39.

22 De Genova and Ramos-Zayas, "Latino Rehearsals," 45.

23 Cindy Rodriguez, "Latina's Voice Silenced before We All Knew Her," *Syracuse Post-Standard*, 26 March 1997, B1.

24 The film's soundtrack used Selena's own voice in Jennifer Lopez's performances of Selena's music. Emma Pérez and Rosa Linda Fregoso, both critics of the film's story line, also noted the palpable sense of connection and community experienced among the movie theater audience in their accounts of attending screenings of *Selena*. E. Pérez, *The Decolonial Imaginary*, 119; Fregoso, introduction to *Lourdes Portillo*, 15–16.

25 Negrón-Muntaner, "Jennifer's Butt," 182.

26 Victoria Infante, "'Coalicion' de dos personas protesta contra productor de *Selena*," *La Opinion*, 10 July 1996, 3D; "Protestas por eleccion de actriz puertorriqueña: Amenazan con boicotear pelicula sobre Selena," *Impacto: The Latin News*, 10 July 1996, 15.

27 Quoted in Mal Vincent, "Lopez Is Bursting into Hollywood Spotlight," *Virginian Pilot*, 22 March 1997, E8.

28 Muñoz, "Feeling Brown," 67.

29 Negrón-Muntaner, "Jennifer's Butt," 185.

30 Ana M. Lopez provides an insightful analysis of del Rio, Velez, and Miranda in "Are All Latins from Manhattan?"

31 Personal interview, 26 February 1999. Italics reflect inflections in speech. Subsequent quotations from my conversation with Claudia are drawn from the interview conducted on this date.

32 Genova and Ramos-Zayas, "Latino Racial Formations," 7. I deploy the term *mexicanidad* in this chapter to refer to Mexican immigrant or Mexican American identity. The term *Mexicana/o* is frequently used as a self-referential term among Mexican American and Mexican immigrant communities in the United States. See, for example, Limón, *Dancing with the Devil*; Zavella, "'Playing with Fire.'"

33 On how latinidad has the potential to operate as an "oppositional stance to majoritarian institutions," see Román, "Latino Performance and Identity," 151–52.

34 Negrón-Muntaner, "Jennifer's Butt," 189. These observations echo Sander Gilman's and Paula Giddings's observations about how the buttocks have historically served as an emblem for racially marked sexual difference, whereby the racialized and sexualized "excessive" buttocks of black women were evoked by hegemonic forces as an emblem for the unrestrained threat of all black people and as the counterweight against which standards of white femi-

ninity was constructed. See Gilman, "Black Bodies, White Bodies"; Giddings, "The Last Taboo."

35 See, for example, Castañeda, "Anglo Images" and "Sexual Violence." In his discussion of Selena, José E. Limón also notes how the construction of Latina sexuality is imbricated within colonial relationships in South Texas (*American Encounters*, 180–81).

36 Fregoso, "Voices without Echo," 146.

37 See, for example, Zavella, "'Playing with Fire.'"

38 Quoted in Hector Saldaña, "Selena Legacy Lives Five Years after Death," *San Antonio Express-News*, 31 March 2000, 1A.

39 Quoted in Vincent, "Lopez Is Bursting," E8. See also Joe Leydon, "Keeping Dreams Alive," *Los Angeles Times*, 8 December 1996, 8.

40 Quoted in *Corpus: A Home Movie for Selena*, dir. Lourdes Portillo, 1998.

41 Stacey, *Star Gazing*, 29.

42 Quoted in Martin, "Aspiran las chicas de Miami," 1A.

43 Comparisons between Elvis and Selena abounded after her death. Ilan Stavans referred to Selena as a "darker-complected Elvis" ("Santa Selena," 181). Both Gregory Nava and Joe Nick Patoski, Selena's biographer, compared the tremendous outpouring of grief over Selena's death to the mourning that attended Elvis's death. Rohter, "A Legend Grows," H39. Similar comparisons pervaded media coverage of Selenidad. For example, the *Minneapolis Star Tribune* reported that thirty thousand mourners had filed by Selena's casket and noted that the same number had paid their respects to Elvis at his funeral. Ramiro Burr, "Selena's Impact Still Felt," *Minneapolis Star Tribune*, 31 March 1996, Metro ed., 9F. A report in the *Chicago Sun-Times* assessed the Selena phenomenon in these terms as well: "It's not a stretch to put this weekend's tributes on an Elvis Presley level. Only 23 at her death, Selena—like Presley—sang in an inspiring range of musical styles. . . . And like Presley, Selena showed that dreams are not impossible to attain. Presley's spirit resounded within the working class South. Selena's music does the same with the Mexican-American community." Hoekstra, "Thousands Vie for Role," 31. The *New York Times* echoed this sentiment three years later: "Selena achieved in death the celebrity of an Elvis Presley or a Marilyn Monroe among Latinos and others, even on the East Coast and in other areas where she was not as well known or Tejano music as popular as in Texas, her home state." Mireya Navarro, "Inspired by Selena, They Seek Her Role," *New York Times*, 8 November 1999, B1.

44 Lott, "All the King's Men," 198–99.

45 Quoted in Portillo, *Corpus: A Home Movie for Selena*.

46 Bettie, *Women without Class*, 61.

47 The Jorge from Channel 66 she refers to is Jorge Barbosa, a news anchor for WGBO, the Univisión network affiliate in Chicago.

48 Phelan, *Unmarked*, 6.

49 Jessica's act reveals how, as Judith Halberstam observes, "preadult, preidentitarian girl roles offer a set of opportunities for theorizing gender, sexuality, race, and social rebellion precisely because they occupy the space of the 'not-yet,' the not fully realized" (*In a Queer Time*, 177).

50 Bettie, *Women without Class*, 61. Bettie discusses the symbolic economies of style such as makeup and hairstyles among working-class girls in high school.

51 Wolf, "*Wicked* Divas," 58.

52 In *Twelfth Night* Viola proclaims, "I my brother know / Yet living in my glass; even such and so / In favour was my brother, and he went, / Still in this fashion, color, and ornament, / For him I imitate" (3.4.344).

53 Ilan Stavans derides young women who impersonate Selena as "countless imitators" who uncritically lose themselves in their attempts to become her ("Santa Selena," 177).

54 Stacey, *Star Gazing*, 159.

55 Their erotically charged embodiment of Selena highlights how, as Stacy Wolf writes, "girls fall in love with performers not because they want to be them in toto but because they want to be them *performing*" (*Wicked* Divas, 58, emphasis in original).

56 Claudia's suspicion that the auditions were a publicity stunt was widely shared by many Latinas who auditioned for the role. This sentiment also surfaced in newspaper accounts of the auditions and grew so pervasive in popular narratives that the film's producers created a mini-documentary, "Selena: The Movie—All Access" (assembled for the special features section of Selena's final concert DVD) in which *Selena* producer Moctesuma Esparza asserts, "The open casting call was truly an authentic, real event—in that we really did go out and search out any possible person that could play the role. And that we, in fact, picked an amateur, a little girl—who had never acted, ever—from south Texas, from Selena's home area to play her as a little girl. And that we had screen tests of—of gosh—over fifty young women." *Selena Live—The Last Concert*, 55 min., Image Entertainment, 2003, DVD.

57 Accounts like this were echoed by an eighteen-year-old Dominican high school student, Nidia Vásquez, who took the day off from her job at a gas station in South Beach to practice her dance moves for the audition in Miami but was never offered the opportunity to show them off: "Practique durante ocho horas seguidas y ellos solo me prequtaron cuales eran mis pasatiempos y me despacharon. Pero está bien. Por lo menos intenté [I practiced for eight hours straight and all they asked me was what were my favorite pastimes and they sent me on my way. But it's fine. At least I tried]." Quoted in Martin, "Aspiran las Chicas de Miami," 1A.

58 I also listened to the unedited interview tapes Claudia and Nancy Updike,

the show's producer, gathered at the auditions. Notably, none of the young women and girls interviewed on these tapes mentioned the potential financial rewards or recognition as motivations for their participation in the audition process.

59 Lott, "All the King's Men," 218.

60 The various relocations that marked Selena's childhood reflect the larger political economic plight of many Tejanas/os as a result of the oil bust in the 1970s and 1980s.

61 As Julie Bettie notes, "The body has long been the only raw material or capital with which impoverished and working-class women have to work" (*Women without Class*, 93). In her ethnography Bettie recalls, "The year I was at the school, the film about the late Tejana music star Selena was being made, and rumor had it that the producers were searching the country for a girl to play the young version of Selena in the film. Las chicas reported stories of younger sisters pleading with their parents to take them to L.A. to try out" (93).

62 Claudia first reported for *This American Life* for the episode "New Year" that aired on 3 January 1996.

63 Nájera-Ramírez, "Unruly Passions," 185, 189.

64 Nájera-Ramírez, "Unruly Passions," 185. Nájera-Ramírez notes that female ranchera singers make interventions through stage charisma, vocal skill, lyrical alterations, costume, and bodily gestures (188).

65 Immediately following her death, numerous mainstream periodicals unfamiliar with Selena mislabeled her bustier-clad, dancing body as a Tex-Mex version of Madonna. For a critical analysis of this trend, see Willis and Gonzalez, "Reconceptualizing Gender."

66 Nájera-Ramírez, "Unruly Passions," 204.

67 Nájera-Ramírez, "Unruly Passions," 188, 192. As Nájera-Ramírez suggests, Selena's alterations were slight, but not insignificant. She changed the opening line from "Mira como ando mujer [Look at the state I'm in, woman]" to "Mira como ando mi amor [Look at the state I'm in, my love]" (192).

68 E. Pérez, *The Decolonial Imaginary*, 116.

5. "Como la Flor" Reprised

1 Grrl Action Showcase, Austin, Texas, 24 July 2005. DVD recording courtesy of Rude Mechanicals.

2 I identify Melissa by first name only, as that is how she and the other "grrls" identified themselves in the performance. My analysis of her performance is shaped by conversations with Sarah Myers, whose dissertation on her work with Grrl Action includes an analysis of the showcase in which Melissa's song was featured. Myers and I were working on our projects at the same time,

and my work has benefited from our intellectual exchange. I thank Sarah for bringing Melissa's performance to my attention and for sharing the DVD recordings of the Grrl Action showcase with me. My re-creation of Melissa's act is drawn from these recordings and from Sarah's memory of the event.

3 Wolf, "*Wicked* Divas," 54.

4 Sarah Myers, "'But I Am the Average American Girl': *Grrl Action* and the Performance of Adolescent Female Identity," Ph.D. dissertation, University of Texas, in process.

5 Alexander Doty writes about the expansive spatial and sexual dimensions of queerness as a "flexible space for the expression of all aspects of non- (anti-, contra-) straight cultural production and reception" in "There's Something Queer Here," 73.

6 For more on queer counterintimacy, see Lauren Berlant and Michael Warner, "Sex in Public," 561.

7 Horacio N. Roque Ramírez borrows from Ricardo A. Bracho's and José Mineros's notion of *latinaje* as the "multilayered hybrid process of creating Latina and Latino worlds and cultures from below" (275) in "'Mira, yo soy boricua y estoy aquí.'"

8 DVD recording of the 23 July 2005 performance courtesy of Rude Mechanicals.

9 "To be queer," Jill Dolan writes, "is not who you *are*, it's what you *do*. It's your relation to dominant power, and your relation to marginality, as a place of empowerment." Introduction to *The Queerest Art*, 5, emphasis in the original. David Savran concurs, understanding queerness as "a performative designation, one that privileges doing over being, action over intention," in "Queer Theater and the Disarticulation of Identity," in *The Queerest Art*, 154.

10 Disidentification, as José E. Muñoz has theorized, operates as "a performative mode of tactical recognition," or a politicized recuperative act, wherein "a stigmatized identity is simultaneously decomposed and recomposed" in efforts to create "minoritarian counterpublic spheres" (*Disidentifications*, 31, 196, 5).

11 Berlant and Warner elaborate on the notion of queer world-making: "The queer world is a space of entrances, exits, unsystemized lines of acquaintance, projected horizons, typifying examples, unspecified routes, blockages, incommensurate geographies. . . . Making a queer world has required the development of kinds of intimacy that bear no necessary relation to domestic space, to kinship, to the couple form, to property, or to the nation" ("Sex in Public," 558). For applications of this theory to dance club culture and performance, see Buckland, *Impossible Dance*; Vogel, "Where Are We Now."

12 *Corpus: A Home Movie for Selena*, dir. Lourdes Portillo, 46 min., Xochitl Films, San Francisco, 1998, premiered as part of the PBS-sponsored *P.O.V.* series on 13

July 1999. The companion video, *A Conversation with Academics about Selena*, dir. Lourdes Portillo, 60 min., Xochitl Films, San Francisco, 1998, was created and distributed in large part as a response to the struggles Portillo faced against Selena's father's efforts to disavow the queerness of and to delegitimize queer affiliation with Selenidad. For an elaboration on the production process of *Corpus*, see Fregoso, introduction to *Lourdes Portillo*.

13 See chapter 1 for a detailed analysis of some of the queer elements of Selena's performance style and persona.

14 Leonardi and Pope, *The Diva's Mouth*, 57.

15 Selena was no doubt not the only diva (consider Lena Horne, Grace Jones, Tina Turner, Mary J. Blige, Whitney Houston, and Celia Cruz, to name a few) to disrupt these assumptions, but there is something about her bubble-gum-pop-meets-world-weary-vocal-stylings and her explicit working-class markings that distinguished her from these established black and brown divas.

16 In "Tears and Screams" Vanessa Knights writes, "Through the explicit emphasis on deliberate performance, *filin* provides a queer cultural space in which gender identities and sexual roles can be destabilized" (87).

17 Vargas "*Las Tracaleras*."

18 My thanks to Deborah Vargas for helping me develop this insight.

19 Tomás Ybarra-Frausto, "Rasquachismo: A Chicano Sensibility," in *Chicano Art: Resistance and Affirmation, 1965-1985*, ed. Richard Griswold del Castillo, Teresa McKenna, and Yvonne Yarbro-Bejarano (Los Angeles: Wight Art Gallery, UCLA, 1991), 155, 162.

20 Alina Troyano/Carmelita Tropicana, *Chicas 2000*, 72.

21 Muñoz, *Disidentifications*, 182.

22 Muñoz writes, "Chusmas, like queers, have managed a spoiled identity by disidentifying with shame" (*Disidentifications*, 194).

23 La Fountain-Stokes, "La politica queer."

24 Doty, Introduction, 2. Doty writes, "Divas offer the world a compelling brass standard that has plenty to say to women, queer men, blacks, Latinos, and other marginalized groups about the costs and the rewards that can come when you decide both to live a conspicuous public life within white patriarchy and to try and live that life on your own terms" (2).

25 E. Pérez, *The Decolonial Imaginary*, 116.

26 Quoted in *A Conversation with Academics about Selena*. All subsequent quotations from Moraga are drawn from her comments on this video.

27 Duggan, *Sapphic Slashers*, 29.

28 Personal interview, 12 June 2004. All subsequent quotations from Herrera are drawn from this interview.

29 Description of death scene drawn from Obituary, *Variety*, 10–16 April 1995, 58; Patoski, *Selena*; Sue Anne Pressley, "Friends Warned Selena about 'Posses-

sive' Aide," *Washington Post*, 2 April 1995, A3; "Thousands Mourn Slain Singer Selena," *New York Times*, 2 April 1995, 18. All quotations are taken from Patoski, 195–205.

30 Duggan, *Sapphic Slashers*, 2, 4–5.

31 Personal interview, 23 October 2007.

32 José Quiroga used this phrase to describe the legendary diva and queer icon La Lupe in "The Devil in the Flesh," *San Juan Star*, 22 January 1995, 30.

33 Berlant and Warner, "Sex in Public," 561.

34 "The Truth about the Rumors," *Estylo*, April/May 2000, 73, emphasis (in bold) in the original. This column can also be understood as an explicit critique of Maria Celeste Arraras's sensationalist book, *Selena's Secret*.

35 Andrew Ross, "Uses of Camp," in *Camp*, 321; Caryl Flinn, "The Deaths of Camp," in *Camp*, 434.

36 Flinn, "The Deaths of Camp," 434, 443, 448.

37 Portillo, *Corpus*. Malissa Mychaels is the stage name of Mike Garza, a Corpus Christi resident who began impersonating Selena years before her death in 1995.

38 The strident policing of queer engagements with Selenidad emerged most forcefully — and publicly — in the making of Lourdes Portillo's documentary, *Corpus: A Home Movie for Selena*. For more on the controversy, see Fregoso, introduction to *Lourdes Portillo*, 15–21.

39 Ellen Bernstein, "House Divas," *Corpus Christi Caller-Times*, 6 August 1999.

40 Como la Flor program, collection of author.

41 "Call for Submissions of Art Works for an Exhibition of Selena Tributes," courtesy of Ixchel Rosal, ALLGO.

42 Como la Flor Participant Invitation, 3 January 2002, courtesy of Ixchel Rosal, ALLGO.

43 Como la Flor Letter of Invitation to Area Agencies, 18 March 2002, courtesy of Ixchel Rosal, ALLGO.

44 Como la Flor program.

45 Moraga, *Heroes and Saints*, 75.

46 See, for example, Anzaldúa, *Borderlands*; Mora, *Nepantla*.

47 Personal interview, 17 August 2004. All subsequent quotes from Kline are drawn from this interview.

48 Muñoz, *Disidentifications*, 108.

49 Gamson, *The Fabulous Sylvester*, 146.

50 *Paris Is Burning*, dir. Jenny Livingston, 76 min., Academy Entertainment, New York, 1991. For an analysis of the racial and gendered politics of the film, see hooks, "Is Paris Burning?"; Phelan, *Unmarked*, 93–111.

51 E-mail correspondence, 27 July 2004.

52 Jiménez, "Selena out of a Coffin."

53 Martin F. Manalansan IV notes the class and racial distinctions between cross-

dressing among queers of color (in their aspirations for "femme realness") and white drag in *Global Divas*, 126–51.

54 E. Pérez, *The Decolonial Imaginary*, 120.

55 Manuel Guzmán defines sexiles as individuals forced to leave their nation of origin on the basis of sexual orientation. "'Pa' la escuelita,'" 227. In "'That's My Place!'" Roque Ramírez expands Guzmán's notion of sexiles to include "those who left their home state, region, or family base for another place in their own country. Just as crossing national boundaries can expand one's sexual horizon and provide radically new opportunities for queer collective belonging, so too can regional moves" (225).

56 Personal interview, 14 June 2004. Rosal's memories were echoed by all of the Como la Flor organizers who, in separate interviews, noted how moved or awed they were by the diversity of Latina/o community members the event drew.

57 Roque Ramírez, "*Mira, yo soy boricua*," 303.

Epilogue

Epigraph is from Avery F. Gordon, *Ghostly Matters: Haunting and the Sociological Imagination* (Minneapolis: University of Minnesota Press, 1997).

1 Cobo, "Latin Notas"; *Selena ¡VIVE!*, Univisión, 7 April 2005.

2 Casse Carling, "Baseball Fans Groove to Latin Beat," *Stuart News* (Florida), 21 March 2005 A1; Carlos Galarza, "Chamber Brings Fiesta to Mets Field," *Fort Pierce* (Florida) *Tribune*, 19 March 2005, B1; personal interview, 2 October 2005.

3 "Queens for a Day," *Ugly Betty*, ABC, 12 October 2006.

4 Morrison, "Unspeakable Things Unspoken," 3.

5 Agosín, "Memorial," unpaged.

6 Cheng, *The Melancholy of Race*, 175.

7 Phelan, *Mourning Sex*, 3.

Selected Bibliography

Newspapers

Atlanta Journal-Constitution
Austin American-Statesman
Chicago Sun-Times
Chicago Tribune
Christian Science Monitor
Columbus Dispatch (Ohio)
Corpus Christi Caller-Times
Dallas Morning News
Fort Pierce Tribune (Florida)
Impacto: The Latin News (New York)
Houston Chronicle
Los Angeles Daily News
Los Angeles Times
Miami Herald
Minneapolis Star-Tribune
El Mundo (Oakland)
El Nuevo Herald (Miami)
New Orleans Times-Picayune

New York Daily News
New York Times
La Opinión (Los Angeles)
Milwaukee Journal Sentinel
Phoenix Gazette
San Antonio Express-News
San Diego Union-Tribune
San Francisco Chronicle
San Juan Star (Puerto Rico)
Sunday Telegraph (London)
Stuart News (Florida)
Tampa Tribune
Toronto Star
Village Voice
Virginian Pilot
Wall Street Journal
Washington Post

Interviews

Cuevas, T. Jackie. Interview by author. Austin, 23 October 2007.
Herrera y Lozano, Lorenzo. Interview by author. Austin, 12 June 2004.
Kline, Kelly. Interview by author. Austin, 17 August 2004.
Medina, Annabelle. Interview by author. San Antonio, 23 March 2000.
Medina, Dennis. E-mail correspondence. 27 July 2004.
Ortiz, Jerry. Interview by author. Chicago, 23 April 2000.

———. Telephone interview by author. 20 September 2005.

Ortiz, Onaney. Telephone interview by author. 2 October 2005.

Pérez, Claudia. Interview by author. Chicago, 26 February 1999, 3 May 1999.

Rosal, Ixchel. Interview by author. Austin, 14 June 2004.

Vara-Orta, Francisco. Interview by author. San Antonio, 23 March 2000, 23 July 2001.

Secondary Sources

Acuña, Rodolfo. *Occupied America: A History of Chicanos*. 3rd ed. New York: Harper Collins, 1988.

Agosín, Marjorie. "Memorial." In *Circles of Madness: Mothers of the Plaza de Mayo*, trans. Celeste Kostopulos-Cooperman. Fredonia, N.Y.: White Pine, 1992.

Anzaldúa, Gloria. *Borderlands/La Frontera: The New Mestiza*. San Francisco: Aunt Lute, 1987.

———, ed. *Making Face, Making Soul = Haciendo Caras: Creative and Critical Perspectives by Women of Color*. San Francisco: Aunt Lute, 1990.

Anzaldúa, Gloria, and Cherríe Moraga, eds. *This Bridge Called My Back: Writings by Radical Women of Color*. 2nd ed. New York: Kitchen Table, Women of Color, 1983.

Aparicio, Frances R. "Jennifer as Selena: Rethinking Latinidad in Media and Popular Culture." *Latino Studies* 1, no. 1 (2003): 90–105.

———. "La Lupe, La India, and Celia: Toward a Feminist Genealogy of Salsa." In *Situating Salsa: Global Markets and Local Meaning in Latin Popular Music*, ed. Lisa Waxer, 135–60. New York: Routledge, 2000.

———. *Listening to Salsa: Gender, Latin American Popular Music, and Puerto Rican Cultures*. Hanover, N.H.: Wesleyan University Press, 1998.

Aparicio, Frances R., and Wilson A. Valentín-Escobar. "Memorializing La Lupe and Lavoe." CENTRO *Journal* 16, no. 2 (2004): 79–101.

Arraras, María Celeste. *Selena's Secret: The Revealing Story behind Her Tragic Death*. New York: Simon and Schuster, 1997.

Asquith, Christina. "Researching Latinas in Crisis." *Diverse Issues in Higher Education*, 21 September 2006, Spectrum sec.

Baez, Jillian M. "From Hollywood and Back: Dolores del Rio, a Trans(national) Star." *Studies in Latin American Popular Culture* 17 (1998): 5–33.

Barthes, Roland. "The Grain of the Voice." In *Image Music Text*, trans. Stephen Heath, 179–89. New York: Hill and Wang, 1977.

Belejack, B., and P. Plagens. "Frida on Our Minds." *Newsweek*, 27 May 1991, 54–55.

Beltrán, Mary. "The First 'Latin Invasion' and Hollywood's Transition to Sound." *Aztlán: A Journal of Chicano Studies* 30, no. 1 (2005): 55–85.

Berlant, Lauren, and Michael Warner. "Sex in Public." *Critical Inquiry* 24, no. 2 (1998): 547–67.

Bettie, Julie. *Women without Class: Girls, Race, and Identity.* Berkeley: University of California Press, 2002.

Bronfen, Elisabeth. *Over Her Dead Body: Death, Femininity, and the Aesthetic.* New York: Routledge, 1992.

Buckland, Fiona. *Impossible Dance: Club Culture and Queer World-Making.* Middletown, Conn.: Wesleyan University Press, 2002.

Burr, Ramiro "*Selena Forever* Premiere Should Boost Catalog Sales." *Billboard,* 25 March 2000, 89.

———. "'Selena' Show's Producers Sue HOB." *Billboard,* 1 July 2000, 40.

Cantu, Tony. "Cashing In on Selena." *Hispanic,* 30 June 1996, 18.

Carlson, Marvin. *The Haunted Stage: The Theatre as Memory Machine.* Ann Arbor: University of Michigan Press, 2001.

Castañeda, Antonia. "Anglo Images of Nineteenth Century Californianas." In *Between Borders: Essays on Mexicana/Chicana History,* ed. Adelaida Del Castillo, 213–36. Los Angeles: Floricanto, 1990.

———. "Sexual Violence in the Politics and Policies of Conquest." In *Building with Our Hands: New Directions in Chicana Studies,* ed. Adela de la Torre and Beatríz M. Pesquera, 13–33. Berkeley: University of California Press, 1993.

Castillo, Ana. "Selena Aside." *Nation,* 29 May 1995, 764–66.

Cepeda, Maria Elena. "Columbus Effect(s): Chronology and Crossover in the Latin(o) Music 'Boom,'" *Discourse* 23, no. 1 (2001): 63–81.

———. "*Mucho loco* for Ricky Martin; or the Politics of Chronology, Crossover, and Language within the Latin Music 'Boom.'" *Popular Music and Society* 24, no. 3 (2000): 55–71.

———. "Shakira as the Idealized Transnational Citizen: A Case Study of Colombianidad in Transition." *Latino Studies* 1, no. 2 (2003): 211–32.

Certeau, Michel de. *The Practice of Everyday Life.* Berkeley: University of California Press, 1988.

Cheng, Anne Anlin. *The Melancholy of Race: Psychoanalysis, Assimilation, and Hidden Grief.* London: Oxford University Press, 2001.

Choi, Heeseung. "Ethic Differences in Adolescents' Mental Distress, Social Stress, and Resources." *Adolescence* 41 (2006): 263–83.

Cleto, Fabio, ed. *Camp: Queer Aesthetics and the Performing Subject.* Ann Arbor: University of Michigan Press, 1999.

Clum, John. *Something for the Boys: Musical Theater and Gay Culture.* New York: St. Martin's, 1999.

Cobo, Leila. "Latin Biz Sets Sights on Teens New." *Billboard,* 2 October 2004, 1, 24.

———. "Latin Notas: Selena's Appeal Still Strong." *Billboard,* 23 April 2005, 21, 26.

Colino, Stacey. "The Fallout from Proposition 187." *Human Rights* 22, no. 1 (1995): 16–17.

Connerton, Paul. *How Societies Remember*. London: Cambridge University Press, 1989.

Conquergood, Dwight. "Rethinking Ethnography: Toward a Critical Cultural Politics." *Communication Monographs* 58 (1991): 179–94.

A Conversation with Academics about Selena. Dir. Lourdes Portillo. 60 min. Xochitl Films, San Francisco, 1998.

Coronado, Raul. "Selena's Good Buy: Texas Mexicans y Selena Meet Transnational Capitalism." *Aztlán: A Journal of Chicano Studies* 26, no. 1 (2001): 59–101.

Corpus: A Home Movie for Selena. Dir. Lourdes Portillo. 46 min. Xochitl Films, San Francisco, 1998.

Cusick, Suzanne G. "On a Lesbian Relationship with Music: A Serious Effort Not to Think Straight." In *Queering the Pitch: The New Gay and Lesbian Musicology*, 2nd ed., ed. Philip Brett, Elizabeth Wood, and Gary C. Thomas, 73–76. New York: Routledge, 2006.

Daniels, Douglas Henry. "Los Angeles Zoot: Race 'Riot,' the Pachuco, and Black Music Culture." *Journal of Negro History* 82 (1997): 201–21.

Davidson, Miriam. "The Mexican Border War." *Nation*, 12 November 1990, 557–60.

Dávila, Arlene. *Latinos Inc.: The Marketing and Making of a People*. Berkeley: University of California Press, 2001.

Davis, Mike. "The Social Origins of the Referendum." NACLA *Report on the Americas* 29, no. 3 (1995): 24–29.

De Genova, Nicholas, and Ana Y. Ramos-Zayas. "Latino Racial Formations in the United States: An Introduction." *Journal of Latin American Anthropology* 8, no. 2 (2003): 2–17.

————. "Latino Rehearsals: Racialization and the Politics of Citizenship between Mexicans and Puerto Ricans in Chicago." *Journal of Latin American Anthropology* 8, no. 2 (2003): 18–57.

Deverell, William. *Whitewashed Adobe: The Rise of Los Angeles and the Remaking of Its Mexican Past*. Berkeley: University of California Press, 2004.

Diamond, Elin. Introduction to *Performance and Cultural Politics*, ed. Elin Diamond, 1–14. New York: Routledge, 1996.

————. *Unmaking Mimesis*. New York: Routledge, 1997.

Diaz, Gwendolyn. "Making the Myth of *Evita Perón*: Saint, Martyr, Prostitute." *Studies in Latin American Popular Culture* 22 (2003): 181–92.

Dietz, James L. *Economic History of Puerto Rico: Institutional Change and Capitalist Development*. Princeton: Princeton University Press, 1986.

Dolan, Jill. *Geographies of Learning: Theory and Practice, Activism and Performance*. Middletown, Conn.: Wesleyan University Press, 2001.

————. *Utopia in Performance: Finding Hope at the Theater*. Ann Arbor: University of Michigan Press, 2005.

Doty, Alexander. "Introduction: There's Something about Mary." *Camera Obscura* 22, no. 2 (2002): 1–9.

————. "There's Something Queer Here." In *Out in Culture: Gay, Lesbian, and Queer Essays on Popular Culture*, ed. Corey K. Creekmur and Alexander Doty, 71–90. Durham: Duke University Press, 1995.

Drewel, Margaret Thompson. "The State of Research on Performance in Africa." *African Studies Review* 34 (1991): 1–64.

Duggan, Lisa. *Sapphic Slashers: Sex, Violence, and American Modernity*. Durham: Duke University Press, 2000.

Dyer, Richard. "In Defence of Disco." In *Only Entertainment*, 151–60. London: Routledge, 2002.

Echols, Alice. *Shaky Ground: The Sixties and Its Aftershocks*. New York: Columbia University Press, 2002.

Ehrenreich, Barbara, Elizabeth Hess, and Gloria Jacobs. "Beatlemania: Girls Just Want to Have Fun." In *The Adoring Audience: Fan Culture and Popular Media*, ed. Lisa A. Lewis, 84–106. New York: Routledge, 1992.

Eng, David L., and David Kazanjian. "Introduction: Mourning Remains." In *Loss*, ed. David L. Eng and David Kazanjian, 1–28. Berkeley: University of California Press, 2003.

Escobedo, Deborah. "Propositions 187 and 227: Latino Immigrant Rights to Education." *Human Rights* 26, no. 3 (1999): 1–15.

Fabre, Geneviève. "African American Commemorative Celebrations in the Nineteenth Century." In *History and Memory in African-American Culture*, ed. Geneviève Fabre and Robert O'Meally, 72–91. New York: Oxford University Press, 1994.

Farmer, Brett. "Julie Andrews Made Me Gay." *Camera Obscura* 22, no. 2 (2007): 144–53.

Flores, Juan, and George Yudice. "Living Borders/*Buscando America*: Languages of Latino Self-Formation." *Social Text* 8, no. 2 (1990): 58.

Foley, Neil. "Mexicans, Mechanization, and the Growth of Corporate Cotton Culture in South Texas: The Taft Ranch, 1900–1930." *Journal of Southern History* 62, no. 2 (1996): 275–302.

Fregoso, Rosa Linda. Introduction to *Lourdes Portillo: The Devil Never Sleeps and Other Films*, ed. Rosa Linda Fregoso, 15–21. Austin: University of Texas Press, 2001.

————. "Voices without Echo: The Global Gendered Apartheid." *Emergences: Journal for the Study of Media and Composite Cultures* 10, no. 1 (2000): 137–55.

Fusco, Coco. "Better Yet When Dead." Performance installation, Toronto and Medellín, 1996.

Gamson, Joshua. *The Fabulous Sylvester: The Legend, the Music, the 70s in San Francisco*. New York: Henry Holt, 2005.

Garofalo, Reebee. *Rockin' Out: Popular Music in the USA*. Boston: Allyn and Bacon, 1997.

Gaspar de Alba, Alicia. *Desert Blood: The Juárez Murders*. Houston: Arte Publico, 2005.

―――. "The Maquiladora Murders, 1993–2003." *Aztlán: A Journal of Chicano Studies* 28, no. 2 (2003): 1–17.

Giddings, Paula. "The Last Taboo." In *Race-ing Justice, Engendering Power: Essays on Anita Hill, Clarence Thomas and the Construction of Social Reality*, ed. Toni Morrison, 441–70. New York: Pantheon, 1992.

Gilman, Sander. "Black Bodies, White Bodies: Toward an Iconography of Female Sexuality in Late Nineteenth-Century Art, Medicine, and Literature." *Critical Inquiry* 12 (autumn 1985): 204–42.

Gordon, Avery F. *Ghostly Matters: Haunting and the Sociological Imagination*. Minneapolis: University of Minnesota Press, 1997.

Gordon, William. "The Implementation of Desegregation Plans Since *Brown*." *Journal of Negro Education* 63, no. 3 (1994): 310–22.

Grossberg, Lawrence. "Is There a Fan in the House? The Affective Sensibility of Fandom." In *The Adoring Audience: Fan Culture and Popular Media*, ed. Lisa Lewis, 50–65. New York: Routledge, 1992.

Grosz, Elizabeth. *Volatile Bodies: Toward a Corporeal Feminism*. Bloomington: Indiana University Press, 1994.

Gutiérrez, David. "Significant to Whom? Mexican Americans and the History of the American West." *Western Historical Quarterly* 24 (November 1993): 519–39.

Guzmán, Manuel. "'Pa'la escuelita con mucha cuida'o y por la orillita': A Journey through the Contested Terrains of the Nation and Sexual Orientation." In *Puerto Rican Jam: Rethinking Colonialism and Nationalism*, ed. Frances Negrón Muntaner and Ramón Grosfoguel, 209–30. Minneapolis: University of Minnesota Press, 1997.

Halberstam, Judith. *In a Queer Time and Place: Transgender Bodies, Subcultural Lives*. New York: New York University Press, 2005.

Haraway, Donna. *Simians, Cyborgs and Women*. New York: Routledge, 1991.

Hewitt, Bill, Joseph Harmes, and Bob Stewart. "Before Her Time." *People Weekly*, 17 August 1995, 48–53.

Holland, Sharon. *Raising the Dead: Readings of Death and (Black) Subjectivity*. Durham: Duke University Press, 2000.

Holmlund, Chris. *Impossible Bodies: Masculinity and Femininity at the Movies*. New York: Routledge, 2002.

hooks, bell. "Is Paris Burning?" In *Black Looks: Race and Representation*, 145–56. Boston: South End, 1992.

Hughes, Walter. "In the Empire of the Beat: Discipline and Disco." In *Microphone Fiends: Youth Music and Youth Culture*, ed. Andrew Ross and Tricia Rose, 147–57. New York: Routledge, 1994.

Hurtado, Aída, Norma Klahn, Olga Nájera-Ramírez, and Patricia Zavella, eds. *Chicana Feminism: A Critical Reader*. Durham: Duke University Press, 2003.

Hutchinson, Sydney. "Mambo on the 2: The Birth of a New Form of Dance in New York City." *CENTRO Journal* 16, no. 2 (2004): 109–37.

Jackson, Shannon. *Lines of Activity: Performance, Historiography, Hull-House Domesticity*. Ann Arbor: University of Michigan Press, 2000.

Jiménez, Joe. "Selena Out of a Coffin." In *Skin.Icon/Media/Myth*, 25. Austin: Tanto Tinto, 2001.

Johnson, Richard. "Exemplary Differences: Mourning (and Not Mourning) a Princess." In *Mourning Diana: Nation, Culture, and the Performance of Grief*, ed. Adrian Kear and Deborah Lynn Steinberg, 15–39. New York: Routledge, 1999.

Jones, Landon Y., Jr. "Inside People." *People Weekly Tribute*, commemorative issue, spring 1995, 2.

Kear, Adrian, and Deborah Lynn Steinberg. "Ghost Writing." In *Mourning Diana: Nation, Culture and the Performance of Grief*, ed. Adrian Kear and Deborah Lynn Steinberg, 1–16. New York: Routledge, 1999.

Kearney, Mary Celeste. *Girls Make Media*. New York: Routledge, 2006.

Kleinhaus, Chuck. "¡Siempre Selena!" *Jump Cut* 42 (1998): 28–31.

Knights, Vanessa. "Tears and Screams: Performances of Pleasure and Pain in the Bolero." In *Queering the Popular Pitch*, ed. Sheila Whiteley and Jennifer Rycenga, 83–100. New York: Routledge, 2006.

Koestenbaum, Wayne. *The Queen's Throat: Opera, Homosexuality, and the Mystery of Desire*. New York: Poseidon, 1993.

Kooijman, Jaap. "Turn the Beat Around: Richard Dyer's 'In Defence of Disco' Revisited." *European Journal of Cultural Studies* 8, no. 2 (2005): 257–66.

Krasnow, Carolyn. "Fear and Loathing in the Seventies: Race, Sexuality, and Disco." *Stanford Humanities Review* 3, no. 2 (1993): 37–45.

Kropp, Phoepe. "Citizens of the Past? Olvera Street and the Construction of Race and Memory in 1930s Los Angeles." *Radical History Review* 81 (fall 2001): 35–60.

Kun, Josh. *Audiotopia: Music, Race, and America*. Berkeley: University of California Press, 2005.

LaFountain-Stokes, Lawrence. "La politica queer del espanglish." *Debate feminista* 17, no. 33 (2006): 141–53.

Laó-Montes, Agustín. "Mambo Montage: The Latinization of New York City." In *Mambo Montage: The Latinization of New York*, ed. Arlene Dávila and Agustín Laó-Montes, 1–54. New York: Columbia University Press, 2001.

Lawrence, Tim. "'I Want to See All My Friends at Once': Arthur Russell and the Queering of Gay Disco." *Journal of Popular Music Studies* 18, no. 2 (2006): 144–66.

———. *Love Saves the Day: A History of American Dance Music Culture, 1970–1979.* Durham: Duke University Press, 2003.

Leonardi, Susan J., and Rebecca A. Pope. *The Diva's Mouth: Body, Voice, Prima Donna Politics.* New Brunswick, N.J.: Rutgers University Press, 1996.

Lessoff, Alan. "Public Sculpture in Corpus Christi: A Tangled Struggle to Define the Character and Shape the Agenda of One Texas City." *Journal of Urban History* 26, no. 2 (2000): 190–223.

———. "A Texas City and the Texas Myth: Urban Historical Identity in Corpus Christi." *Southwestern Historical Quarterly* 100, no. 3 (1997): 305–29.

Limón, José E. *American Encounters: Greater Mexico, the United States, and the Politics of Culture.* New York: Beacon, 2000.

———. *Dancing with the Devil: Society and Cultural Poetics in Mexican-American South Texas.* Madison: University of Wisconsin Press, 1994.

Lipsitz, George. *Dangerous Crossroads: Popular Music, Postmodernism and the Poetics of Place.* New York: Verso, 1994.

———. *Time Passages: Collective Memory and American Popular Culture.* Minneapolis: University of Minnesota Press, 1990.

Livingston, Jessica. "Murder in Juárez: Gender, Sexual Violence, and the Global Assembly Line." *Frontiers: A Journal of Women Studies* 25, no. 1 (2004): 59–76.

Lopez, Ana M. "Are All Latins from Manhattan? Hollywood, Ethnography, and Cultural Colonialism." In *Unspeakable Images: Ethnicity and the American Cinema*, ed. Lester D. Friedman, 404–24. Urbana: University of Illinois Press, 1991.

Lorca, Federico Garcia. "Play and Theory of the Duende." In *In Search of Duende*, trans. Christopher Maurer, 48–62. New York: New Directions, 1998.

Lott, Eric. "All the King's Men: Elvis Impersonators and White Working Class Masculinity." In *Race and the Subject of Masculinities*, ed. Harry Stecopoulous and Michael Uebel, 192–227. Durham: Duke University Press, 1997.

Manalansan, Martin F., IV. *Global Divas: Filipino Gay Men in the Diaspora.* Durham: Duke University Press, 2003.

Marchevsky, Alejandra. *Not Working: Latina Immigrants, Low Wage Jobs, and the Failure of Welfare Reform.* New York: New York University Press, 2006.

Martin, Philip. "Proposition 187 in California." *International Migration Review* 29, no. 1 (1995): 255–63.

Mazón, Maurizio. *The Zoot-Suit Riots: The Psychology of Symbolic Annihilation.* Austin: University of Texas Press, 1992.

Mazzarella, Sharon R. *Girl Wide Web: Girls, the Internet, and the Negotiation of Identity.* New York: Peter Lang, 2005.

McClung, William Alexander. *Landscapes of Desire: Anglo Mythologies of Los Angeles.* Berkeley: University of California Press, 2002.

McRobbie, Angela. *Feminism and Youth Culture.* New York: Routledge, 2000.

McWilliams, Cary. *North from Mexico: The Spanish-Speaking People of the United States.* New York: Praeger, 1990.

Méndez, Juan M. "Selena *por siempre.*" *Latina Magazine,* March 2000, 30–32.

Miller, D. A. *Place for Us: Essay on the Broadway Musical.* Cambridge: Harvard University Press, 1998.

Miller, Susan. "Selling Evita to the Masses." *Newsweek,* 11 November 1996, 92.

Molina Guzmán, Isabel, and Angharad Valdivia. "Brain, Brow, Booty: Latina Iconicity in U.S. Popular Culture." *Communication Review* 7 (2004): 205–21.

Monarrez, Julia. "Serial Sexual Femicide in Ciudad Juárez, 1993–2001." *Aztlán: A Journal of Chicano Studies* 28, no. 2 (2003): 153–78.

Montejano, David. *Anglos and Mexicans in the Making of Texas, 1836–1986.* Austin: University of Texas Press, 1987.

Montgomery, Charles. *The Spanish Redemption: Heritage, Power, and Loss on New Mexico's Upper Rio Grande.* Berkeley: University of California Press, 2002.

Mora, Pat. *Nepantla: Essays from the Land in the Middle.* Albuquerque: University of New Mexico Press, 1993.

Moraga, Cherrie. *Heroes and Saints and Other Plays.* Albuquerque: West End, 1994.

Morales, Pablo, and Clara E. Rodríguez. "Latinos and the 'Other Race' Option: Transforming U.S. Concepts of Race." NACLA: *Report on the Americas* 34, no. 6 (2001): 40–46.

Morrison, Toni. "Unspeakable Things Unspoken: The Afro-American Presence in American Literature." *Michigan Quarterly Review* 28 (1989): 1–34.

Most, Andrea. *Making Americans: Jews and the Broadway Musical.* Cambridge: Harvard University Press, 2004.

———. " 'You've Got to Be Carefully Taught': The Politics of Race in Rodgers and Hammerstein's South Pacific." *Theatre Journal* 52, no. 3 (2000): 307–37.

Muñoz, José E. *Disidentifications: Queers of Color and the Performance of Politics.* Minneapolis: University of Minnesota Press, 1999.

———. "Feeling Brown: Ethnicity and Affect in Ricardo Bracho's *The Sweetest Hangover (and Other STDs)*." *Theatre Journal* 52, no. 1 (2000): 67–79.

Nájera-Ramírez, Olga. "Unruly Passions: Poetics, Performance, and Gender in the Ranchera Song." In *Chicana Feminisms: A Critical Reader,* ed. Gabriella Arredondo, Aída Hurtado, Norma Klahn, Olga Nájera-Ramírez, and Patricia Zavella, 184–210. Durham: Duke University Press, 2003.

Nathan, Paul. "Travels with Evita." *Publishers Weekly,* 4 September 1995, 20.

Negrón-Muntaner, Frances. "Jennifer's Butt." *Aztlán: A Journal of Chicano Studies* 22, no. 2 (1997): 181–95.

Nevins, Joseph. *Operation Gatekeeper: The Rise of the "Illegal Alien" and the Making of the U.S.-Mexico Boundary.* New York: Routledge, 2002.

Nora, Pierre. "Between Memory and History: *Les Lieux de Mémoire*." In *History and Memory in African-American Culture*, ed. Genevieve Fabre and Robert O'Meally, 289. New York: Oxford University Press, 1994.

Noriega, Chon A. "Fashion Crimes: Chicano Identity and Clothing." *Aztlan: A Journal of Chicano Studies* 26 (2001): 1–12.

Oboler, Suzanne. *Ethnic Labels, Latino Lives: Identity and the Politics of (Re)presentation in the United States*. Minneapolis: University of Minnesota Press, 1995.

Ortiz, Altagracia, ed. *Puerto Rican Women and Work: Bridges in Transnational Labor*. Philadelphia: Temple University Press, 1996.

Padilla, Felix. *Latino Ethnic Consciousness: The Case of Mexican Americans and Puerto Ricans in Chicago*. Notre Dame, Ind.: University of Notre Dame Press, 1985.

Patoski, Joe Nick. "The Queen Is Dead." *Texas Monthly*, May 1995, 110.

———. *Selena: Como La Flor*. Boston: Little, Brown, 1996.

Peña, Manuel. *Música Tejana: The Cultural Economy of Artistic Transformation*. College Station: Texas A&M Press, 1999.

Perea, Juan. *Immigrants Out: The New Nativism and the Anti-immigrant Impulse in the US*. New York: New York University Press, 1999.

Pérez, Claudia, narrator. "1000 Women Become Selena." *This American Life*. Narr. Ira Glass. Prod. Nancy Updike. NPR. 19 April 1996.

Pérez, Emma. *The Decolonial Imaginary: Writing Chicanas into History*. Bloomington: Indiana University Press, 1999.

———. "So Far from God, So Close to the United States: A Call for Action by U.S. Authorities." *Aztlán: A Journal of Chicano Studies* 28, no. 2 (2003): 147–51.

Pérez, Gina. *The Near Northwest Side Story: Migration, Displacement, and Puerto Rican Families*. Berkeley: University of California Press, 2004.

———. "Puertorriqueñas Rencorosas y Mejicanas Sufridas: Gendered Ethnic Identity Formation in Chicago's Latino Communities." *Journal of Latin American Anthropology* 8, no. 2 (2003): 96–125.

Phelan, Peggy. *Mourning Sex: Performing Public Memories*. London: Routledge, 1997.

———. *Unmarked: The Politics of Performance*. London: Routledge, 1993.

Prado, Jose M. "English for the Children: The 'Sentencing' of Spanish Speaking Students." *Latino Studies Journal* 11, no. 3 (2000): 100–130.

Ramírez, Catherine S. "Crimes of Fashion: The Pachuca and Chicana Style Politics." *Meridians: Feminism, Race, Transnationalism* 2, no. 2 (2002): 1–35.

Rivera-Servera, Ramón. "Choreographies of Resistance: Latina/o Queer Dance and the Utopian Performative." *Modern Drama* 47, no. 2 (2004): 274–86.

Roach, Joseph. *Cities of the Dead: Circum-Atlantic Performance*. New York: Columbia University Press, 1996.

Rodman, Gilbert. *Elvis after Elvis: The Posthumous Career of a Living Legend*. New York: Routledge, 1996.

Rodriguez, Clara. *Heroes, Lovers, and Others: The Story of Latinos in Hollywood.* Washington: Smithsonian, 2004.

———. *Latin Looks: Images of Latinas and Latinos in the U.S. Media.* Boulder: Westview, 1997.

Román, David. "Latino Performance and Identity." *Aztlán: A Journal of Chicano Studies* 22, no. 2 (1997): 151–67.

Roque Ramírez, Horacio N. "'Mira, yo soy boricua y estoy aquí': Rafa Negrón's Pan Dulce and the Queer Sonic Latinaje of San Francisco." *Centro Journal* 19, no. 1 (2007): 274–313.

———. "'That's My Place': Negotiating Racial, Sexual, and Gender Politics in San Francisco's Gay Latino Alliance, 1975–1983." *Journal of the History of Sexuality* 13, no. 2 (2003): 224–58.

Rúa, Mérida. "Colao Subjectivities: PortoMex and MexiRican Perspectives on Language and Identity." *Centro: Journal for the Center for Puerto Rican Studies* 2 (2001): 116–33.

Sánchez, George. "Face the Nation: Race, Immigration, and the Rise of Nativism in Late Twentieth Century America." *International Migration Review* 31 (1997): 1009–30.

Sánchez Korrol, Virginia E. *From Colonia to Community: The History of Puerto Ricans in New York.* Berkeley: University of California Press, 1994.

Sandoval-Sanchez, Alberto. *José Can You See? Latinos on and off Broadway.* Madison: University of Wisconsin Press, 1999.

Schechner, Richard. *Between Theatre and Anthropology.* Philadelphia: University of Pennsylvania Press, 1985.

Scheiner, Georganne. *Signifying Female Adolescence: Film Representations and Fans, 1920–1950.* Westport, Conn.: Praeger, 2000.

"Selena ¡VIVE!" Univisión, 7 April 2005.

Singer, Mark. "Texas Shipwreck." *New Yorker,* 27 November 2000, 78.

Solomon, Alisa, and Framji Minwalla, eds. *The Queerest Art: Essays on Lesbian and Gay Theater.* New York: New York University Press, 2002.

Stacey, Jackie. *Star Gazing: Hollywood Cinema and Female Spectatorship.* New York: Routledge, 1994.

Stavans, Ilan. "Santa Selena." In *The Essential Ilan Stavans,* 176–81. New York: Routledge, 2001.

Sturken, Marita. *Tangled Memories: The Vietnam War, the AIDS Epidemic, and the Politics of Remembering.* Berkeley: University of California Press, 1997.

Taylor, Diana. *The Archive and the Repertoire: Performing Cultural Memory in the Americas.* Durham: Duke University Press, 2003.

———. "Downloading Grief: Minority Populations Mourn Diana." In *Mourning Diana: Nation, Culture and the Performance of Grief,* ed. Adrien Kear and Deborah Lynn Steinberg, 187–210. London: Routledge, 1999.

————. "Opening Remarks." In *Negotiating Performance: Gender, Sexuality, and Theatricality in Latin America*, ed. Diana Taylor and Juan Villegas, 1–16. Durham: Duke University Press, 1994.

Telfer, George F. W. "Barge Accident Damages Columbus Replicas." *Journal of Commerce*, 18 April 1994, 7B.

Troyano, Alina / Carmelita Tropicana. *Chicas 2000*. In *I, Carmelita: Performing between Cultures*, 72–122. Boston: Beacon, 2000.

Valdivia, Angharad N. *A Latina in the Land of Hollywood and Other Essays on Media Culture*. Tucson: University of Arizona Press, 2000.

Vargas, Deborah R. "Bidi Bidi Bom Bom: Selena and Tejano Music in the Making of *Tejas*." In *Latina/o Popular Culture*, ed. Michelle Habell-Pállan and Mary Romero, 117–26. New York: New York University Press, 2002.

————. "*Cruzando Frontejas*: Re-mapping Selena's Tejano Music Crossover." In *Chicana Traditions: Continuity and Change*, ed. Norma Cantú and Olga Nájera-Ramírez, 224–36. Urbana: University of Illinois Press, 2002.

————. "*Las Tracaleras*: Texas-Mexican Women, Music, and Place." PhD diss., University of California, Santa Cruz, 2003.

Vogel, Shane. "Where Are We Now: Queer World Making and Cabaret Performance." GLQ: *A Journal of Lesbian and Gay Studies* 6, no. 1 (2000): 29–60.

Wald, Gayle. "'I Want It That Way': Teenybopper Music and the Girling of Boy Bands." *Genders* 35 (2002): 1–22.

Williams, Raymond. *Marxism and Literature*. Oxford: Oxford University Press, 1977.

Willis, Jennifer L., and Alberto Gonzalez. "Reconceptualizing Gender through Dialogue: The Case of the Tex-Mex Madonna." *Women and Language* 20, no. 1 (1997): 9–16.

Wilson, Chris. *The Myth of Santa Fe: Creating a Modern Regional Tradition*. Albuquerque: University of New Mexico Press, 1997.

Wolf, Stacy. *A Problem Like Maria: Gender and Sexuality in the American Musical*. Ann Arbor: University of Michigan Press, 2002.

————. "'We'll Always Be Bosom Buddies': Female Duets and the Queering of Broadway Musical Theater." GLQ: *A Journal of Lesbian and Gay Studies* 12, no. 3 (2006): 351–76.

————. "*Wicked* Divas, Musical Theater, and Internet Girl Fans." *Camera Obscura* 22, no. 2 (2007): 39–71.

Wright, Melissa W. "The Dialectics of Still Life: Murder, Women, and Maquiladoras." *Public Culture* 11, no. 3 (1999): 453–73.

Yarbro-Bejarano, Yvonne. "Crossing the Border with Chabela Vargas: A Chicana Femme's Tribute." In *Sex and Sexuality in Latin America*, ed. Daniel Balderston and Donna J. Guy, 33–43. New York: New York University Press, 1997.

Ybarra-Frausto Tomás. "Rasquachismo: A Chicano Sensibility." In *Chicana Art: Resistance and Affirmation, 1965–1985*, ed. Richard Griswold del Castillo, Teresa

McKenna, and Yvonne Yarbro-Bajarano, 155–62. Los Angeles: Wight Art Gallery, UCLA, 1991.

Zavella, Patricia. "'Playing with Fire': The Gendered Construction of Chicana/ Mexicana Sexuality." In *Gender/Sexuality Reader: Culture, History, Political Economy*, ed. Roger N. Lancaster and Micaela di Leonardo, 342–408. New York: Routledge, 1997.

Index

Page numbers in italics refer to illustrations.

auditions for *Selena* biopic (*continued*)
and, 126–30; massive turnout for,
126–27, 220n2; power dynamics at,
145–46, 224n57; as publicity stunt,
146, 224n56; self-creation and, 139;
sexuality and, 140–42; as showcase,
129–30; subjectivities and, 147–49;
visibility and, 141
authenticity: co-optation and, 148;
in drag performances, 181, 183;
imaginative space for, 120; Mexican
middle-class and, 205n43; minorities' burden of, 12–13, 133, 135, 183;
mourning and, 118–19; religion and,
195n27; self-fashioning vs., 160. *See
also* self-fashioning

Barrio Boyzz, 25, 198n64
Barthes, Roland, 51
Behar, Jose, 51
Berlant, Lauren, 169, 226n11
Better Yet When Dead (Coco Fusco),
26, 27
Bettie, Julie, 141, 143, 224n50, 225n61
biography. *See* narratives of Selena's
life
blackness. *See* Afro-diasporic influ-
ences; race
body, Selena's. *See* Latina bodies
Bonilla, Frank, 207n22
Bracho, Ricardo A., 226n7
Brandesky, Betty, 81, 210n62
Bronfen, Elisabeth, 9
Burr, Ramiro, 223n43

camp sensibility, in drag performance,
159, 172, 174, 181, 183, 184–85
Cancela, Eduardo, 110–11
Carillo, Leonardo, 79
Castillo, Ana, 212n80
Census (2000 U.S.): commemora-
tion of Selena and, 102–3; Latina/o

citizenship "problem" and, 213n13;
Latina/o market and, 214n19;
Latina/o population growth in, 105,
215nn22–23; Latina/o promotion of,
96, 97, 97–98; Latina/o vs. African
American rhetoric and, 214–15n20;
Los Angeles population in, 123,
219n67; "majority minority" status
and, 100–101, 103–4, 214n18; promotional campaign, road tour of, 103–4;
Selena Forever and, 99, 101–6
Cepeda, Maria Elena, 198n63, 203n41
Cheng, Anne Anlin, 1, 192
Chicana/o identity. *See* Mexican
American, Chicana/o identity
chusmería, queerness and, 160–62,
227n22
citizenship, Latina/o: Census count
and, 213n13; commemoration and,
118; common struggles for, 119;
consumption and, 22; crossover
frames and, 40; cultural norms and,
109, 216–17n38; Howard Stern and,
14; immigration reform and, 15–16;
in/visibility of, 88–90, 92; labor and,
84–85, 93; musicals and, 100; "national affect" and, 212n79; obstacles
to, 136; *People Weekly* and, 22; performance of, 61, 82, 87, 94, 189; *Selena*
biopic and, 105, 133; state-sponsored
tributes and, 17; strengthening of,
120; transnational, 34, 115
class. *See* social class; working class
Coca-Cola, 24, 95, 107, 111, 113, 198n62,
217n49
Coleman, Sherman, 70
colonialism: Corpus Christi's economic structure and, 64; "decolonial desire" and, 153, 198n28; "Disco
Medley" and, 43; Latinas as moving
beyond, 125; Latina sexuality, bodies
in, 135–36, 198n65, 223n35; Spanish,

crossover stardom (*continued*)
representation and, 103; mainstream
culture and, 21–22; Mexican market
and, 203–4n43; queer identity and,
175; from regional to national, international, 24–25; in *Selena* biopic, 48;
Selena biopic auditions and, 149–50;
Selena Forever and, 98
Cuevas, T. Jackie, 169, 171–72
cumbias: audience participation and,
48–49, 156, 173, 188; Colombian vs.
Tejano, 50; crossover appeal of,
37–38, 48–49; freestyling from, 35;
grief juxtaposed with, 51–52, 54–55;
queering of, 161–62; in spectrum
of forms, 216n33; Tejano history
and, 11, 43; in transcultural fusions,
203n41
Cusick, Suzanne, 42

Dako, Peter, 27
dance: assertiveness in, 54–55; *bailes de
negocio*, 41, 202n21; colonial history
through, 43; crossover narratives
and, 39; disco and Latin fusions of,
35, 37–38; flamenco, 52–53, 140, 173;
irreverence toward loss through,
54; survival of tragedy through, 55;
Tejana subjectivity and, 41
Dávila, Arlene, 19, 21, 23, 109, 217n48
dead body as symbol, 27; in asserting
identity, subjectivities, 7–9, 155, 158,
187, 194n17; immortality and, 172;
Iphigenia and, 90, 212n80; Latina
labor and, 26; Latina racialization
and, 132; open casket and, 6; performance as invocational and, 28, 33,
190, 213n11
death, untimely: "Como la Flor" and,
47; disco's structure vs., 46–47;
Latina icons with, 5–7, 9–10, 26, 28,
190; of lesser-known Latinas, 28–29,

190; performers as repositories and,
13, 196n29; present tense and, 151; as
preserving identity-in-process, 134,
142; as preserving vitality, 186
death scene, Latina lesbian readings of:
act of becoming in, 163; coming-out
narrative in, 169–70; femme figure
in, 165; financial duplicity and sexual
transgression in, 167; murder trope
in, 168–69; patriarchy in, 164
de Certeau, Michel, 56
De Genova, Nicholas, 131
De la Cruz, Gloria, 190
Del Rio, Dolores, 134, 160
desire, longing: in "Como la Flor,"
54–55; in death scene readings, 165;
"decolonial," 153; in disco, 42; diva
performances and, 157; identification and, 138, 144, 220n11; at *Mirador
de la Flor*, 83, 85; through performance of mourning, 143; queerness
and, 158; rancheras and, 45, 53, 152;
at *Selena* biopic auditions, 149–54
Deverell, William, 61
Diamond, 176, 177–78
Diamond, Elin, 200n71
Diaz, Arlene, 191
disco: black/Latina/o collaborations
in, 46; claims of social space in, 40;
"Como la Flor" and, 54; dance as
central to, 201–2n14; future as open
in, 203n39; future staged in, 46–47;
queer identity and, 41–43, 202n18;
race and, 202n15; as strategic choice,
38–39; Tejana/o identity and, 41, 44;
transcultural mixing in, 39
"Disco Medley": affective space of,
34–35; Afro-diasporic sound and,
45; Astrodome performance details
of, 35–37, 36; crossover narratives
and, 39–40; as expansive, 46; list of
songs from, 201n7; performances

tion, subject formation through, 143–44, 156–57; loss of self through, 224n53; pathologization of fans and, 150, 153–54; performer/spectator relationship in drag, 181–82; resistance through, 128; revering vs. replacing and, 139–40; "self-validation" through, 148; sexuality *sin vergüenza* and, 140–41; as staging iconization, 157; in Tejano music, 195n24; vitality in drag, 184. *See also* disidentification

intergenerational affiliation, 108, 110, 131–33, 173, 176

"I Will Survive" (Gloria Gaynor), 35, 40, 42, 45, 203n40

Jackson, Janet, 41, 160
Jackson, Michael, 45
Jimenez, Flaco, 203n42
Jiménez, Joe, 176, 184
Jimenez, Miriam, 214n17
Jimenez, Nick, 85–86, 88
Johnson, Richard, 14, 196n34
Juárez murders, 28–29, 190

Kahlo, Frida, 5–7, 9–10, 26, 28, 190
Kazanjian, David, 194n16
Kear, Adrian, 213n11
Kleinhans, Chuck, 201n8
Kline, Kelly, 176, 177, 180–83
Knights, Venessa, 205n51, 205n55, 227n16
Kooijman, Jaap, 39
Krasnow, Carolyn, 201–2n14
Kun, Josh, 34, 51, 201n5

labor: citizenship and, 84–85, 93; in Corpus Christi history, 61, 66–67, 79, 87–89, 93; gender and, 62, 119; in/visibility of, 61, 64, 93, 130, 148–49, 179; Latina bodies and, 136;

leisure in statue of Selena vs., 92; *Selena Forever* and, 105–6; vocal power and, 106

La Fountain-Stokes, Lawrence, 162

La Lupe, 42, 53, 205n55, 228n32

La Monte, Diane, 211n67

Laó-Montes, Agustín, 23

Lara, Jessica (as young Latina), 142–44, 151, 224n49

"Last Dance" (Donna Summer), 37, 42, 45, 55

Latina bodies: critical mimesis and, 116–17; entertainment industry representations of, 130; exoticism and, 9–10; in fantasies of obsession and identity, 25; in Howard Stern's comments, 14; identification and disidentification with Selena's body and, 130–39; in/visibility of Latina/o culture and, 122–23; *morena* appearance and, 12–13; in narratives of Selena's life, 198n65; ownership, control of, 118; as raw material, capital, 225n61; Selena's costume measurements and, 4; Selena's rear end and, 4, 25, 46, 134–35, 137, 222–23n34; Selena's reshaping of Tejano music and, 11; sexuality-in-process and, 140–41; validating labor of, 148–49; vitality vs. decay and, 172; working-class struggles and, 91–92

Latina identity: advocacy and, 145; agency and, 136; assertion of subjectivities and, 146–48; colonialism and, 135; "Como la Flor" and, 144; dual approach to, 131; effect of imitation on, 129; emergent sexuality and, 141–42, 224n49; entertainment industry representations of, 146; failed crossover and, 149–50; generative excess and, 153–54; health, educa-

Latina identity (*continued*)
tion and, 129, 221n12; heterosexual
family constraints and, 163–64; identification and, 128, 132, 139–40, 147;
in-process, 143; labor as valued and,
130; oppositional history and, 151–52;
queerness and, 157; ranchera used in
negotiating, 153; *Selena* biopic audition details and, 126–27; self-love
and, 137–38; shared racialized markings and, 133; visibility/invisibility
and, 134, 144–45, 149
Latin Grammys, 25, 198–99n67
latinidad, Latina/o identity, 1–30;
definitions of, 23–24; homogenizing
constructions of, 133; *latinaje* and,
226n7; representational range of,
98–99, 104–5, 117–18, 120
Latin music: boom in, 7, 22, 25, 28,
118, 204n41; influence of, on pop
music, 38; influence of, on Selena's
music, 50; Mexican rancheras, 45, 53,
152–53, 185, 199n67, 225n64; Spanish
language and, 19, 21, 198n63. *See also*
cumbias; Tejano music
Lawrence, Tim, 42
Leonardi, Susan J., 160
Lessoff, Alan, 70, 208n33
Limón, José E., 87, 196n28, 207n19,
211–12n78, 223n35
Lincoln, Abbey, 51
Lipsitz, George, 95
Little Joe y La Familia, 203n34
Lopez, Jennifer, 4, 7, 132–33, 136–37, 183
Lott, Eric, 139, 148

Madonna (pop star), 12, 41, 116, 122–23,
152, 160
"majority minority" status of Lati-
nas/os, 100–101, 104
Makeig, John, 196n33
Manalansan, Martin F., IV, 228n53

market, Latina/o. *See* consumption,
commercial culture
Martin, Ricky, 203n41
Martinez, Julio, 219n70
Martinez, Sylvia, 136
Martinez-Cannon, Margarita, 111
McGarrity, Tom, 214n19
McWilliams, Carey, 61
media: Chicago inner-city youth and,
221n13; Latina/o representation
in, 107, 130, 199n67; reactions to
Howard Stern by, 14; *Selena* biopic
auditions and, 127; at *Selena Forever*
premier, 95; Selena's death coverage in, 223n43, 225n65; Spanish-
language, 21, 25, 111, 198n63, 204n43;
2000 Census and, 103–4
Medina, Annabelle, 122–23
Medina, Dennis, 176, 179–80, 183–85
Melissa, Grrl Action performance of
"Como la Flor," 155–59, 182, 225–
26n2
memory, official vs. unofficial: commemorative acts and, 4, 8, 21;
as contested terrain and, 93–94;
"emotional message centers" and,
86; messing up, cleaning up, and,
87–88; *Mirador de la Flor* controversy
and, 57, 61; selective forgetting and,
62–63; "spontaneous" environments
and, 206n4; whitewashing and, 61
memory circuits, 9–10, 33–34, 194n16
Mendoza, Lydia, 41, 202n22
Mercado, Jessica, 191
Merman, Ethel, 106, 215n26
Mesa-Bains, Amalia, 161–62
Mexican American, Chicana/o identity: appearance as transcultural
bridge and, 133–34; in Corpus
Christi vs. San Antonio, 79; dual
sense of, 135; *mexicanidad* and,
222n32; narratives of Selena's life

and, 164; *rasquachismo* and, 161; re-appropriation of term in, 205n44; sexual repression and, 169; Spanish roots and, 208n27; "working-class postmodernism" and, 207n19

Mexican Americans/Anglo tensions. *See* Anglo/Mexican American tensions

Mexican American working class. *See* working classMexican rancheras, 45, 53, 152–53, 185, 199n67, 225n64

middle class, 67, 205n33, 207n19, 213n14

Mineros, José, 226n7

Mirador de la Flor (Selena memorial), *58*–60, *68*, *83*, *87*–88, *90*–91, *93*; controversy about, 57, 61; description of, 56–57; interactive design of, 82–83; memory, forgetting unbalanced by, 94; off-balance composition of, 90–92; othering at, 84; *Paseo de la Flor* message walkway at, 83; productive misbehavior of, 93; promise and challenge of, 80–81; race, class conflict and, 62; "role model" inscription at, 82; as semiotic interruption, 64; signs prohibiting marking of, 57, 85; steel barrier at, 56–47, *58*, 86, 88–89, 91, 94; visitor markings at, 84–86, *87*–88, 88–90, 92–94, *93*; white rose sculpture at, 56, 82, 89. *See also* statue of Selena, *Mirador de la Flor* memorial

Miradores del Mar project, Corpus Christi (8 miradors on bay front), *14*, 62–64, 68, 88–89

Miranda, Carmen, 134

Montalban, Ricardo, 111

Mora, Pat, 179

Moraga, Cherríe, 28, 140–41, 163–64, 168–69

Morales, Ramona, 29, 190

Morales, Sylvia, 86

morena appearance (complexion, hair color), 10, 12, 103, 134, 137, 143, 204n43

Moreno, Gilberto, 198–99n67

Moreno, Rita, 134

Morrison, Toni, 190

mourning, memorial practices: becoming Selena compared to Viola in *Twelfth Night*, 143, 223n52; embodied, 142–43; imitation as, 143–44; irreverence toward loss and, 54; Latina lesbian readings of death scene as, 159; *Mirador de la Flor* and, 79, 84–88, 211n67; performing grief through ranchera as, 152; queer Latina/o drag performances as, 159; Selena as generative force and, 190; *Selena Forever* attendance and, 108; Selena tributes, 21st-century, 187–89; spaces of surrogation and, 99–100; vocalization and becoming the future as, 124–25

mourning or grief, collective: of accretion of losses, 192; as bridge for "crossover" dreams, 179; classical tragic model and, 102, 213n11; "Como la Flor" as anthem for, 51; cultural differences in, 79; decisions about participation in, 14–15, 196n29; devaluation of Latina body and, 139; future staged in, 219n71; as massive force, 15, 19, 79; *Mirador de la Flor* and, 79, 85; palimpsests and, 4, 93–94, 119, 194n16; Selena/Elvis comparisons and, 223n43; shaping latinidad and, 8–9; through *Selena Forever*, 122; tragedy as narrative framework and, 101; vocal performance of longing and, 53–55

Muñoz, José Esteban: on affect, 90, 200n2, 204n4; on *chusmería*, 162; on disidentification, 226n22; on drag,

circulation of, 203n40; dual temporality of, 33; emotional present of, 53; interactive moments at, 50–51, 144; queering of boundaries by, 158; *Selena Forever* and, 107

performance and spectatorship. *See* spectatorship and performance

performances, as affective mode, 31–55; audiotopic space and, 34, 40, 44, 51–54, 201n5; diva fandom and, 157; expansiveness and, 55; imitation and, 129; Latina/o "excessiveness" and, 90, 212n79; queer expressive space and, 158; rancheras and, 152; utopian performatives and, 31, 33–34, 46–47, 201n4

performance studies, theories: agency in, 28; ethnography and, 212–13n8; methodology in, 26–28, 212–13n8; process in, 200n71; repertoire in, 200n71; revision in, 199–200n71; surrogation in, 200n71

Perón, Eva Duarte (Evita), 5–7, 9, 26, 28, 190

Phelan, Peggy, 28, 118, 192

Phillips, Michael, 219n70

political resistance: disruption of classism and, 160; to nativism, 44; oppositional, dissident stances, 23–24, 116, 135, 152, 155, 223n33; spaces of surrogation as, 99; subversive gestures, 220n8; through Tejano music, 11

Pope, Rebecca A., 160

Portillo, Anuta, 140

Portillo, Lourdes, 137, 159, 227n12

Presley, Elvis, 2, 13, 46, 127, 139–40, 196n29, 223n43

Proposition 187 (1994), California, 15

Proposition 227 (1998), California, 15

public commemoration: absence evoked in, 4, 115; Astrodome concert circulated as, 32–33; "Como la Flor" as inspiring, 47, 144; contested arenas and, 8, 79, 118; cultural memory and, 26–28; family-approved, 21; future staged in, 83–84, 102; irreverence toward loss at, 54; latinidad as negotiated in, 23, 98–99, 103; as messing up and cleaning up, 87–88; *Mirador de la Flor* as stage and, 83, 92; nineteenth-century African American ceremonies and, 100; palimpsests and, 4, 93–94, 119, 194n16; public memory created by, 61; *Selena* biopic auditions as, 146–47; *Selena Forever* and, 95–96, 122; speaking names of dead as, 190–91; spectator misbehavior at, 94. *See also* drag performances, queer Latina/o

Puerto Ricans, 119, 132, 133, 218n60, 218–19n61

purple pantsuit, *3*; at Astrodome concert, 35, 42, 44–45; in impersonation, 126; measurements of, 2, 4, 136, 160; in *Selena* biopic, 32; voice as carrying, 55

queer identity: agency and, 158, 226n9; class, race, and, 228–29n53; cumbia and, 161; disco and, 41–42, 54–55, 202n18; expansiveness of, 226n5; heteronormativity and, 42, 55, 159–60; impersonation and, 185; Latina lesbian readings of death scene and, 163–65, 167–70; rumor in, 170–72; "sexile" and, 185, 229n55; world-making and, 226n11. *See also* drag performances, queer Latina/o

Quintanilla, A. B., 31, *36*, 49, 50

Quintanilla, Abraham: barrier at *Mirador de la Flor* and, 86; in death scene description, 166–67; disavowal of queerness by, 227n12; in Latina

31–32. *See also* auditions for *Selena* biopic

Selena Day, 16–17

Selena Forever (musical's first run): convergence of capitalism and patriarchy in, 113–14, 218n51; corporate sponsorship of, 107; description of, 95–96, 106–11; early cancellation of, 106, 108–11, 216–17n38, 217n39; expansiveness of, 99–100; Latina subjectivities in, 115–23; mainstream views vs. subjectivities in, 99–100; mother-daughter attendance of, 218n52; neophyte theatergoers at, 108; patriarchal narrative in, 98–100; press release for, 105; production details of, 106; program cover from, 107; surrogation and, 121; symbolism of American musicals and, 100; ticket cost and attendance at, 110; value of labor and, 105–6. See also *Selena: A Musical Celebration of Life*

Selena Live — The Last Concert (DVD, 2003), 34, 37, 78, 224n56

Selena Museum, 1–5, *3*

"Selena out of a Coffin" (Joe Jiménez), 184

Selena's body. *See* dead body as symbol; Latina bodies

"Selena Sites," tourist map of, 80, *81*

Selena's Secret (Maria Celeste Arraras), 228n34

Selena ¡Vive! (Univisión broadcast), 187–88

Selenidad: as anthem, 189–90; definition of, 7–8; memory as uncategorizable and, 191–92

self-fashioning: analyses of, 195nn28–29; authenticity and, 13, 182–83; entrepreneurial endeavors and, 114–15; "good girl/siren" dialectics

within, 12; nativist discourse vs., 7; *Selena Forever*'s music and, 216n33; "star as brand" and, 12; Tejana identity vs. cross-Latina popularity in, 25; young Latina identification with, 218n52

settlement narrative, Spanish and Anglo: Columbus ship exhibit and, 72–73, 77, 208n33, 208–9n37; Friendship Monument and, 71, *71*; in/visibility of Tejanos in, 61, 67, 69–70, 80, 84; unsettling of, 64, 82

Shelton, Don, *36*, 37

Shirley, Don, 217n44

Silva, Chelo, 41, 202n22

Singer, Mark, 208–9n37

social class: civic identity and, 61–62, 67, 69, 81–82, 87–89, 206n3; crossdressing and, 229–30n53; crossing of, negotiation of, 23–24, 131, 143, 160, 176, 179, 213n14; divaness and, 160, 182; drag performances and, 174, 182–83, 185; image in Mexico and, 204–5n43; inter-Latino tensions and, 199n67, 206n3; *rasquachismo* and, 161; realness and, 181; *Selena Forever* attendance and, 109–10. See also working class

Spanglish, 37, 40, 52, 162

Spanish American Genealogical Association (SAGA), Corpus Christi, 62, 69

Spanish language: acculturation and, 22; in American latinidad, 19, 21; in Astrodome performance, 37; English-only campaigns and, 101–2; fluency and, 48; linguistic categories and, 119; marketing and, 23–24; media views on, 204n43; queerness and, 157; in stereotypes, 143; transnational reach of, 25, 52

Deborah Paredez is an assistant professor of theater and dance at the University of Texas, Austin.

Library of Congress Cataloging-in-
Publication Data
Parédez, Deborah, 1970–
Selenidad : Selena, Latinos, and the performance
of memory / Deborah Paredez.
p. cm.
Includes bibliographical references and index.
ISBN 978-0-8223-4489-6 (cloth : alk. paper)
ISBN 978-0-8223-4502-2 (pbk. : alk. paper)
1. Selena, 1971–1995. 2. Hispanic Americans—
Ethnic identity. I. Title.
ML420.S458P36 2009
782.42164—dc22 2009004161